# Unconditional

# Unconditional

*How a Mother's Love Rescued
Her Rebellious Son*

## Suzanne J. Roragen

Forefront
BOOKS

Published by Forefront Books.
Distributed by Simon & Schuster.

Library of Congress Control Number: 2023917784

Print ISBN: 978-1-63763-245-1
E-book ISBN: 978-1-63763-246-8

Cover Design by Mimi Bark
Interior Design by Bill Kersey, KerseyGraphics

# Dedication

*To my son, Nick, the only one who calls me Mom.*

*And to all the courageous mothers loving their*

*sons and daughters unconditionally.*

# Contents

PART TWO
# Just in Time

# Prologue

" *These teenagers who veer off course might strain up against the bound-aries* for several years before flying straight and getting serious about their lives," the headmaster drawled, his words measured and careful. "Or," he paused, his piercing gaze meeting mine, "they completely derail, losing all self-control in what I know to be the point of no return."

Is that why we were in his office? Was his little train analogy a pointed warning to me and my husband about my son?

He continued sharing his deserved wisdom developed over some twenty-seven years mentoring his rotating flock of K–12 students. He said that once they enter high school they settle on their peer group—and this group defines their performance at school and in extracurricular activities. Many students at Franklin Prep respect adult authority figures, keeping to a minimum the sporadic forays into minor rebellion. Other, more fringe students at the elite school ferret out all manner of ways to break free of the authoritarian grasp, or to measure up to it.

Girls trend inward during their natural growth process. Inevitable stumbles commonly result from insecurity with body image and appearance, spiraling for some toward unhealthy choices. I had once mentored a Franklin Prep alumnus who'd disguised her emaciated body for over a year with bulky sweatshirts. Finally, when her periods ceased and her hair began falling out in clumps, she outed her eating disorder to her stunned mother.

The headmaster lobbed more tidbits our way, explaining that boys typically opt for a more physical, and dangerous, expression in the awkward attempts toward developing their unique identity. *Physical*, on that day, I assumed meant sports or, I don't know, pumping iron? The headmaster did not elaborate and, I suppose, I wanted to pretend Nick was still on track to a brilliant future.

"I have sat behind this desk for years tellin' parents that their child must have a course correction." Ken and I sat in rapt attention on the other side during this third visit to the headmaster. The first appointment two years prior ended with advice on how to keep Nick awake in class—a cold shower in the morning. As far as wisdom is concerned, that sanguine tip was perfect for a fourth-grader, but missed the mark for a pimply teen like a guided missile with broken radar. Last month, on our second meeting in this office, it was because Nick had shouted obscenities at a Franklin Prep employee. On the table then was a threat of a multiple-day suspension. This time, in a sick flashback to Nick's third-grade year when he carved his name in his desk with a pocket knife, he had just ditched school and forged my signature on an excuse note. The time for pointed warnings was up, and now, there would be more than some gentle counseling.

Before his sophomore year, our only visit to this office was as proud parents walking in with folders full of proof as to why Franklin would benefit from having our son among the future class of ninth-graders. Boy Scout! Honors Program! Golf Champion! Now, it was four years later and four months until graduation from this campus, and the headmaster conveyed his real concern.

"Let me be frank with y'all. Nick is running around with a questionable group of boys. My advice to you? Encourage him away from attending university here in South Carolina. I encourage pullin' him far away from this current path—with boys who seek out trouble—and away from the local universities. I know some folks at Arizona State. It's a fiiiine school with a fine engineering program, and a great option for Nick."

"But he has already been accepted to both Clemson and USC. He is dead-set on staying local, with his friends," I stated.

"I understand. Your son, Nick, could have a very promising future. But, as I said earlier, he has gotten all twisted around." Here he paused and leaned in over the papers on his desk. The motion spurred his orange Clemson Tiger bobblehead desk ornament into a spastic nodding fit.

"What you should want to avoid, and what you cannot control, is a sort of 'past the point of no return.' I call it the *Epic Fail*. Kids don't often recover well, if at all, from the *Epic Fail*."

Was it a high school pregnancy he meant? A DWI? Or perhaps an arrest or car accident? Sitting stone-still, I felt pity for the parents who went down the "epic fail" path. Poor things that were unable to self-arrest in an avalanche raging toward the very village where they lived! Wake up and smell the weed, naive parents!

I would prefer this book was a short story where wisdom kicked in to harness the powerful words of the headmaster that day. The story ahead would be a quick retelling of how the visit culminated with whisking Nick off his misguided path to the University of Arizona to tackle his coursework in engineering. How thrilling to report, the day after graduation, we loaded up the moving van and rolled right past Clemson, South Carolina, with Nick riding sulky shotgun all the way out West. Once safely ensconced in our sturdy New Mexico nest for a summer reset, he would heal his miscreant ways and repair our fractured mother-son bond. The long, hot days of guiding golfers out of sand bunkers and perfecting his handicap at the country club as a full-time caddy would leave him joyfully exhausted. After three months of kumbaya we would load up his SUV mid-August for the six-hour drive to Tempe, Arizona.

We should have been bold enough. That fantasy plan is still a balm to my soul to imagine. Should, should, should. An awful word filled with regret, shame, guilt, and remorse. We should have taken to heart the intel that day from the headmaster, whose perfect clarity predicted the vignettes of Nick's isolated actions coming together in an *Epic Fail*.

God hands us intel as well. All too often we block out His whispers intended to guide us toward a quick lesson, growth, and a speedy course correction. If we listen, our obedience lands us back on a smooth path with an intact soul, armored up to slay the purpose laid before us. In forging forward under our own will, the messy, drawn-out process is fraught with tumbles and heartbreak, as God chisels away at the stubborn preferences eroding our firm foundations. I had dabbled with God all my life, grown up in the Lutheran Church and made a point to introduce Nick to all things Jesus. He was baptized in the Presbyterian Church in Alexandria (more on that later). We said blessing prior to digging into the sumptuous feast overflowing on every holiday table. Once Nick had mastered his vocabulary at two years old, a nightly recitation of the spooky prayer, "Now I lay me down to sleep, I pray the Lord my soul to keep, If I should die before I wake, I pray the Lord my soul to take," became ritual. Whispers? Our family loved God, but we sure never heard heavenly roars, let alone godly whispers. I wish I had tuned in to one of the many "hotline calls" attempting to rescue me and my son with a speedy solution to the impending trouble. What does it take for God to get our attention?

Perched that day in the hard and unforgiving parent's chair, my hubris and denial set in motion a scenario 180 degrees removed from all the "should have" course-correction options that, over time, would garner every ounce of my attention as we headed toward an epic fail.

# Introduction

*I* *was visiting my son in Orlando. My child had leapt at the opportunity to* continue living about as far away from his parents as possible and still remain in the country. He had just logged four solo years on the East Coast. Four long years. Then a month ago he'd signed a contract with a major financial corporation to be all-in for more six-hour flights away from family—indefinitely. I felt bitter—robbed of the geographical reunion I assumed would come after my kiddo graduated from college. But alas, there would be no wavering from the unconditional, and possibly enabling, support patterns I had laid down since his birth. I flew from our post–Air Force, desert-Southwest retirement casa to the mosquito coast in August 2020 to help settle my son into his apartment. I would make the best of it and enjoy our well-oiled groove for one-on-one time together. I also had something to talk to him about, an idea that had been percolating for three years.

Could I write a book about us and what I saw as the worst season of my life? We chatted away through Home Goods and Pottery Barn, Publix and Chick-fil-A, about what that would look like, spewing his worst decisions out into the world for all to see. (Would anyone even read my cathartic confessional, other than a handful of loyal family and friends?) Finally, the last day of my week-long trip loomed ever near its end before he joined me on the curry-smelling couch we had picked up from an out-of-business Indian restaurant.

"Yes, you can write about all that happened," he said, locking his gaze with mine, eyes as familiar to me as my own—my DNA apparent in their shape and color.

"Will you write too, from your perspective? I will write what I think happened, then you can swoop in with, 'Here is what really happened'?" I asked slowly.

Nick thought it over with his customary reflection for only a moment before bravely answering, "Yes." He would lay bare all his dance-with-the-devil misadventures. Why on earth would he *let me* write this thing?

"I wish I could change some of the things I will tell you. But I am not ashamed. I would not be the person I am now if my life had unfolded differently, or with less struggle," he continued. "You want to write this book and I want you to be happy. Hey— God's got a plan. I love where I am, where He has brought me, and people should not be ashamed of the past that brings them to a bright future."

In life, grace says we don't have to share our terrible mistakes with strangers, new friends, or trusted family members. They can forever be oblivious to the idiotic choices made in our life, and believe us to be the hero in our own story. Nick was agreeing to out himself. The jig would be up on the perception he owned a charmed past once he revealed the tough journey to this glorious new career. He would let anyone who cared to know and understand in on the facts. I call that courage.

Somewhere between anticipation of the therapeutic process ahead of me and terror to dig up the shameful past of the person whom I loved beyond measure, lay peace. I could do this. We would do this book together. We would heal our relationship together.

Shortly after returning home from Orlando I was sitting on my patio, sipping coffee, staring at a blank computer page. How would I start this memoir and, by the way, why? Why the strong urge to bare my soul? Then I caught sight of a family of finches on my neighbors' roof. The tiny gray mama finch perched on the edge of the stucco, with movement of her little head the only clue she was alive and well. A small chick sat to her left. Three other chicks were gleefully launching off the roof, taking shaky flights before a crooked return to their mother's side. Off they would go, one or two at a time, always returning to the roof. The fourth chick remained fixed in place, watching the others dip and swoop. My coffee grew cold as I fixated on nature unfolding before me.

When the lesson drew to a close, mama tipped her torso toward the wary chick. The beak that had certainly crafted their nest and provided infinite meals for them poked him so well that he launched off the roof. After a precipitous drop, his wings a blur in his frantic effort to take flight, he rose up and around in a shaky circle, returning to his mother's side. Then he did it again, of his own volition, joining his siblings in their forays into the nearby trees.

I thought of my own incessant and urgent poking of my son. Unlike Mama Finch, I fell short in the courage department. Perched at the edge of my chair on my sun-filled patio, I saw clearly what went wrong in the rearing. I couldn't poke him enough. Missing in the rearing of my kid was a good dose of weed-killing tough love to prod him out of his waning self-discipline and proclivity toward all things fun, leading to misguided choices. Transitioning to adulthood requires a careful plan and persistent execution to navigate the inevitable rough air. An internal moral compass is a necessity in locating stable, solid ground for weary or broken wings. I couldn't shove him fully off the roof. I couldn't stomach the *splat* on the other end of the shove, because my finely honed mama instincts *knew* he was not equipped for flight—not just yet. And—shocking was this news to me—*I* was sorely unprepared as well.

Also, the more words that rose up out of me and spilled onto the keyboard, the clearer it became what a terrible transition I had made from mothering a child who could almost do no wrong, tell no lie, to mothering one that in a span of a few months had secretly been wrongdoing and lying all over the place. My child, who I knew better than I knew myself, executed a behavioral 180 and needed some tough, drill-sergeant-type discipline. The response I conjured up was a familiar spirit of teamwork to work toward his goals. As a daughter of an alcoholic I had worked the self-help aisles at Barnes and Noble for ten years to obliterate any trace of the enabler role I subconsciously acquired in my youth. But that dysfunctional spark, still glowing somewhere in my emotional toolbox, would ignite like a wildfire as my child blindsided me with his terrible Jekyll-and-Hyde about-face. The chronic stress of helping my son nose-dive while simultaneously poking at rescuing him leveled quite a blow to my emotional and physical good health.

Military families build nests quickly, with an understanding of the impermanence inherent in a two-year assignment. Despite the fleeting nature of each home, I nurtured Nick with layers of love among hastily hung pictures. Furniture arranged in the new house to mirror the previous address offered hope to assuage the plaguing sense of homesickness. I worked hard to craft some sturdy wings. But, have you noticed in your own life that soaring is easy when the skies are mostly clear? Have you ever bustled around, thinking you have nailed parenting, that your child's wings are strong, only to discover during a rough patch that they aren't? I was blindsided when my remarkable son suddenly...wasn't.

I am taking my messy season of parenting and laying it out on the pages to follow, to bear witness to a sometimes-inept process of raising up and letting go of a most precious blessing—my child. When we share our heartaches and successes, when we are brave enough to tell our unvarnished stories, we offer a chance at a smoother path for someone else. When you gut it out and make it to the top of a mountain, reach down behind you and offer a hand to those who have a similar journey ahead of them.

Laid out in the chapters to come is a time-honored story of an unconditional love of a mother for her child. It is natural to love your children fiercely. All mothers could write chapter after chapter about the many ways they have devoted themselves to their family. But the tragic loss of my friend's child when Nick was a baby muddied the years of childrearing with a messy illusion: If I was vigilant enough, standing guard as a sentinel to ward off all things awful, I alone could keep my child safe and alive to thrive into adulthood. Perhaps you have a story that has colored how you parent? I plan to put the shame of my actions aside and come clean about the awful ways I attempted to "protect" my son from himself. Move into my life and hear my story, and maybe you will gather hand-me-down wisdom and insight that helps your child steer clear of epic fails. And be reminded of the courage you need to be the drill sergeant in response to your child's reckless actions. The certain clarity gained via writing for myself and for you, dear reader, urges my efforts onward. Enduring passion, deeply carved into the plasticity of my brain and the chambers of my heart, flow onto these pages with three defining reasons I discovered for my unyielding motivation in toiling at this project.

First, we parents with rebellious children are not alone. From the time of a child's birth, parenting entails a wicked and delightful cha-cha of on-the-job training to keep that child alive. Every parent has bumped up against the scary, shadow side of parenting. The awkward dance is a jumble of missteps creating callouses on our hearts and minds. Often, our own upbringing by equally unskilled parents, whose parents often fumbled even worse, bears heavily on the efforts we muster on our journey. As a flawed mother, I perpetuated the cycle. Perhaps my revelations will allow your eyes to open wide early on in your progenies' shenanigans and might steer you clear of mistake and regret. Despite your missteps, separation between you and your child often yields terrible results. Sharing stories is a time-honored method to distill a jumble of facts and emotions into a purified drink which goes down smoothly to nourish and inform the body and soul. For the reader, the message has the power to guide the course of choices to avoid a sickening likeness or emulate the grace given by the bold storyteller.

Second, I am a writer. From the first time I saw double-pink lines on a stick, all things pregnancy, birth, and parenting occupied a quest to know, which crowded my mind and bookshelves. Many parental guides exist for the birth-to-middle-school stages. During Nick's teen years, I found a dearth of adolescence-to-adulthood parenting books. Barnes and Noble offered the following subjects: *how to win your teen with love, how to set boundaries, practical consequences in parenting,* and *how to turn your teen around.* Then there was the more horrific: *how we survived my child's addiction, my child was a mass murderer, my child ran off and joined a cult,* and *my child joined the Taliban.* Navigation guidance was scarce for *on-the-edge but isn't it normal? How bad is weed?* type of trouble. Percolating in my subconscious over the three toughest years of my life was this book that began while I was watching the baby finch, then continued into chapters that accumulated hardship and volume faster than I could retroactively pray them away.

My own childhood revolved around riding my daisy-print, banana-seated one-speed barefoot and the places it took me. That cushy-seated bike would transport me to the hundreds of stories filling the pages of thousands of books shelved at our local library. My anticipation mounted as I found a spot in the bike rack out front. Heaving all fifty pounds of my spindly frame into the heavy door, with a whoosh, it gave way to musty, cold air welcoming my hot and sweaty eagerness. The adult racks beckoned always, as I strolled first through the Dewey decimal aisles, imagining a day when I could read *those* books. Shelving temporarily my bubble of anticipation, I would head over to the children's books and check out Dr. Seuss (no coincidence that my son's graduation gift was *Go Dog Go*, by Dr. Seuss). The day soon came when in elementary school I devoured big-girl books like *Black Beauty*; *The Diary of Anne Frank*; *All Creatures Great and Small*; *Are You There God? It's Me, Margaret*; and *My Friend Flicka*. Then, in high school, it was Leon Uris, Ayn Rand, John Jakes, and Elie Wiesel. The words of gifted authors happily tangled up over the decades with my passion for stories. The roots of my desire to someday translate my intangible thoughts into words that would fill the pages in a physical presence nestled on a shelf began with reading books. Something tangible and lasting out of mere thoughts astounds me to this day—the potential of words to impact a life transfixes me still in their power to cure, ignite, and make wise all who encounter them.

The power of words combined with the courage of the writer to clarify and make sense of intimate thoughts through sentences, brings me to do the same. I won't attempt a weighty fiction novel like those I visited in that deliciously chilled Texas library, though the inspiration spawned while strolling the aisles, with my six-year-old hand bouncing from one textured spine to the next, was formative. The other side of the library housed the tough stuff; this I knew, even then. The truth, the facts, the history loomed intimidating to my intact young soul a few aisles over from the fiction I understood. Here in this decade, I reveal a book that houses the tough stuff, a work in memoir form of my bitter and harsh three-year season of unwanted lessons culminating in painful and heartbreaking truths. I know this book, in your hands now, will proudly rest, spine tall, among those austere works on the other side. Inspired by fiction and motivated by facts, I lay it all out here on the pages to come.

Laughter feeds the soul, and who wants to read a story devoid of occasional humor? I promise you some respite from the tough stuff through humor. I want to share how I came to take the door off Nick's bathroom to stop his early bad habits. Why was the screen off of his window? How did I actually *help* (enable!) my child to find places to hide alcohol in the crevices of his SUV? I write, my head shaking in disbelief at my stupidity and shame as my son reveals how much worse it all really was.

We humans are shaped by those that raise us up and by the actions of random people. They leave their imprint on our psyche and help shape our personality in both positive and negative ways. A myriad of news stories tell of miraculous survival at the hands of fate or despite the agendas of evil people. One such story belongs to a boy named Charlie. Growing up in his native Uganda, he was sent to a witch doctor for removal of his male organs for a ritual ceremony. Bob Goff in his book *Everybody Always* talks about his persistence and dedication to Charlie, and others in similar situations. Despite all the unspeakable acts he suffered at the hands of deplorable adults, the boy is living well, by all public accounts. Trauma well-managed has potential to create grit and pluck, and the all-crucial element of stable emotional health. Trauma comes at the hands of evil, as endured by Charlie, or inadvertently through the mishaps in life which don't register as trauma, but burrow into our psyche, creating pervasive fear to show up later in the form of dysfunction. Fear is powerful, and has an agenda all its own, outside of our conscious control, and morphs easily into a pattern of worry.

How do you move forward when you are mired in quicksand, when surrendering to the muck that inevitably life will hand you seems the only option? Stories abound in the Bible of disciples who were stuck and waiting on the Lord for rescue. Some, like John the Baptist, made good use of their relentless suffering. He turned out some letters while in prison, trusting and staying in faith. Others were in a scary holding pattern made worse by doubting: think Peter in the boat. If we dig in and wait while patching together a plan with tools at our disposal, and with our face to Jesus, moving through the muck passes. Or we can stay stuck, muscle it out on our own, and will die a hundred small deaths until our souls fizzle out. What bold parenting did I actually put into play, that may have ameliorated what played out? Mine is a good story, sure to hold your attention as you ingest my lessons and avoid some of the same for yourself.

Lastly, the colossal reason to chronicle my tough journey is my son. He has agreed to sit alongside me and amend my knowledge for the first time on the events that led to our near destruction. In humble agreement, with unadorned truth and full disclosure, he will reveal the awful facts that birthed this memoir. What I thought was awful, we will discover through his confessions, was far, far worse.

I don't know that I am ready to relive it all through the telling or to hear the inner machination of a teen hell-bent on destruction, let alone my precious son. But here we go. Hold on and let's do this.

PART ONE

# WAKE-UP CALL

# Chapter 1

# In The Beginning

*M*others of infant children hang in a subconscious limbo awaiting the unequivocal proof that God has blessed them with a healthy child. Physical wellness can often be determined right at birth, giving your baby the once-over for ten fingers and ten toes. Mental wellness can be a bit trickier to assess. Clues were plenty early on with Nick meeting growth and milestones as expected. But crying seemed to be his comfort zone, and he balked with mighty resistance at complying with that to which he was opposed.

"Is he okay?" I would ask my doctors at each checkup. Finally, indisputable validation of his "smarts" arrived at age two.

Nicholas and I stood at the same height thanks to the dining room chair. Cooking side by side in our tiny beige-and-brown galley kitchen in our apartment in Crystal City, Virginia, Nick stirred the boxed, neon-orange mac and cheesies. Clad in a blue T-shirt and Thomas the Tank Engine undies, he happily embraced his sous chef gig. Then my elbow brushed the opened foil "cheese" packet, sending it hurtling toward the floor in a dinner-ending tumult. With lightning speed, I arrested the impending crisis with a swoop of my hand, catching the ingredient, with no spill in sight.

"Just in the nick of time!" I cheered.

Nick looked over with a steady gaze, his chubby hand stirring the boiling pasta from his perch, and assessed the action.

"No! Just in the Mommy time!"

Silence. The world stopped spinning. The pasta stopped boiling. Tears pooled in my eyes, while I absorbed fully this split-second flash of intellect. I hugged my little Einstein chef in this moment of pure joy and relief.

"Mommy! I have to stir!" He squiggled free and I went to fetch the strainer with a spring in my step. This parenting was going to be a cinch now that I had a wise and gifted child. It had been, mostly, a breeze since conception. Despite the scary stories circulating in the mom world of first-time pregnancies fraught with anxiety and the births dragging on for an entire day or two, my birth story with Nick was one of ease.

All first-time parents must move through various stages of shock and disbelief, maybe different levels of fear, as they enter the hospital as a couple and discharge with an extra human and instructions on how not to kill them. The world pivots permanently within the space of duo to trio. It's a good shifting that occurs. Birth was Nick's first milestone moment, and also the last time my son and I worked so perfectly at the exact same goal, as though we were one person. I understood at some bittersweet level, with a heavy belly and life inside of me, that all other milestones would belong solely to him. The last one for us would be the first for him alone. As we gently labored prior to the epidural, the freedom to walk the cold linoleum surfaces in the thin cotton hospital gown was a respite offering a sense of control over my circumstances. I was there with two intertwined lives of concern to me, and had been for nine months: nine wonderful months. Wandering off and away into the world has characterized me since my own birth. True to form on the day of Nick's grand entrance, I escaped the confines of the room and wandered, with Ken in tow. Darting my gaze left and right for nurse patrol, we strode outside the boundary where Labor and Delivery oozes into the sick part of the hospital. Spotting a corner waiting room which overlooked Twenty-Fourth Street at the precipice of Georgetown in Washington, DC, we saw the coast was clear and entered the empty space. Dodging the cheap coffee tables littered with rumpled AARP magazines, I shuffled toward the perimeter of chairs below the windows.

"Ken, open that window!" I pleaded, hunching into the next contraction.

He strolled over and struggled with the suicide-proof window, cranking the stiff handle out to its maximum ten-inch gap. Ahh... enough room to stick my head through. With Nick protruding into the wall I leaned into the crisp air, like a floppy-eared pooch slobbering out a car window for joyful gulps of blowing air.

This 10th day of October 1997 was a bitter one. The biting air was medicine to my soul, sustaining me and Nick, fueling us for the long journey ahead. Down below were intrepid joggers and bikers. I envied them, with the freedom to tussle along with the colors of autumn, alive in the trees. The yellows, browns, and vibrant reds responded to the mighty bluster in a chorus of tinkles and shudders. Closing my eyes, I drank in the musty, fragrant world readying for hibernation. But alas, inside the hospital was a time of birth and renewal.

"Suz, the nurse is looking for you." Ken shook me from my autumnal reverence. "She just put out a search party; we better head back to the room."

"Just one more minute. Don't you wish we were out there running?"

"Nope, I want to get in there and have this baby. Let's go," he stated in his usual get-down-to-business mandate.

For nine months Nick and I had sailed in tandem. First trimester had handed me constant nausea as I struggled to nourish Nick with more than pudding. Second trimester brought loads of energy and long runs into Georgetown along the GW Parkway Trail—sometimes past the very spot below this hospital window. We would set out, Ken and I, from our apartment in Crystal City to catch the trail by Reagan National Airport and, usually, jog to the Key Bridge where it crossed over the Potomac into Georgetown. My hand checked in on my bulging belly from time to time, assessing and assuring Nick as we began the two-mile uphill on Thirty-Third Street, then crossing over to Wisconsin at some point to reach Starbucks. After lattes, muffins, and reading the Sunday paper, we would walk down Wisconsin and into DC via M Street, passing Columbia Women's Hospital (our hospital), to catch the Metro at Foggy Bottom or Farragut.

I'm normally prone to bouts of hypochondria, such that every real or imagined ache or sniffle is a terrible disease in my mind, but my pregnancy was the complete opposite. I knew not only that I was in perfect health, but that being perfectly healthy was my full-time job for the good of my growing baby. I imagined Nick floating to and fro, nestled in his undulating aquatic world, loving the activity of the day. During third trimester, with the mounds of delicious and healthy cuisine, classical music, and exercise, in utero Nick kicked and punched his strong body into my belly. He was fierce and strong, almost seeming impatient to meet the world. Massaging his foot or elbow through my ever-expanding skin quieted the ruckus.

Turning away from the window, pausing as another contraction squeezed me back to the moment we had long awaited, I embraced with renewal and strength the birth ahead. Eight drama-free hours later, an angry squall and Apgar score of 10 out of 10 confirmed his stubborn nature and excellent health, qualities we'd already sussed out over the course of the pregnancy. Breathing outside of fluid for the first time, my baby inflated his tender pink lungs with the medicinal air in that private delivery room at Columbia. What a bittersweet hello and farewell in the celebration, blending loss with blessed elation.

A gift at a baby shower prior to Nick's arrival was a milestone journal offering an abyss of blank pages to record the new child's pivotal events from baby to six years old. Setting the wrapping paper aside I recall flipping through the tabula rasa, wondering what happened after six years old. Was it all plateau and no milestones? With Nick safely incubated for eight months at the time of the shower, it was a stretch to even imagine his birth milestone. What happened when I wasn't physically connected to his well-being every single second? I wonder if the ubiquitous tears of new mothers herald not just joy, but heartache at the sudden removal of perfect, umbilically linked, protection of their children.

Later that night, alone in the quiet of the maternity ward, a nascent nocturnal alertness infiltrated my attempts to sleep. Earlier, I had acquiesced to the insistence of a bossy nurse delivering a full-stop explanation of the great reasons to put Nick in the infant nursery instead of bedside in a bassinet for our hospital overnight. Now, I was unsettled, restless, and worried.

"This will be your last night for a long while to get a good night's sleep! You have the rest of your life to get awakened in the middle of the night by your child!" Nurse Ratchet presciently stated.

I adhered to the suggestions of those who knew better, and Nicholas slept down the hall away from my semi-private room where I lay wide awake. Enough, I thought. Swinging myself out of the hospital bed, I padded down the silent hallway to the nursery. I yearned to hold him, but he was bundled up and sleeping alongside six other swaddled infants in their plastic bassinets. Other trusting moms had complied as well, it seemed. I returned to my room with tears of frustration for not knowing—for the first of many times—how to best parent my son. Cocking my ear toward the silence of the nursery, I settled my focus on my overnight bag. I reached down to pull out the blank journal and pen. I returned to the bed and began to write: "I pushed like a champ! Ken relayed his fear as he saw Nicholas' head pop out the size of a baseball and white as snow. He was coming to terms with preparing for a disabled child. Then his head sprung to full size, his mouth and nose were cleared and he wailed. Ken told of his amazement at watching the tiny shoulders twist out, then the rest of Nick's squirming body! Wailing cries from his sweet, swollen mouth filled the room as the doctor put Nick on my stomach. My child was shocked to be in the world, and to be honest, I was shocked too! One moment, he was alive in my belly, then *BAM!* Instantly breathing air, like he had been doing so all his life. At this first breath, and to my shocked surprise, the comfort of his presence within me immediately shifted to a fierce maternal urge to protect him. Though I loved being pregnant, I constantly wondered about my ability to parent. I didn't know how I would adapt to this new role, as a first-time mother at thirty-five. I was very emotional alone—but not—in the hospital. Nicholas was so small and delicate, coming out at six pounds, eleven ounces. I had woken up that morning as the nurse wheeled in a crying Nick—I immediately responded with an intense urge to comfort him. *Whew, I might be okay at this mothering gig.*

Our Crystal City fifth-floor apartment was arguably more pro than con when considering a location to raise up a baby. The balcony was large enough to settle into our plastic Adirondack chairs for a choice, albeit peek-a-boo viewing spot of the Jefferson Memorial, ablaze at night across the Potomac River. Come summertime, when the snow and wind calmed, we set up Nick's playpen on the balcony to enjoy summer nights "out" after Ken returned from the Pentagon, eight blocks to the south. Ken would call with a heads-up that he was leaving his office in the E Ring. Nick, who slayed the walking milestone at nine months, would toddle in front of me to the balcony to await his approach. Ken would quicken up his Pentagon shuffle when spotting Nick wildly jumping up and down, waving his pudgy arms in greeting.

Oblivious to the apartment rules forbidding a junk-strewn balcony, I focused on keeping Nick safe with a brilliant plan to line the perimeter of the rail with green plastic fencing, secured with zip ties. Soon enough though, containing my toddler's high energy caused a niggling guilt; an apartment was not a suitable place to raise a child. This seed of doubt wormed its way into my joyous bubble. The solution: I needed to replicate a suburban landscape. I added a plastic wading pool which provided some measure of a backyard atmosphere. The "front yard" was our hallway. Ken or I would empty our car of groceries or other purchases into one of the liberated shopping carts someone had stolen from Best Buy or Costco. We brought everything up the elevator in one trip, then transformed the empty buggy from workhorse to favorite toy. I'd scrunch up an old pillow to serve as a cushion for Nick on the dirty thatched metal bottom of the cart and race him up and down the long corridor, propelling the cart until the wheels wiggled and Nick giggled with joy.

Once, a fierce snowstorm dumped a foot of snow in one day on the Metro area. When the winds died down and the snowfall ceased, we located some discarded cardboard boxes from the garage and made our way to the adjacent hotel to take advantage of the sloped parking lot for hours of perfect sledding! Nick happily embraced his concrete world morphing into his urban playground.

Quality adventures requiring less imagination existed not only within but outside our apartment property, on all the paved trails spiraling at all compass points mere steps from our apartment. The Mount Vernon Trail offered eighteen miles of asphalt with the choice to head south, toward George Washington's Mount Vernon Estate or north, to Georgetown. Runs where Nick had once nestled in utero were now an event requiring mounds of baby gear. Our red three-wheeled baby jogger held a removable insert, keeping his floppy head and body stable. With wheels the size of small bike tires this thing took up its share of the running path. My hands almost resting on the jogger's handle while running, rather than pumping gently at my sides, presented yet another adjust-ment to life with baby and one which I happily embraced. Once I was cleared for exercise, training for the Marine Corps Marathon ensued. Familiar runs outside our building grew ever longer, with the Georgetown option a favorite as it offered flats, hills, and history. The back of the jogger offered a net storage area perfect to tote drinks, snacks, and diapers. Often, our weekend runs flowed into a tourist day visiting monuments on the Washington Mall.

I loved my new mom-life. I continued to embrace the banquet of pre-baby outdoor pursuits, but now, with my new companion, every outing was richer, filled with a deeper purpose. I savored sharing with Nick the feast of art and culture housed within the cool halls of the world-class museums a few Metro stops from Crystal City. Most shocking, for the first time in my life, was a thrill at stepping away from pursuit of a career and earning a living. Yet—I hesitated to pivot mentally to full-time mom and wife. I feared a dusty resume and losing credibility as a smart person. The kindest man and still the greatest teacher of my life, my former boss, offered up a part-time side hustle where I could make phone calls from home when I decided to stay on permanent maternity leave from the athletic club. Earning money—staying "relevant"—offered a modest salary and the fringe benefit of dropping Nick off at the Kids Klub while I utilized the exercise classes and equipment. Keeping one foot in my former life while loving the mom job eased me gently out of my career path. But the fringe benefit? It proved useless in another clue to Nick's personality. My workouts ceased twenty minutes in when, inevitably, one of the staff members from the Klub would hunt me down. Nick would not stop screaming.

I enjoyed working and for over fifteen years had thrived in managing my solo life. Two qualities I valued and clung onto, independence and diligence, heavily influenced all my significant life choices. Looking for options to put into action those values and secure Nick in a peer group presented incompatible goals. If an hour at a daycare in a gym was too much, what options existed for someone else to care for my kiddo while I invested my energy into a career? But an emerging truth ripping apart my rock-solid concept of my "value" created a strike-slip fault across ingrained priorities and goals. I was divided in the upheaval between identifying as wife/mother or career professional. Leaping over the divide from career to stay-at-home mom stirred up my stereotypes, all negative, of minivan moms watching daytime television. The inevitable getting-to-know-you question, "What do you do for work?" had me shying away from the truth. "I am in health and wellness at Worldgate Athletic Club." Rarely did I reveal I worked fifteen hours a week at a fun side hack that brought me a few bucks to blow on running shoes and got me out of my 900-square-foot apartment where mastering explosive-poop cleanup was a rubric for success.

Was I fooling myself? Did I really want to get back on track to resume a career? My nonlinear career path resembled nothing like that of many of my friends and family, where a college degree led to a career they stuck with for decades: teaching, human resources executive, lawyer. Perhaps this mom-job was my wheelhouse, what I did really well? As this combined with the role of Air Force spouse and traveling the globe, this tectonic shift of an ever-expanding chasm between former goals and reality left me firmly in the land of *Mom* with *Career* growing further and further away from possibility. I never fully surrendered my ego to the unexpected stumble into a land of motherhood and domesticity. When were the career police going to bust me for the transgression of *enjoying* "Stay-at-Home-Mom."

This slowing down brought a vacation aspect to our outings and adventures, contributing to the "cinch" of early parenting. We had help too. Extended family nearby contributed to an ideal start to our new life. Ken's parents lived two hours north in Pennsylvania in the home where Ken was raised, and my cousin Karen and her partner, Bill, lived thirty minutes away, just outside the Beltway. Ken's parents could pop down for the day, and often did, or we would drive up for a day or weekend. A better summertime option was the family cabin perched on five tree-filled acres, five hundred yards from an inlet of Raystown Lake, in the bowels of Pennsylvania. The largest lake in the state at 8,300 acres hosted boaters and fishermen to Raystown. The less obvious, albeit critical, existence for the lake was the electrical benefit of hydropower which sustained the communities spiraling out around the lake and state. Underneath the pristine waters lie homes and parks, landmarks and historic sights, all intentionally swamped for the sake of the residents and tourists in the area. In later years, we would gather friends for weekends of waterskiing. I still recall gently releasing the towrope after a long turn on skis around one of the lake's many fingers. I loved the feel of my full weight pressing the skis slowly into the depths, always wondering as I bobbed in wait of my ride if I was above someone's lost home, or a park where children had once played. Always, I wondered what ghosts lay beneath our oblivion.

The point of each day when staying at the in-laws' modest cabin in those early years was time on the lake. Strapping Nick into the tiny orange life vest with the attached float for head support was priority one. Should pre-toddler Nick fly out of my arms into the deep lake waters, the baby PFD (personal flotation device) was weighted in such a way as to flip him onto his back, jutting the cranial float out like a little raft for his head. He would remain bobbing above the flooded town, awaiting a circle-back of the boat and a safe rescue. This never happened, though we were always prepared.

Once Nick was older, the PFD offered no cranial support. Then, after we had moved and come back and moved and come back again to DC, the life jacket was mandated only when being pulled behind the boat for waterskiing or knee-boarding. Craggy stone walls, carved out millions of years ago, fortressed the placid, clean water, creating twists and coves and adventure. Lunchtime we would pull into one of the fingers and drop anchor for an hour or so of eating, sunning on the deck, and quick swims out and back from the boat. Often, Ken would pull out the fishing rig and try his luck at catching dinner. The lake was about unwinding, activity, and soaking up nature. Back at the cabin, the only real comfortable seating option was a futon handed down from Karen and Bill, who lived with Karen in Fairfax. Without traffic we could drive from Crystal City to their house in thirty minutes. Bill and Karen were our family. Holidays, birthdays, and trips to Raystown naturally included them.

Karen also hustled up from Fairfax for trick-or-treating because she enjoyed Halloween candy. I would fashion a costume for Nick a few days before the 31st—always, it was last minute and superior to ones found on a plastic hanger in a store. Once we outfitted him, we would drive four miles down the GW Parkway to the Fort Meyer Army Base, located adjacent to Arlington National Cemetery. Our first year, Nick wore the uniform of a train conductor. I painted a swirly mustache on his upper lip with eyeliner, and around his neck hung his plaid, denim bib. Settled at a jaunty angle upon his soft, blond curls rested a striped conductor hat. He peddled his feet as he sat astride his toy choo-choo, punching down on the horn to clear the way with an authentic, *WOO-WOO!* We strolled among the throngs of children and parents through the neighborhood with historic senior officer housing, walking house to house. Most of the residents were out on the steps in front of their houses checking out the scene, chatting and handing out candy. In under two hours, Nick's plastic pumpkin bucket brimmed with baby Snickers, Milky Ways, and Junior Mints. The following year he was a pilot, same drill as the previous year with Karen joining us—only this time, once back at the apartment, she lay on the carpet brokering candy handouts with a very involved Nick. Early on, these deals highlighted his innate talent at the art of business. The following year, our last before our PCS (Permanent Change of Station) to Portugal, the costume reverted back to a train conductor. I had other costume plans, but as a stubborn three-year-old his preferences weighed in firmly and often, this time with the insistence to go as Thomas The Tank Engine's Mr. Conductor. Bill never joined us for the annual trick-or-treating: the first few years he and Karen dated he had a young son of his own, a sweet boy who shot himself when he was just eleven years old.

Bill and his ex-wife were civil enemies after a contentious divorce and custody battle over Bobby, Bill's son. Once Karen joined in the mix, she welcomed Bobby in her life much like she would a stepson. She took the futon that had served as a bed for Bobby to the Raystown Lake cabin—and replaced it with a proper double bed for his bedroom. Bill's house became more of a home, rather than a weekend hangout for Bobby, with the addition of Karen. Bobby was an amazing eight-year-old when I first met him. He was bubbly, engaged, smart, and curious. We turned to Bill often for tips and tactics on raising Nick. Having successfully treaded those waters a few short years before us, his wisdom was a beacon for me—the sometimes-frazzled parent sinking in a sea of stinky diapers, colic, and rashes.

"When will Nick finally stop crying and sleep through the night?" I asked Bill at Sunday brunch following yet another sleepless night of howling. Nick already had a bent for noncompliance; struggling through life the hard way started early.

Bill would shake his thick black hair, throw his head back, and laugh.

"Bobby got his first good night of sleep last week!" he chortled. "No seriously, Bobby slept through the night after we discovered the sound of running water put him to sleep. Have you tried one of those CDs with nature music?"

"No! We have not! But we are headed to Barnes and Noble right after this meal!"

Bill influenced our parenting. A glimpse into our possible future existed in watching his incredible eleven-year-old son—his apparent success in raising Bobby made clear the wisdom of heeding Bill's mentoring.

But then, perfect Bobby; straight–A Bobby; never-a-moment's-worry Bobby; seemingly well-adjusted Bobby, ended his own life—and not a single clue existed as to why. There were no notes or journals and no best friend with insider information.

Bobby did so with Bill's gun, in Bill's closet, while Bill was traveling with Karen. One last time as a duo, Karen and Bill set out for France. When they returned, Bill would officially be granted full custody of his son, and the trio would move into their new home, now under construction. How remarkable it was to witness this "well-adjusted child." Bobby was a blessing and joy. But he wasn't adjusted, he had not adjusted within the fractious attempts at co-parenting between Bill and his ex-wife. He wasn't fine. *And his suicide was the first clue he wasn't fine.* Here's what happened on Bobby's final day, and the facts preceding it.

Given Bill and his ex-wife's agreement to honor Bobby's desire to reside full time with his father, Bobby would attend the first day of sixth grade at the district elementary school assigned to the address of the future home. He knew not a soul at this school. But all this transitioning coincided with the European travel plans. The practical choice as understood by all parties was to begin the year at the new school. His mother refused to shuttle Bobby in rush hour traffic each day, therefore Bobby could not live in her house anymore, if he was committed to attending school far from her home. It was decided that Karen's parents, my aunt and uncle—whom Bobby did not know—would stay with Bobby at the condo, until the return from abroad of Bill and Karen. My aunt and uncle would drive him to Broad Run Elementary and pick him up each day. These "strangers" would usher in this new life for Bill's son. Bobby agreed to the plan.

Dropping off his father and Karen with the new "grandparents" at Dulles Airport on the day of departure, Bill was surprised when his typically affectionate son deflected a farewell hug.

"Bob? What's up buddy?" Bill asked quietly.

No answer.

"Bob? We will be back in two weeks; you know that time will fly by. Mr. and Mrs. Peters will take care of everything." Still no response. Bobby furrowed his brow.

Bobby turned and walked away, and Bill attempted one last time to connect with his child. He was a hands-on father—present— and a positive role model, nailing this thing called parenting. If anyone had connected perfectly with their son, it was Bill.

"Bob!" he called out in the terminal, standing stock still among throngs of hurried travelers, in wait of a response. Watching his son walk away from him, I imagine his stomach dropping, or some looming feeling. Knowing his son's resilience, he turned to board his flight, sure Bobby would bounce back immediately.

Four days later, Bobby placed a frantic call to his mother. It was day two of the new school year and he was done pretending. He bellowed out eleven years of grief in a plea for rescue.

"Mom. Come and get me. Now!" Bobby sputtered over the phone to his mother. With luck and an unclogged flow in traffic, she could have reached her child within thirty minutes of his call for help. Unfortunately, his unusual desperation crashed up against Tuesday's rush hour on the outer Beltway ring.

After questioning Bobby on his angst and receiving no clarity, her concern for him amped up. "Bobby, the traffic is heavy. It will take me an hour to get there, but I will leave right now."

Immediately after the phone call, my aunt knocked on Bobby's door in what I learned was a third attempt to get him to join them, this time insistently, for dinner.

"I'll be right there!" Bobby said under his breath.

Aunt Pearl heard the familiar squeak of hinges to Bobby's room down the short hallway. Good...he was on his way. Then another door slammed.

A loud pop rang out, like a large firecracker, reverberating through the small condo. Uncle Leroy, a seasoned hunter, recognized only too well the sound of a gun. A sick feeling roiled in his gut.

Rushing down the hall, my uncle first peered into Bobby's empty room before checking Bill and Karen's bedroom. Finding the door locked, Aunt Pearl ran into the kitchen for a toothpick to use as a makeshift key. The lock popped and the door opened without a fight.

"Bobby?!" My Uncle Leroy called out. No answer. Bobby was not in sight. Leroy closed the door several inches to step to the right and peer into the closet. Up against the wall, propped up on a pile of shoes, was Bobby.

Uncle Leroy dashed over to his still, almost peaceful form, lying lifeless beneath shirts and pants hung with precision above his precious body. My uncle screamed for his wife, then pounced into lifesaving mode. CPR was nearly impossible. Bobby had shot himself in the chest. Compressions were impossible, and blowing into his mouth created tiny bubbles of proof that Uncle Leroy's efforts were useless. He screamed at my aunt to stay away, protecting her from the unimaginable scene.

"PEARL!" He paused long enough to shout to her outside the bedroom. "Call for help!! NOW!"

She rushed to the kitchen phone to dial 911. Moments unfolded with the harried rescue attempts until, finally, emergency crews filled the room. Their efforts were futile as Bobby, true to form, had done an excellent job. He stopped the pain of his fractured life. He'd learned perfectly how to shoot a gun from his father, a former Army Green Beret. They enjoyed the occasional target practice at the shooting range.

Bobby's mother pulled into the complex forty-five minutes after the paramedics. Seeing the emergency vehicles, she bolted up the two flights of stairs, awash in dread and fear. This perfect child, this amazing father, my cousin—all decimated in this single desperate instant.

I learned of the tragedy and all the cruel details that night, when I arrived home from work at 10:15 p.m. Ken was still up, waiting for me in our bedroom.

"Suz...Aunt Pearl called an hour ago. I didn't want to bother you at work."

"Oh heck. I forgot to call them today. I want to have them all over for dinner this weekend." I moved to the closet, readying for bed.

"Suz...it's not good news."

My heart sped up...That feeling. The one I had when my mom called me at work one day to inform me of my father's death. No warning, just a phone call while I was at work on a busy Saturday at the retail store. Boom. "Your father is dead."

"What? Just tell me," I demanded, moving in to pick up my baby, sleeping next to Ken.

"Bobby is dead. He killed himself tonight, with Bill's gun."

Sinking to the bed, wrapping Nick into my chest, I shed no tears, I made no sound. In pre-cell phone 1998, tracking down Bill and Karen would be tough. This was their travel day from Paris. They had no plans for lodging. A call was placed to the next night's hotel and a message left for them to call Bobby's mother immediately. One last night of normal—of utter ignorance—they enjoyed lodging somewhere in the French countryside.

We spent a long, sleepless night, Ken and I, as we lay alert and sturdy on either side of Nick. We three geared up early the next morning and headed to Reston.

Walking up the flight of stairs to Karen's condo as I had many times before, I paused at the landing before knocking softly, then gazed left and right for signs of the night before, only to find everything quite normal. The doormat beneath our feet shouted WELCOME! The shining sun was heating up the day, promising only good things with its steady warmth. Maybe this was all a mistake.

Aunt Pearl swung open the door.

"Suzie!" she cried as she reached out and clung to me.

Ken walked over with Nick on his hip to the chair where Uncle Leroy sat, a nearly empty coffee cup at his place belying the seriousness of the day. Sobbing now, he rose up to his imposing six-foot-six stature to embrace Ken, then me. I walked back to the bedroom to grasp what had unfolded the night before.

The closet was freshly scrubbed, I was told, by a hazmat crew. As with the morbid rubbernecking at a twisted interstate pileup, I was unable to stay away from the scene of a final desperate struggle of a boy barely more than a decade old. What could be so awful to end it all before even getting launched in the world? There was a magazine sitting on the chair outside the closet—outside the closet—smattered in dried blood. I paused, then took a deep breath.

I stepped into the closet. Clothes hung on all four sides of the walk-in area, some piled on the floor in what looked like a struggle to pack for two weeks in Europe. The shoes, in silent witness, refused to speak as they perched on metal racks around the periphery of the space. All that was left after the suicide were a few smatterings of blood on a magazine. The pain of a hidden sadness of an eleven-year-old boy who in either anger or despair no longer wanted his life should have been reflected in chaos and devastation. Where were the clothes all akimbo, shoes tangled and uncoupled, and carpet irreparably stained? I fell to the ground, and sat soaking in all the nothing. Unable to cry or process, I sat still scanning the small space for a few minutes.

"Mommy! Mommy! Where are you?!" the beatific voice of my child beckoned, breaking my stupor.

Rising up and out of the closet, I reached for the magazine, concerned that Karen and Bill would find it upon their return. I stashed it in my purse to throw away later. The tragedy sits with me still today. Disbelief still hums in the periphery of my psyche, twenty-plus years later, that a pre-teen boy, straight-A student, devoted son would succumb to an inescapable hopelessness. I spoke to an esteemed Marriage and Family Therapist specializing in youth and child trauma therapy and was told, "When anyone commits suicide with a weapon, it is surely an act of not only violence, but anger." I suspect that boy had a lifetime's worth of anger stored up in his soul.

I never sought out more than one therapy session to help process this tragedy. I never processed fully the answers as to why an individual, a young boy, felt his life was no longer worth living. Instead of understanding this was an unusual, isolated response to pain, it bloomed in my mind as almost normal. Bill had raised Bobby well—in my mind. I soaked up, for over a year, much of his wisdom on parenting. I came to believe that anyone, anytime could be filled up with unexpressed emotions and say, "To hell with it all" and chuck their life for good. That faulty reasoning became a slow cancer gobbling up my healthy coping patterns garnered from hundreds of secular chapters authored by self-help gurus Stephen Covey, Deepak Chopra, and James Redfield.

The ensuing months of conversation with Bill, where I inquired why but never landed on a reason, embedded this belief deep into my psyche. The deafening fear whispered initially in that closet became, over the years, a silent scream. *If Bobby, then why not Nick... why not Nick?* This burrowed into my subconscious and danced an evil jig when all the millions of opportunities arose over my son's early years to hold him accountable for his actions. *If Bobby, then why not Nick* taking up space in my soul where fearlessness and courage once resided. A nonstop, all-access pass, granted through Bobby's suicide, opened me to the shadows of darkness and vigilance.

Sadly, Bill died five years later, as he was evolving out of the darkness from that loss. A deadly blood clot took him down. Doctors discovered that Bill had a hole in his heart. The blood clot became lodged between the chambers, and during surgery, Karen was told, he just seemed to stopped fighting. Bill was beyond saving as he bled out of his chest midway through the open-heart surgery.

A mother's heart ceases to be exclusively her own upon the birth of her child (or I imagine at the point of adoption as well). Perhaps in addition to DNA, shards of heart tissue break off and attach in utero—giving a piece of a mother's heart to their baby—leaving it forever with the child. I read once a quote attributed to Miriam Adeniyi: "You will never be completely at home again, because part of your heart always will be elsewhere. That is the price you pay for the richness of loving and knowing your [children] are in more than one place." I understand this at a cellular level and wonder now how many other parents feel this bittersweet fallout of loving their children.

I know my son very well; I know the circumstances that shaped his character and personality. It turns out, I am entwined not only in his DNA, but he in mine, as several reputable scientific studies prove, in a process called *fetal microchimerism*. During pregnancy some of the cells of the fetus travel to the mother's various tissues and organs, to either remain for a short time or for her lifetime. It is thought the mother's body kills off most circulating fetal cells shortly after pregnancy, but some evade the immune system and can stay for long periods of time in the mother's body. "If [the cells were] integrated into tissue...they can be around for a lifetime," claimed University of California biologist Amy Boddy.[1]

It gives me pause to wonder: Do those who soak up more of these cells have a stronger intuitive bond with their child? And if so, is my body still flush with these fetal cells and thus, does that help explain my fierce connection and innate desire to protect my son long past the point of necessity?

# Chapter 2

# Portugal Is an Island

W hen Nick was three years old, Ken was selected an Air Force commander in Portugal. The outgoing commander's tour was cut short at the hands of his struggle with alcoholism on this remote island. With no resources to assist his addiction, he was heading back to the States and we were stepping in midyear to take over. The Azores is a small island chain nine hundred miles off the coast of the mother country of Portugal. Lajes Air Force Base was located on a strategic archipelago in the mid-Atlantic, and hosted a small contingency of Air Force personnel and their families. The US military's millions of dollars of investment into housing, schools, and infrastructure ramped up significantly during our three-year tenure on the island. Oddly though, and with reasons shrouded in sound bites and military jargon, a gradual base drawdown occurred. What had originated as a post–World War II outpost that pressed the sleepy community into service, and had done so during every mid-Atlantic crisis since, was slated to become a virtual ghost town and "airfield" for a smattering of locals and American military folks.

While devoid of activity most of the year, there were reasons to maintain a sense of purpose during our assignment. Lajes was an alternate landing site for the occasional NASA space shuttle orbiter and a key diversion airport for any type of medical or mechanical emergency for any aircraft in the vicinity. Mostly, Lajes existed to fuel fighter jets passing through, and as an outpost for NATO's war-fighting capabilities. In short, we lived for the excitement to serve in the next aviation, naval, or political crisis. Once, while back in the States with Nick, a Canadian Air Transat Airbus A-330 ran out of fuel and diverted to our runway to attempt an engines-out landing. Tires popping and catching fire on impact, the massive plane clawed up the Lajes runway, spraying debris, and resulting in an airport closure. While civil engineers repaired the airport's one runway, Nick and I remained stranded in Virginia for ten days.

Our most exciting event was President George W. Bush, British Prime Minister Tony Blair, and Spanish Prime Minister Jose Maria Aznar convening for a one-day emergency summit on our isolated island. The meeting, officially to examine prospects for a UN resolution on Iraq, transformed Lajes from one of waiting, preparing, and military dinners to one of high-stakes diplomacy. My husband had just deployed to the war zone in Kuwait for the Shock and Awe invasion of Iraq, which was formalized before our eyes during this Azorean summit. I had the pleasure, at the time, of shaking President Bush's hand. He looked me in the eye as I implored him to do the right thing. I am pretty sure sitting where I am now that he lied in promising me he would keep my husband safe.

I would later watch the battle unfold in our on-base townhome. This was the first time a war had been televised live. I was power-less to turn it off. Perhaps I thought watching it would keep my husband, who was in Camp Pennsylvania stationed with the 5th Army, safe if I was vigilant enough. A week after the summit, a deranged soldier lobbed three grenades into the tents of fellow soldiers at the very camp where he was living. The report at the time claimed one life was lost among the twelve that were attacked. Life on Lajes was one of contrasts. Like parenting, it vacillated between sleepy and bucolic and high-stakes management of emergent crisis. These opposites would unfold in our Azorean future, but going in that first day, we were flying blind.

On the blustery pre-Christmas introduction to our new home, the chartered wide-body jet sparred with island crosswinds as it bucked through the driving rain on its way to a safe-ish predawn touchdown. The roughest landing of my life confirmed my dread about our existence on this tiny spit of volcanic residue. Soon, I would know peace at these sideways takeoffs and landings, as I ventured off-island almost bi-monthly on military "hops." I had a friend in Italy stationed at the Vicenza army base, the second stop on this weekly "rotator" transport to Lajes. Nick and I would spend a week, rather than a night, exploring Italy, before catching the rotator on its way back. It was these trips from Portugal, I am certain, where Nick developed a fearless attitude toward fun and spontaneity and became the adventurous traveler he is today.

On our maiden flight, I knew nothing of future trips for spaghetti or how often I would escape off island. Upon landing, Nick, Ken, and I eased up out of our seats hesitantly, wondering at the sparse numbers deplaning with us. We were among ten or so people of two hundred making our way into one of the two aisles. I would come to know that in winter that rotator dropped off only a few Lajes-bound passengers. Because who of sound mind chooses wintertime to conduct official business on, let alone tour, Terceira Island? The stiff wind, horizontal rain, and bleak, persistent cold leave the musty indoors as the only reasonable wintertime recreational choice. The summer experience is a one-eighty from winter when the island chain's villages come alive.

That winter day, my first glimpse of Terciera Island offered up a rainy smack in the face as I poked my head out the exit door of the aircraft. No jetway, only a set of steep and slippery stairs resting up against the fuselage, comprised my transition from "normal" to Azorean. I instinctively took hold of Nick's hand and launched into our new life.

"Ma'am?" At the landing of the stairs waited a uniformed enlisted airman.

"Yes!" My eyes widened at his recognition of me.

"Let me liberate a few of your bags, ma'am, if I may?"

"Well, sure. Thank you!" I responded, stunned at the offer.

The salty, frigid, and musty air whipped around us as we made our way gingerly down the steps to the tarmac. A young officer saluted Ken and shook my hand.

"Welcome to Lajes, sir. You arrived just ahead of the squall. Come with us—we will get your bags and settle you into the TLF." Wow...what a greeting. And this wasn't a squall that we landed in?

"Grab hold of your son, ma'am. Small children have been known to get swept off their feet in these winter gusts." I popped Nick up into my arms, and held him close.

The airman heaved his weight into opening the terminal door, revealing over twenty people in rain slickers awaiting us with warm greetings. Names I don't recall now, but souls I came to know well, rose early to start their day in this organized welcome committee. Touched and overcome...I have not since that day experienced such an emotional reception. One kind stranger after the other took their turn introducing themselves and offering help. One dinner invitation for that night and an offer for lunch the next day, with a time and a place, was authentic and genuine. Their joint desire to wrap us into the community as soon as possible pulsed out a palpable energy throughout the terminal that left me...confused.

Shuttling the short drive up the hill in the blue Air Force van to our Temporary Living Facility (TLF), my first real glimpse at this agrarian outpost was of lava rock walls and narrow streets, amplifying a distant roar from the churning Atlantic Ocean. This stark nature greeted us with a simple, unbridled hello. An hour after landing and less than two days since being ensconced in the thrum of the bustling outskirts of Washington, DC, we stood alone in a 400-square-foot, one-window apartment looking out over the ocean, three days before Christmas.

I recall the bittersweet gut punch of spending the holidays far away from family and the traditions that defined the season. All our holiday decorations and items collected over our short time as a family—the stockings, heirloom ornaments, precious macaroni Christmas balls made in church—all were on a boat, lurching and tossing their way to Portugal. With any luck, they would reach us by Valentine's Day.

Ken's new deputy commander and his spouse understood more than us the harshness of the coming season—the isolation from the familiar. We were moved to tears upon stepping into our sterile one-bedroom unit. Not because it was quite awful, which it was, but because of the special decorations festooning our new home away from home. On an end table in the corner sat a spunky, twenty-inch-tall, fully decorated faux Christmas tree. Green felt stockings dangled from the TV cabinet. Framing the lone window, strands of tacky red-and-green garland struggled against determined thumb-tacks. I tear up still today at the efforts of Kelly Jenner in this special welcome to personalize our space and remove a bit of the sting at being plunked in the midst of the holidays on this frigid island. She reached out and made a difference. All of the people of Lajes, our new home, reached out and made a difference.

So life began. With a dearth of career opportunities, what would I do with the three years ahead of me? From the get-go,

I was left to consider applying for some odd job, hold down the home front, and care for my child. Days were spent juggling meetings with the spouse group, volunteering at my husband's squadron, and inventing occasions to gather at The Top of The Rock Club with the other commanders and their spouses, while our kids were in the care of someone's teenager. This small community would become our family, and other military airmen and their dependents would come, with us offering similar loving welcomes and departures.

When revealing our new assignment to people in the US in the months leading up to our departure, a quizzical raise of the eyebrows and gentle cock of the head signaled their ignorance on the geography of Portugal.

"Isn't that a tiny island in the middle of the Pacific? Whoaaaa, sorry brother!" A soft look of pity had flashed in our friend Paul's eyes before an attempt to redeem his poorly shared insight.

"But hey! I had a friend of a friend whose commander's wife stopped, quite by accident, when their flight landed with some mechanical issue a few years back. She raved about how friendly the locals are!" Paul cooed.

I boned up on the island chain at the library the next day. This volcanic chain of nine islands off the coast of the mother country was home to a mostly agrarian population. The farmers and shop-keepers resided still with limited electricity and financial means. Likening this archipelago to the volcanic chain of the Hawaiian Islands, I would attempt to assuage the curious stares: Our island was the "Lanai" of the Azores, except with 50,000 more people in the same nearly 150-square-mile space! Both islands required only a drive of about twenty miles to get from one end to the other. The future, unknown to us as we landed in Portugal, would allow Nick claim to living two-thirds of his life on islands. Three years at Lajes, then a follow-on of three more on the Hawaiian island of

Oahu. By the age of nine, Nick's life sat nestled on spits of land in the sea. But once we moved to California, two hours into a drive to Las Vegas, he was perplexed.

"Mom!" Nick said, looking up from his Gameboy, straining against his seat belt to peer out the window. "We sure have been driving for a long time. When do we run out of island?!"

An off-cycle move brought housing challenges for any military family, especially on a tiny island with limited housing options where desirable rental homes across the island were occupied. We found one contender, recently renovated, in the nearby village of Fontinas. The lovely, updated three-bedroom stone house was in the tiny town plaza, perched a short walk across from the Catholic church. A lack of central heat and air did not seem a big issue at the time we signed the lease with our twenty-five-year-old land-lord, Carlos—all older homes lacked heat and air, we were told.

"The base provides you with two propane heaters. It is all you will need!" Carlos said in his heavily accented English. "You will find they work well on the colder days!"

After howling winds calmed with the light of day, Ken would scramble out of bed to fire up the heater. This contraption was a hollow, black, three-foot-tall metal housing with a mesh screen in front. The opening in the back allowed the easy insertion of a propane tank. Sitting atop four small skateboard-type wheels, it has a few knobs in front to start it up and regulate the outflow of heat. To be effective in the most frigid cold, R2-D2, as we called it, must be no more than ten feet away from the desired area to warm. Firing up the first heater, Ken would roll it into the bathroom and head back to bed for fifteen minutes, while the thing warmed up the space. Before his shower, he would fire up the second heater and place it in the kitchen and then wheel the first one into our bedroom for my comfort. Later in the morning, I would wheel the one in the bathroom to the living area, right next to the couch.

The wobbly wheel often caught on a floorboard, nearly upending it and shooting the propane tank out the back end. The furniture for most of us stationed at Lajes was on loan from the housing office. This low-quality couch and chair certainly resisted stains. The unintended consequence was the combination of cheap fabric and Scotchguard made this stuff a magnet for flames. One extremely cold January day, the heater set the couch on fire. Luckily, I was *on* the couch when I smelled the acrid fume of burning polyester. Springing up, I grabbed my glass of water and doused the tiny fire just in the nick of time.

Fontinas ranked as the last choice of places for Americans to live; they preferred the town of Praia, closer to the ocean and home to a downtown replete with shopping and cafes. We had a church and one tiny store in our square. Despite a few spouses making their way up the winding one-lane road (so narrow that once, I bashed into the jagged rock wall, scraping off the side mirror of our SUV) to our home for a quick visit, I was lonely. My next-door neighbor, though kind, gracious, and generous, spoke zero English and I knew only how to say hello and goodbye in Portuguese. "Ola! Bom Dia! Adeus, Amiga!" *If* I braved the weather to venture to her house for some smiling and nodding, January had winds peaking at 40 mph, making the short walk slightly dangerous. If Nick and I arrived unscathed, we stayed only a moment due to not only the lack of conversation but because her house was dark and freezing in her quest to save resources. I suspect they couldn't afford their own R2-D2. Bleak skies and daily rain coupled with spotty electricity and a chilly, musty house offered me little to do in those early months. Nick had the cows out back, whom he unilaterally named Friend Moo-Cow, for his playmates when the winds calmed down. We reached out to engage with base life and on weekends toured the soggy island. I was ready for the move to the American community on base when an offer of a duplex with an ocean view became available in April.

Our half of the thirty-year-old duplex, indistinguishable among the other houses and nondescript duplexes in the "on-base" housing, hunkered mid-center of the enclave right outside the base security gate. Two streets of bland beige units, with an occasional cul-de-sac, dead-ended into the Lajes commander's home at our street's terminus. Children rode bikes, families gathered, and gossip spread like a tsunami rolling into shore in our tight-knit community.

We were hungry for people after three years in apartment living followed by the isolation of Fontinas. Nick rarely lacked for playmates. There were frequent informal gatherings, celebrations, Pampered Chef parties, and friendly pleasantries in passing. Porch parties in the summer were a highlight. After hearing the hype all winter long about how fun they were, I didn't want to miss the first of the season's porch parties and planned on kid-free time to enjoy. I wanted to usher in the brief summer after the funk of a long winter, just sitting on a porch, free from chasing after my three-and-a-half-year-old child in a dark and cold neighborhood.

Gathering a bottle of Dao Grasco wine and two canvas Little League chairs, we put Nick to bed and trekked two doors down. Rather than reveal to my son that we would be leaving the house to gather with friends for drinks and conversation, I made do with a sketchy plan of pretending we were downstairs. I would skulk back home to check up on Nick every fifteen minutes or so. The third check-in was about thirty minutes from the last look. Nick didn't like to be left alone, still he doesn't to this day. He loves people and being included! But with him, the porch party would not have happened for me in the sense of sitting, chatting, and sipping wine.

I quietly pushed open the front door, which I had left slightly ajar, to the sound of Nick howling. The cracked walls echoed the soul-curdling anguish of my child in panic. I bolted from the threshold of the front door and up the stairs to our bedroom, where I had put Nick down to sleep with a read from *Jamberry* and a kiss. The door was wide open, bedroom lights ablaze. His tear-soaked face and rigid arms fisted alongside his playful choo-choo-train pajamas told of his torment. Scooping him and his pain into my arms, I held on tight, shushing his fear. Three or four long minutes later, he told his story.

"Ma-Ma-Mommy!" He struggled to get the words out through his hiccups. "I looked everywhere for you...and you *weren't here!*" Where were you?!" he implored.

"Oh, Nick, I am so, so sorry. Daddy and I were just next door at the porch party. I have been checking on you every few minutes," I fibbed, twisting the facts to ease this new distrust of me.

"No, Mommy, I looked downstairs and I even opened the front door and you were *not* next door. I looked all over the house! You left me!" he spat through quieting hiccups.

"I am so sorry baby, I would never just leave you. I would never leave you alone!"

"Stay, Mommy. Don't you leave!" Sobs gone, anger was moving in.

I quickly changed into shorts and a T-shirt and burrowed under the covers with my little boy. I held him close, the smell of his freshly washed blond hair a balm to my shame. This little blip should have been a "shush-shush, you are fine," and back I go to the gathering. Should have been...but this moment struck me hard. This event for Nick is one of his first solid memories. A few hours before, my child had never really known fear. A few hours earlier, his world was safely patrolled by a "perfect" mother. Scary moments are unavoidable and after a brief shock, not a big deal for most kids. The next morning, we woke up, joyfully, and just moved on with our regular routine.

But still, I couldn't help stewing on Bobby, who had been gone for only a few years then. Bobby's entire little life must have consisted of parental mistakes. That type of mistake we get to hide from everyone in our inner circle, the type of mistake that Nick is now sharing with me, must have rattled Bobby to the point where he felt abandoned and unsafe. For years, probably until writing this book, I believed it was possible to achieve perfect, protective parenting. Because that is what I thought about Bill. I blamed his death initially on the "crazy ex-wife." At the time, I thought I set up this scenario for Nick to learn that people he trusted would let him down, cause him fear and distress, and that was a tough lesson to swallow. Had Bill let Bobby down so often that it led to a truly epic fail for them both?

I get it, any judgment someone might make for this obsessiveness where tragic possibilities always lurked just behind my common sense. But I was driven by a steadfast declaration: "I will parent my kids differently..." Differently than Bill and his ex-wife. And differently from the ubiquitous parental mismanagement during my own upbringing. I was a latchkey kid because my folks worked full-time careers with odd hours. I literally wore my house key on a string around my neck. My younger siblings and I took turns as keeper of the key. Once, when it was my day, I lost it at school recess. Getting locked out was not uncommon so we knew what to do. My brother created a human escalator with his clasped fingers, where I would place one of my dirty tennis shoes in his little hand hammock. He would hoist me up, up, up until I could open the window and crawl through to unlock the door. I waffled between feelings of bravery and isolation in the independence thrust upon me. Growing up as the youngest child, my common fears were never resolved, only blown off by exhausted parents. Once, while the folks were working, I followed a crawdad into the storm drain near our house—and got stuck. Now, I wonder, is that why I experience claustrophobia in rooms with no windows? Like the constant swirl of Texas dirt, which came to settle on my bike tires and bare feet, so did squirmy fears come to settle in my soul.

Despite the inevitable negatives, the overarching Texas imprint left strength and grit for the bedrock upon which my life rests. The sturdy foundation layered year upon year through many trips with extended family in Minnesota and camping trips to Galveston; Easter dresses pressed and new every year, worn to church after hunting for Easter eggs in the yard and baskets hidden in the house; nightly, delicious homecooked meals around the dinner table; and a constant carefree spirit passed down from my father are all qualities I intentionally included in Nick's own foundation. Still, splattering into all the goodness, tainting my roots with a permanent sludge, was that ever-present and unmanaged fear and loneliness from managing my struggles alone. Mismanagement and overcompensation in raising Nick flittered in through word and action that *my* kid won't ever feel...alone, scared, unwanted, or stupid.

So, instead of hiding under cover, I see in hindsight the option to yank him out of that scary moment. Walking him over with me to finish the porch party, to see our friends next door, could have unmasked the fear and kept intact his safe construct of a trusting world. Nick is standing by, chomping at the proverbial bit to chime in—here is his input:,

——————————— **Nick's Perspective** ———————————

*All I really remember is that I woke up and I think I went into y'all's room and you were not there. I looked all around the house for you or Dad. And then—I freaked out. I don't totally remember; it was more a sense of fear. I remember how I felt—terrified. That is what sticks with me. I remember you coming home at some point and staying with me.*

# Chapter 3

# Crazy Mama

*T*he first notable event that called out my unconditional devotion to my child occurred when Nick flunked out of ski school. The inception for this first life expungement occurred at The Top of The Rock Club three months after our Lajes arrival. An offer to travel together to Austria came from our still-good friends, Jason and Mary Hunt. Mary had done a great job as the boss's spouse organizing our welcoming committee. Jason and Ken, as colonel and subordinate, hit it off almost immediately.

"We go every year, when we can, to Austria to ski! You should join us!" Mary said, as we sat watching our spouses play a game of Crud. Crud is a form of pool, with no cue sticks, only hands and bodies, where a pair of teams of two bash into each other to avoid allowing the cue ball to be launched into the hole to score a point. The rules are sketchy to me now, and really don't matter, but it is not unlike the rugby of pool, where someone always winds up on the ground and lots of drinking is involved.

We barely knew Jason and Mary, yet in a short week came to view them as friends. What was I to say? "We would love to go!"

The Hunt family with their two children and Nick, Ken, and I claimed seats on the rotator in early March. Renting a minivan at

Aviano Air Force Base Terminal, we made our way to Austria with this seasoned family of travelers.

I had skied in France, having traveled to Europe a few times prior to living in Portugal. With Nick in tow now, considerations for his well-being conflicted with the carefree selfishness known only to those traveling without children. I was still selfish, possessive of "my time" after thirty-five years in pursuit of my habitual predilections. I wanted to ski the way I wanted to ski on the slopes of my choice. Nick, at just three and almost a half, was technically permitted for inclusion into ski school at Obergurgl Ski Resort. It was a fine ski school, and perfect to guide a young first-time skier into the basics. This would be a great place to drop off my child. With all the ropes, carpets, and state-of-the-art instruction on the frozen white element, we were satisfied he was in good hands and would learn to ski. We promptly checked him into the Skischule one day after we arrived.

Dozens of exuberant children milled about the flat expanse that was the Skischule section of the resort. Jason and Mary's children were in a higher-level class for elementary-age skiers, and would be skiing the mountain with their group. We lingered on the mushy snow along the fringe for a half hour until Nick was settled and engaged, then skied off to a bluebird day and excellent conditions.

Day two of Skischule drop-off presented a reluctant and clinging Nick. This was familiar. A reluctant Nick at drop-off to the Kids Klub at my health club, at Ikea kids care, or the church nursery was normal. Drop-off at the daycare on the military base while I attempted to reenter the work force full-time resulted in a stiff-bodied, screaming Nick, who refused to return. At thirty-five, the age I gave birth to Nick, my established patterns of alone time jibed poorly with his very shy nature. He thrived on intense amounts of interaction but was reticent to pursue attachments with those who didn't interest him or were unfamiliar. There was enough selfish single in me to say, "I am not going to miss a day of skiing because of his fear." We fake-laughed and smiled as we plucked him off our legs and left him at the *schule*.

We skied the entirety of the mountain until, with exhilaration at the finale of another day on the slopes, we roared off the slopes and into the fray of the adjourning ski classes. Ken maneuvered on skies to collect Nick from his group. The sky was blue, the air perfectly crisp, and my child was munching on gross, used-up snow as Ken and a lovely lady on skis were chatting.

"Hey!" I shussed up, spraying snow on the little meeting. "How did it go today?"

"Well, Hilda is telling me that she thinks Nick should not come back to ski school for his last day," Ken almost stammered.

"What? We are all paid up through tomorrow." My gaze darted to the ground. "Nick, please don't eat the dirty snow, sweetie."

"Ma'am...your child, he is not responding to the lessons. It is best he must not return to Kinderschool," Hilda explained in Austrian-accented English.

"But, that is why he is here...to learn to ski. I'm sorry, what is your name?" I can't imagine a ski school that can't teach a child to ski.

"I am called Hilda, Frau Roragen. The class...it is a group class. We work to be certain all the children have a nice day and learn the basics," she explained, with every *w* sounding like a *v*.

"Suz...it's fine. I will stay with Nick tomorrow and you guys can ski," Ken offered, keenly aware of my passion for my signature sport.

"No, it's not fine!" I shouted. "We paid for ski school. This is a great time for Nick to learn to ski and the private classes are all booked up. If he can't learn in Austria, where can he learn?!" I shouted to no one in particular.

"I saw him barreling down the mountain this morning and he can't turn yet!" I continued. Nick had no fear. I had skied one run down the bunny slope with him earlier. He pointed his skies downhill and killed a turn-free run to the bottom, stopping when the ground leveled off. I knew this was good for him, and I knew he only needed more instruction to learn the turns. I know he learns best when instruction moves quickly, and at this slow pace, I am sure his excitement morphed to boredom while waiting for the other students to catch up.

"Hilda, can you just spend more time with him tomorrow?" I asked.

"Ma'am...your son is a poor boy. He will not be able to return."

Crazy made its way through my cells, and out of my mouth.

"*Poor boy?!*" The class was obviously the problem—filled with children who took longer to catch on.

"What are you saying?! My gosh. My son is *not* a poor boy!" Shaking my ski pole at her in agitation threw me off-balance, and like a one-legged table, I toppled over, tumbling on to the tips of Hilda's skis. Shaking my pole at her throughout the fall, my words flowed without pause.

"You ought to be ashamed of yourself. This is an AUSTRIAN SKI SCHOOL for small children. You should not market to three-year-olds who need your attention if you merely exist to babysit!" Digging my accusing pole into the snow I attempted to rise. Plop... back down, the side of my face and helmet smacking Hilda's ski.

"Really! I can't believe this!" I bleated, wiping snow off my goggles.

"Suz, it is not Hilda's fault," Ken interjected.

"Really?!" I squeaked. "You are defending these people?!" My son was getting kicked out of school, and it just didn't compute for me. Writhing around on the ground and two more futile attempts to rise left me spent and surrendered.

In a moment filled with grace, Hilda bent down, took my arm, and guided me back to an upright stance on my skis. Her lovely blue eyes bore into me with kindness.

"I am sorry. We just have so many children." Hilda's accent oozed compassion now. In a show of goodwill, she agreed to allow Ken in the children's area the next day as sort of a butler/ski instructor for Nick. Ken reported back to me later that Nick was distracted and bored with the class, not engaged, as the momentum often wandered from instruction to fiddling with the physical needs of the fifteen children in the class. But a broader and invasive reason existed that contributed to his expulsion from ski school.

Enter the Austrian ski mascot, Bobo Penguin. A large human bedecked in a massive black, white, and yellow fuzzy penguin costume, schussing erratically down the small, frozen white element, darting around among the mostly delighted little children. The anticipation—no—*dread* of the ubiquitous presence at ski school of the feared Bobo presented a scary distraction for Nick. It was Bobo the Penguin, I suspect, with his fits of exuberance and bursts of unexpected play, that most intimidated Nick. We wondered later, if we had requested Bobo remove his giant beaked facade, showing the man underneath to reveal that there was nothing to fear, would Nick have—despite the slow pace of the class—blossomed at ski school? If we unmask fear, will our "Bobo" present as more sanguine than our crazy minds invent, harmless in the real? If we unmask our Bobo, will we often find a friend on the other side of the scary mask?

Still, my mama crazy was winding up.

Another pair of lifelong friends to us and a touchstone in Nick's oscillating youth was Don and Kristie Ohlemacher. They showed up in Lajes halfway into our three-year tour. As a civil engineer, Don was assigned the task of determining the viability of constructing a new wing onto the Family Support Center. The FSC was the central gathering place for indoor trick-or-treating, music lessons, conferences, and local art festivals. Don came equipped to collaborate with Ken and me on options for the build. The collaboration bubbled up from the successful meeting in to an instant connection with he and Kristie over love of food, wine, and winter sports. Though they were a decade younger and without children at that point, our friendship had no choice but to blossom. Nick loved the Ohlemachers, but equally so, he loved their German Shorthaired Pointer named Meagan. Nick's love affair with dogs had begun with Ken's Beagle, Peanut. Nick would put Peanut in an old wagon at Ken's parents' house and pull him along the bumpy grass. Meagan patiently indulged similar play while Nick perched hats on her head, brushed her smooth coat, and chased her around the yard.

My first adventure with Kristie was to Rota, Spain, on a military medevac flight—or "rotator" with one flight a week in each direction—for a mammogram and biopsy. Kristie understood my apprehension and offered to come along for support. The medical appointment lasted a few hours, but the tour of Spain unrolled joyfully over the course of five days. A trip to Sevilla to tour the Moorish Alcazar; to Gonzalez Byas Winery for a sherry tour and tasting; and in another show of teamwork during a near arrest for an illegal turn, we cobbled together rusty Spanish and brainstormed ways to stay out of the gulag. After negotiating with the Policia Nacional through a crack in the window, in the safety of our locked car, we laughed our way through the windy cobblestones to grab some cash at an ATM to pay off the officers. Last stop before heading back to Rota was a trip to Gibraltar. We spent an afternoon hiking the town and playing with the wild urban monkeys. We closed out the evening walking the town hunched over for a full hour with a pee-your-pants, belly-laughing fit that remains a remarkable, top-twenty, hysterically funny moment. Then, there was another ski trip to Austria.

I planned to take Nick on the rotator flight to Baltimore for a stay with his grandparents, while I flew alone on a commercial flight from Baltimore to Munich to meet up with Ken, Don, and Kristie in Innsbruck. They were taking "the spaghetti run" from Lajes to Aviano, which was only a few hours south of our ski destination. Despite having no cell phone and a vague plan to meet outside the train terminal, we easily met up about an hour after my train had arrived from Munich. We drove to Lech, in the Arlberg Region of the Alps, to enjoy record snowfall, amazing food, and unencumbered time away from our responsibilities at Lajes.

The final day, upon checkout at Hotel Bergkristall, an avalanche roared into the nearby town. The Arlbergpass, the only route out of the area and back to Munich for my return flight to Baltimore, was at least a day away from clearing by the army of snowplows parked in town. We returned for one more night in Lech. If the mountain pass had opened early that morning and if the traffic had flowed unfettered, we could've caught our departing flights.

I had spoken to Nick during our ski trip. Each time the conversation was similar.

"Mommy! I miss you! When are you coming back?" He sounded excited.

"I miss you too, Tiger! We are having 'snow' much fun with the Ohlies! But we wish you were here too!" I said.

Each call he implored me further about my return. "*Mommy!* How many days now until you come?" he would ask.

"Two more days, Nick. I will be there when you wake up on Saturday morning. Then we will go to see Grammy in Missouri— together," I said before hearing his stories about playing with Sarah, the Amish girl next door, helping Papa shovel snow, and sledding down the small hill in front of the house.

Each opportunity to fly back to the States was an opportunity for Nick to see my mother, his aunts and uncles, and cousins. I committed to providing family—one of several sturdy pillars— before his birth. He would know his extended family, and the support of those relationships would plant indelible, sturdy roots. He would not know the nagging tug of persistent loneliness, of not belonging. I knew the ache—from moving around attaching and detaching—for four decades. Bobby knew that ache, too. I was always proactive for Nick to be grounded and connected, to know he could approach me with any woe or question and if not me, then his relatives.

With mounds of avalanche snow to relocate off the road, it was afternoon before the snowplows cleared the pass into Innsbruck. We drove like banshees to avoid the avalanche of negative outcomes should I have missed that flight. Ken, Don, and Kristie were anxious as well; their flight would depart a few hours later, and they were counting on its dismal 30 percent on-time record to save them from a night in a hotel. We arrived intact and with my reluctant agreement, they left me and my baggage at the curb of the Innsbruck train station to fend for myself.

Gasping for air after a mad sprint to catch my train, I stood heaving, watching it chug away from me and out of the station platform. Glancing up at the departure board, I saw the next one scheduled for four hours later. I would certainly miss my afternoon flight on United Airlines. Nick would wake up to find me *not* where I said I would be, and a flight change to my mother's the following day would carry a few hefty fees. Trouble can morph from bad to good though. I was in trouble, hoping for transportation back to my son by morning. Dragging my suitcase up the stairs from the platform into the main terminal and out into the chilly day, a possible solution greeted my desperate self. A line of black taxi cabs awaited. Though shocked at my request,

I found one who could take me to Munich for the bargain price of 250 euros.

Relief! I would board my flight home, fulfilling my promise to my son, while avoiding delays and change fees on the second half of this adventure. I soaked up the last hours in Europe, the majestic Alps a backdrop as my ride zoomed free of speed limits down the Autobahn toward Munich International Airport. I jerked my gaze away from the scenery as the cabdriver locked up his brakes, halting the taxi for a line of stalled traffic.

"What is the problem?" I asked slowly, as one does, despite coming off as patronizing with children and people who don't know our language.

"Crash," came his response, thick and heavy with traces of German and years of cigarettes. He squawked a few more guttural words into a radio mounted on his dash, and then silence.

After a restless hour of waiting, unable to endure another minute of this awful abyss, I hopped out of the back of the car. I walked over to the median in time to watch as a medical helicopter ascended in the distance. Assuming traffic would start to flow, I ran back to the cab. Twenty minutes later, the stalled cars and trucks moved forward. I arrived to the airport hours later than planned, grabbed my luggage, and ran to the arrivals and departures to board. Amsterdam—Abu Dhabi—Bangkok—and on down to Baltimore: departed.

With zero travelers at the ticket counter, I pressed into action the three agents, who busied themselves immediately with investigating my alternative departure options. I could wait for the next United flight, and pay no penalty or extra airfare. This would require an overnight in a hotel, and I would not arrive in time to fulfill my promise to my son to be there when he woke up the next morning. Not an option. Buying a ticket on Lufthansa seemed a logical next step, but I was reluctant to use our family credit card for a foolish, expensive purchase, and this "splurge" to leave Germany within the hour rather than wait another eight seemed impulsive. I dug into the back of my wallet for my emergency Chase Visa card. My shiny, silver ace in the hole, dependable helper, had faithfully absorbed my hefty tuition charges for over two years with nary a complaint. Ahhhh, my old friend, pressed into action once again after a ten-year hiatus, would see me through this financial hopscotch just as it had all through my courses at UNLV. I resisted the tears of relief that accompany solutions to harried struggles, when support, both human and inanimate, shoulder the burden for a minute, allowing a moment of peace to recharge and regroup. I collected my luggage and, calmly, made my way to my gate.

A smooth flight, wonderful service, and a tasty meal, all enjoyed in a bulkhead seat, brought the fun back into my adventure. We landed in darkened skies, on time, at New York/LaGuardia, allowing a full hour to connect with my flight to Baltimore, where my father-in-law would pick me up. I trotted up to the departure board. Amarillo—Albuquerque—and on and on it went until Baltimore: cancelled. *WHAT the ever loving WHAT?!* I tracked down a stressed airline representative. LaGuardia was shut down until further notice—no flights in or out due to a winter storm barreling its way to New York—and the airline was looking for alternatives.

Instead of stranded travelers waiting days for the storm to clear, strange solutions erupted all around me, and I was apparently one of the lucky recipients of some late-night airport executive brainstorming. Instead of flying the quick hop to BWI, I and my fellow passengers would be squeezed onto two Greyhound buses to journey ahead of the storm on slick roads the three-plus hours to Baltimore. *Seriously?* Yes! Coming to our rescue, the buses rumbled up to the tarmac outside the jetway and jolted to a stop with angry brakes squealing. These retired Greyhounds were infrequent stand-ins for the new ones rolling smoothly along on their way out West, I intuited. Filing down a set of solid stairs and out the security door into the frigid night, a miasma of toxic smoke fumes choked out any chance of grabbing my first breath of outdoor oxygen since Munich. But, we would make it to BWI in time for my father-in-law to pick me up and in plenty of time for me to catch five hours of sleep. We rolled out of LaGuardia onto the freeway—home free.

Or not. The wheezing bus broke down—twice. The second time, the driver managed to sputter into a rest stop more than halfway to BWI, but only forty-five minutes' distance from where my in-laws lived—and where my son was now sound asleep. The snow, spitting out of the midnight sky, pelted me as I ventured into the tired rest stop in search of food and a map of the surrounding area. The food counters were closed, but I found a pay phone and called my in-laws. It was one o'clock in the morning. My mother-in-law, Gert, picked up on the first ring before handing the phone to my father-in-law, Chuck. After over forty years of traveling to New Jersey from Pennsylvania to visit family, he was overly familiar with my location. He hung up the phone and hurried out the door, on his way to rescue my tired and sorry self. The Greyhounds were still stalled in the parking lot as his Dodge Caravan minivan glided into the lot. The sun was considering peeking up over the gentle hills of Pennsylvania an hour later as we pulled into the driveway. Thank the Lord. I arrived safely. And just in the nick of time.

A hot shower helped melt away some travel stress piled on in the twenty-four hours since departing Austria. Then, I collapsed with heavy relief into bed. Three hours later my sweet child burst into my bedroom. The comforting weight of his four-year-old, pajama-clad body crushed my sleepy form, covering me with kisses and giggles. The exhaustion from my harrowing journey lifted out of my bones, replaced only with the energy of my little boy and the knowledge that all my imperfect, difficult choices had winnowed into a perfect moment. I had indeed followed through in crazy ways on a promise to my son, and now the struggle paled behind a precious memory I hold dear.

"MOMMY!! *You made it!*" he exclaimed, launching in for a big hug. "Let's get up! I want to show you the fort I built for Peanut!"

The Bobo Penguin story and my planes, cabs, and buses debacle illuminates my maiden moments of mama-bear crazy. This maternal fierceness is an ancient instinct. So many years I thought myself passed over as someone who could possess such devotion. But birthed along with my son was this "crazy" which lived now with a singular purpose to protect and defend Nick, with no thought to my own well-being. Other parents have waged all manner of fierce battles for their children—to save them no matter the cost. I recall a story in the news, in 1987, of a mother who shielded her four-year-old daughter with her own body as their Northwest Airlines flight taking off from Detroit hurled back to the runway on takeoff. All on board perished, except Cecilia Cichan, who was found alive beneath her mother's lifeless form. Another dramatic rescue occurred in New Jersey in 2019, when a father sacrificed his own life to save his drowning son. The son was spared. I was pleasantly shocked that imprinted in *my* DNA was the same ability to give my life for someone else.

This new resolute spirit had a life of its own. What had been, for three years, a relentless, quiet devotion crashed into my consciousness with gusto: *The Crazy!* I would come to know it in varying degrees again and again in those early years, in a sharpening of instinct in preparation for larger battles. In a dance between squeezing him tight and letting go, I often erred in squishing him too tight or watching him stumble out of my line of sight.

Simple efforts championing my son, like being certain Nick was treated fairly with a difficult teacher in fifth grade or finding a rental home in the "right" school district, took little to no sacrifice on my part. Greater challenges emerged, rolling in like thunder, as he grew further away from boyhood. God, I later understood, had readied me often for the battle ahead.

Our assignment to Lajes Air Force Base i Portugal came to a close after three years, in 2003. Those three years took us through some milestones both personally and as a nation. Nick started kindergarten at Lajes Elementary school, it was my last year as a thirty-something, 9/11 changed our country while we were living in another one, and Ken served in a combat position in Kuwait and Iraq. Nick arrived to Lajes wearing pull-ups to bed, eating mac and cheesies, and riding a toy train around the house, but he departed as a two-wheel biker/world traveler/rising first-grader whose favorite food was fish with *ojos* (eyes). I hold that season, the close bond forged with my son, and the lifelong friends we met close to my heart.

# Chapter 4

# Aloha—
# Another Island

*S*mooth air on the flight from the mainland US to Oahu coddled us from bumps and jolts. Cocooned in the American Airlines wide body, I reflected on the stark difference from our last PCS. The Pacific Ocean from my vantage point at thirty-two thousand feet appeared placid. Instead of landing in gale-force winds in time for breakfast like three years ago, this PCS we were set to arrive in time for a pau hana (happy hour) mai tai and bask poolside at the Hilton Hawaiian Village before dinner. The Azores shuttle ride in the December driving rain to a lonely one-room unit in base lodging had given our first and accurate glimpse of both the isolation and frigid nature of our new home. In stark contrast on this late-July day in Hawaii, nothing frigid awaited us except a deliciously chilled hotel room.

Descending into Hawaii, excitement mounted. Below us sparkled the azure Pacific, dotted with bobbing boats and cruising cargo ships. We doubled back over Hickam Air Force Base to a gentle landing on its shared runway with Honolulu International Airport (renamed in 2016 as Daniel K. Inouye International Airport). My tense body softened into a serene smile playing at the corners of my mouth. Would the next three years mirror the verdant land sprawling out my tiny airplane window? The abusive Lajes landing was not a foretelling of a similar life. Despite moments of loneliness and the isolation, it was the opposite. The Azores was a season of mostly positive growth, forging lasting friendships, purposeful pursuits, and exploring Europe. Was this serene welcome going to betray us with a harsh existence? I banished that tiny niggle in my gut as we stood, collected our belongings, and joined the tourists and residents (us!) descending the stairs onto the tarmac. Hawaii won me over at that first, fragrant waft of air with its plumeria scent, albeit tinged with a hint of jet fuel.

A welcoming committee of three awaited us in baggage claim, at the bottom of the escalator. They spotted us and waved. Our new sponsor, Joseph, and the couple responsible for this diversion from Germany to the tropics, Ted Patrick and his wife, Tammy, were a welcome sight.

"Aloha! Welcome to Hawaii!" Tammy placed a plumeria lei around my neck then moved over to do the same with Kukui Nut leis for Nick and Ken.

Luggage popped up the chute, spilling onto the rubber conveyer belt. The golf clubs clunked up next, into the oversize-luggage dump zone. Two Smarte Cartes held all the bags, and our small entourage shuffled toward the double sliding doors leading to the parking lot. My hair breezed back as the doors slid open, offering the first of many Hawaiian trade-wind breezes. I instinctively gripped Nick's hand tighter. The humid, tropical air blasted another welcome waft of plumeria and promise of abundance. We felt baptized as *Kama'aina* (locals) already by this sweet, balmy aloha. Traffic was thick as we inched our way onto Nimitz Highway toward downtown Honolulu and the Hilton Hawaiian Village.

It was the tail end of a busy PCS season, and with Ken's Air Force job at Camp Smith rather than Hickam Air Force Base, our chance to secure lodging at the Air Force Inn was zero. Camp Smith is a United States Marine Corps installation but is also home to the headquarters of the US Pacific Command (PACOM), where Ken was assigned a secure office in the building's basement. As an Air Force officer working on a Marine base PCS-ing late in the summer, we rested near the bottom of the housing list. There was truly "no room in the Inn" at Hickam, which forced us into an interim home at a hotel.

I'd chosen the Waikiki Hilton complex, erected at the edge of the tourist zone, out of a few hotel options because it offered a penguin park, shops and restaurants, and three massive ocean-front swimming pools. We stepped out of the Patricks' minivan at the valet station/chaotic passenger drop-off and into a bustling open-air lobby, fronted by massive potted palm trees. Tourists calmly queued up at the busy front desk, heads on swivels at the space that seamlessly transitioned to the main pool before spilling out onto the thrum of people enjoying the Waikiki vibe and sparkly Pacific Ocean. We were not in the Azores anymore, Toto. I couldn't wait to dabble my feet in the ocean.

Isolated on our other island for three years, two out of four seasons forbade outside pursuits, as stiff winds could rip the door off your car or the child out of your grip. But, I had found ways to create a playground in our small two-story duplex in base housing. One of two favorite games was called "Hot Lava!" The object was for Nick to make a circuitous path from the kitchen to the bottom of the stairs without touching the "hot lava" gurgling around the floor. Our other indoor thrill was taking the thin mattress out of the sofa couch and laying it across the staircase. I would scrounge up discarded cardboard boxes—which previously held care packages from our family—to create a makeshift sled for schushing down the mattress slope.

Much relief from the dank winters abounded in the creative indoor time with my son. But I was always hankering for more robust outdoor living. Now, I stood there taking it all in. This was the launch of our tropical lifestyle, here, at a mega resort. The warm sun, the fragrant breeze, and the soothing ukulele sounds piping into my soul served up a Guittard chocolate-cake experience after the harsh, first-island course of Lajes.

There are seasons in life, days and experiences, that rush past us in a blur. We can tend toward being unaware in our taking as normal and expected the myriad inherent gifts existent in near-perfect moments. Only in the absence of these blessings do we realize the best time in our life is over and done, and we are left wishing for another one of those precious times. That was not Nick and I over those six weeks. Not for one minute did I fail to soak up the fact that our home—in a world-class destination hotel in *a tropical paradise,* financed mostly by my husband's job—continued to be our pleasure as the military approved one more week after another in a life-on-pause in paradise.

Stepping onto our balcony at sundown after dinner and showers, we would settle into the metal chairs to watch the nightly tiki torch lighting. Waiting, we sat with feet up on the rail, gazing at the fleeting travelers who would be returning to their homes in Detroit, Des Moines, Dublin, or Tokyo while we remained to carry the torch of an extended luxury so few are ever afforded. Soon, the harmonic bleat of a conch shell ushered in our nightly ritual. A stunning Hawaiian man, bedecked in only a print cloth skirt, ran below us holding high a blazing torch. He would lower the torch down to each tiki, setting it ablaze before racing to the next tiki and so on, then disappear from sight. I came to love the traditional Polynesian ceremony that, for me, marked the closing of the day and lit up with promise the approaching night. This predictable rhythm of the torches—every single night—settled us all with a grounding we lacked in what would become the longest PCS we would ever know. While Nick and I embraced it and flourished within the excitement and fun of our unusual resort life, Ken was moments from losing his mind. He craved resolution and structure, neither of which existed during six weeks of living in downtown Waikiki. We had a real estate agent working hard to find a suitable home for us, who was having no luck, and I couldn't have been more thrilled at the delay.

With normal still somewhere in the future and the first day of first grade still three weeks away, we embraced our freedom and explored the resort and all of Waikiki. I welcomed each day with a solo run along the beach, with its massive resorts fronting the quiet ocean, to the Diamond Head side of Waikiki, near the Honolulu Zoo. The park across the street from the zoo boasted a sprawling, centuries-old banyan tree. Many days, Nick would swing off one of the dangling "roots" and attempt to grab hold of the trampled ground. Turning back from the park I would jog down Kalakaua Avenue, which was slowly coming to life. Stopping at the Moana Surfrider (the terminus of the run portion of my three-mile loop) for a mocha latte at Honolulu Coffee Company was as important a goal as the run itself.

Coffee shops were—and are—our gathering place. I am shocked that now Nick prefers Starbucks! Here is his take on the matter:

*Hey. It is more out of convenience and the fact that I actually like Starbucks. More to the point, Mother, it is because you so kindly allow me use of your Starbucks app until I have children of my own.*

The run to Georgetown for coffee before and after Nick was born defined most of our weekends. The winter DC months often brought inclement weather, prohibiting a run, and offering the opportunity to pile in the car and sample a trendy coffee shop in DC or farther out, in Old Town. For three gloomy-weathered Azorean years, and after many failed attempts to enjoy Portuguese espresso, we purchased a Breville espresso machine and crafted our own lattes. Though a reasonable alternative, our kitchen lacked seating, exciting people, and a thrum of activity. Plus, I rarely crafted a perfect espresso shot, leaving the drinks a far cry from the ones we enjoyed at Misha's or St. Elmo's in Alexandria, Virginia.

The aroma of freshly pulled espresso wafted out the open door of Honolulu Coffee Company, through the hibiscus and palm tree–lined porch, all the way to my starved senses. My Pavlovian response was strong as I bolted up the steps, almost salivating in the welcoming space. The hiss and shush of steaming milk, the clatter-clack of ceramic cups blended with the toasty scent of coffee and yeasty pastries. Screenless windows thrown open to the quiet street invited plumeria smells to mix with the aromas and lively coffee klatches. I queued up, in no hurry at all for my turn to order.

Coffee and pastry secured, I would sit under one of the open windows, or if time was tight, stroll along the porch to the hotel. I would enter the open lobby to meander around for a minute, learning from the exhibits displayed on walls and in cases. Then, hurry out the ocean-facing back doors, as Ken would be ready for work. I'd pass another age-old banyan tree standing guard near the pool as I rushed past the rocking chairs. No time to grab a spot on the lanai and ponder how to make the most of yet another amazing day. My time with Nick beckoning, I would set out with my coffee breakfast and a pastry for him to the Hilton, along the sprawling Waikiki Beach. Honolulu was up and ready too, with early joggers and morning surfers enjoying the new day along with me. With over a mile of thick sandy beach and warm ocean water lapping at my bare feet, the walk sparked a tiny light in my soul. Nick and I still crave the ocean and always yearn for a beach vacation.

This tropical place and the walk back to the Hilton allowed me space to reflect.

The clear demarcation, rather than the typical gentle passage, between the last season and the upcoming one was a poignant leap from a harsh and spectacular three years in Portugal to a deep exhale at the return to our United States. I felt the shift in life seasons physically and emotionally. We would transition from renting to owning our first home together. On the cusp of my fortieth birthday, and the second half of my life, no possibility was off limits to reimagine how the next fifty, God willing, could unfold. Here I was, at a 180-degree pivot point, saying farewell to the past and aloha to my life—volume two. A breathtaking and hopeful aloha standing in the blocks on the sandy starting line, I was eager to run hard and finish this mom race to twelfth-grade strong.

So, coffee cup empty and me ankle deep in the warmth of the encroaching tide, I'd hurry my way back to the Hilton to include my son in a day full of promise and an unfolding season bathed in *Aloha*.

In the middle of our sixth week at the hotel, we at long last closed on our slightly used Hawaiian home. With the moving van summoned and move-in day finally set, Ken was released from the gray abyss of the unknown, just in time to enjoy a final few days as resident tourists staying at a tropical resort. The lifestyle at Hilton Hawaiian Village had burrowed into my heart and indelibly scored my love of Hawaii with a first impression seen through the eyes of a tourist, swiftly becoming a local.

Nick and I waded through some real grief when we relinquished our resort home. The uncomplicated life with the reprieve from the heft and grind of responsibility suited us. But, embracing the drone of daily life—grocery shopping, school plays, church, work, and changing the oil in my car—bore the scent of holiday almost every day. Over our three years in Hawaii, we enjoyed a gradual emergence of becoming local, or Kama'aina. We sank into the "on vacation" vibe with frequent jaunts into Waikiki to play tourist. If it wasn't a Saturday at the beach or zoo (where Nick would later enjoy summer camp), it was an evening adventure to enjoy a nice dinner at the ever-growing number of restaurant options in Waikiki. A just-opened Cheesecake Factory could be counted on for a two-hour wait, leaving us time to browse the shops at The Royal Hawaiian Center. A few times a year, usually for my birthday, we enjoyed Benihana for sushi and teppanyaki. We would always rush outside after our meal to take in the tiki-torch lighting, poolside, at our former home. If we were there on a Friday night, we would stay for drinks, along with (to avoid repetition) the weekly hula show and fireworks display.

We absorbed many local customs. *Slippahs* became our usual choice of footwear, and Hawaiian tradition insists people remove their footwear before entering a residence. We all accumulated quite a slippah collection, piled up at the door from the garage into the kitchen. Nick wore flip-flops everywhere except when playing sports. The only shoes he ever tied were the several pairs of cleats in his shoe arsenal—and Ken and I usually tied these for him. He was well into third grade before he got the hang of tying a shoelace. Both tourist and resident status forever merged together, defining the home of my heart—Hawaii. I wonder if it is the same for Nick, buried inside his subconscious, where it hides even from him yet defines much of who he is. He remembers vignettes of Hawaiian moments, some very vivid. Our first visit to Waimea Bay is a clear memory.

We had limited experience with ocean tides prior to our move. There was a trip to the pink sandy beaches of Bermuda when I was

pregnant with Nick, the Azores North Atlantic inlet in summertime and the brown waters that define the Southern California
Pacific Ocean. Nothing at that point, though, compared to the
currents and waves in Hawaii. On our first visit to Waimea, we
naively allowed a rip current to carry us on our plastic float out
of Waimea Bay, toward the closest dry land, Kauai. We dismissed
a tiny figure on the beach waving his arms and blowing a whistle,
thinking it was for the kids jumping off the nearby rock. Ten
minutes later, a lifeguard paddling out on a surfboard passed all
the swimmers, and kept chugging our way. Still clueless about our
perilous drift, we were a bit shocked when he yelled, "I am here
to rescue you!"

An unappreciative Ken declined the help. The lifeguard told
Ken he could drown but would not be taking his family with him.
He pulled up alongside our ABC convenience store float, barking
orders on how this rescue would occur: Nick in the first position
at the tip of the surfboard, and I was next, followed by "Ron Jon,"
supine on his stomach with his head hovering uncomfortably over
my bikini-clad rear end, paddling his arms like he was ready to
catch a big wave. Ken joined us on the beach a half hour later,
exhausted and irked. We all survived.

## Chapter 5

# Island Fever

*I* *expected the land we purchased in Waipahu to mimic the black volcanic*
residue spewed out of the sea, and still spewing to this day off
the Big Island. But instead, the earth everywhere under our feet
was Hawaiian red dirt. The red stuff stubbornly stuck to our shoes
and bare feet, embedded itself in our clothes, cast a film over our
house, and stained our front porch and driveway a soft shade of
red. The red swirled everywhere on days when dry tropical winds
blew in from the sea. Red soil, I came to understand, is typically
found in hot, humid environments that receive good amounts of
rainfall. In terms of soil classification, most of Hawaii's red soil is
part of an order or group known as *oxisol*. Hawaii is home to ten of
the twelve orders in the soil taxonomy system. Interestingly, oxisol,
always stuck to our cars and now our memories, exists nowhere
else in the United States. Stick with me here—this is interesting.
The beaten-down volcanic rock over time leaves behind this iron-
and aluminum-rich material. Millions of years of continuous
beating snuffed the life out of the once alive volcanic soil, leaving
behind this dead red dirt.

Our house was an easy half mile from Nick's school and more
often than not, we walked to it. Or Nick would ride his Razor

scooter, with me and his dog Maggie following behind. When I rode the scooter back home, it required one hand on the Razor and the other hand looped through Maggie's leash. The sidewalk hosted fragrant plumeria trees all the way home. I recall still the smell of the balmy air, the scooter ka-thunking over the slight cracks in the red-stained sidewalk. On the days I accepted a substitute teaching opportunity at Waikele (that was my new part-time gig) we would drive to school, parking in the teachers' parking lot. The first day of school, we drove up from the Hilton and arrived early. Standing outside as the early morning heated up, we waited for the classroom door to open and the opportunity to meet Nick's first-grade teacher.

Mrs. Kumamoto was her name. Nick and she almost stood eye to eye, and I towered over her diminutive frame. She welcomed us to Waikele and to Hawaii.

"Oh, so nice to meet you," she almost whispered. "I just know Nick and Sean will be best friends! Welcome!" It turns out that Sean was the only other Caucasian boy—*haole* in Hawaiian—in the class, and he was also a military dependent. Later, Sean would come to find Nick a threat to his lone haole status and create scenarios for the other children to ostracize him. At some point in the year, I learned Nick was unhappy and I approached the teacher.

"Welllll...Nick is a smart and likable boy," Mrs. Kumamoto began in her soft voice. "I was sure he and Sean would be fast friends."

Looking up at me from her four-foot-eleven stance she continued. "But we met for several circle times to find out why the children were unkind to Nick."

"You met in a circle? With all the kids in class? To find out why those kids were mean to my child?" My brows knitted together, eyes drawing into mere slits.

"Oh, yes. Circle time!" she beamed as the part in her shiny black hair stared up at me.

I stood straighter to maximize my ten-inch advantage in stature. "That sounds like a scary thing for a first grader. What was the outcome of putting Nick on the spot in your circle time?"

"Well, Sean says all the kids think he is telling stories that aren't true. He tells them stories of skiing in Austria, riding in the cockpit of an Army airplane with propellers, and then the story of Nick taking a GONDOLA in the Venice canals!" Mrs. Kumamoto oozed her own doubt through the retelling of the tribunal results.

"Let me see if I understand," I began slowly. "Nick has been telling these whoppers to all the kids in class. They don't believe him and therefore are mean to him?"

"Yes, I am afraid so. Sean spoke for most of the other children, and he was deeply upset."

"Mrs. Kumamoto. I wish you had let me in on the bullying sooner. Nick has been having anxiety, has not wanted to come to class, and he has been sleepwalking. And the only lie in all of that, Mrs. Kumamoto, is that the plane you mentioned was an AIR FORCE plane, and he didn't spend the entire flight in the cockpit, only a brief five minutes to meet the pilots and lay hands on the instruments.

"Nick does not lie. He is being bullied for BEING HIMSELF and sharing his great experiences and as a result has developed anxiety..." I was beside myself in my empathy for Nick. If I'd had a ski pole, I would have been shaking it at her vehemently.

It is not without merit to point to this rocky transition as cause for a personality shift: from a kid who belonged to a move across the globe to an island where he was different as both a minority and an intelligent child with vast world experiences. Muddying the waters was the bully child who was most similar to him, whom he had sought to befriend—at Mrs. Kumamoto's insistence. Sean held status, as much as one can as a first grader. His throne was threatened, I suspected, in the way that kids seek to be "King of the Hill." Sean apparently led the charge to bully and ostracize Nick.

Mrs. Fukumoto managed the hoopla with the lens of a native Hawaiian insider whose class structure oozed feminine. Her class was nicknamed "The Butterflies" and boys were directed away from physically engaging with each other, thus the circle time to discuss feelings. Nick shunned the spotlight, and just wanted to fit in and have friends. He was now called out as different and would remain so to some extent for all three years at Waikele Elementary.

He found some comfort with his peers in class after I learned of the bullying, but there was a shift in him. The class clown role was there to stay it seemed, as an attempt to endear himself to those who had doubted his remarkable stories. In third grade, he and Sean had found a sort of friendship and bonded over a trip to the principal for carving their names in desks during class. Acting out was better than not fitting in?

If Nick chose to share and embrace his remarkable talent, experiences, and true personality he could have suffered retribution from his peers. Choosing to dismiss the best part of himself and diminish his talents brought, if not acceptance, a tacit agreement to coexistence in their circles. Shaped emotionally and neurologically in our youth through a barrage of external forces, we have a choice during the struggle: to roar and proclaim who we are, or to silence our voice and actions and become less than what God intended. Given a chance to intervene and mentor my son early on that year might have helped avoid laying down some permanent and negative patterns.

Nick found, instead, acceptance with the older boys in the neighborhood. These boys' lack of wisdom and freedom to roam the neighborhood exceeded their years. Melvin and Gabriel, from fifth grade, were headed down a path toward rebellion, their names foreshadowed on blank ledgers at the nearby juvenile detention center. Eager for Nick to find a tribe, I accepted these new playmates with reluctance and a watchful eye while encouraging friendship with the private school student down the street, whose mother taught at an elite academy. A smart, sweet kid Nick's age who gravitated toward Legos and Yu-Gi-Oh! cards, Nick found him lacking in personality. He was not *fun*. Given that Nick's placement in local competitive Junior Golf, Taekwondo, and all Little League sports occupied much of his free time, firm bonds with Melvin and Gabriel and the brainy kid down the block sputtered out before our next PCS rolled around.

But, a few early patterns developed in this three years of first-time jockeying for a position within a peer group. First, fun ruled high as a priority and the fringe crowd won out over the boredom felt with high-achieving children. Next, in school, Nick began to dumb himself down rather than stand out as a smart kid or the cultured kid whose life experiences were more complex than the average kid.

Later, in middle school, Shaw Air Force Base offered tours through many of the Air Force planes. One was a C-130, an aircraft we enjoyed catching a flight on several times. The perk of being a military family—to grab available seats on any variety of aircraft designed to carry passengers—continued beyond Portugal, and Nick mentioned to his skeptical friend, John, that he had ridden in the cockpit on the C-130.

"Funny, Nick!" John responded.

"I did. The pilot invited me into the cockpit during the flight!"

"You are a liar! No way."

I stepped in and told John that we had flown on this plane, and Nick was in the cockpit. John fell silent but the interaction left me wondering how often Nick's incredible stories sounded like tall tales. I suspected he just stopped contributing, and that any special talents or knowledge he held remained unshared to avoid being different or ridiculed as the oddball new kid.

His third-grade teacher, Mrs. Kelly, told me in passing one day on campus that Nick was falling asleep in class. When his first report card arrived a few months into the school year, I grew concerned. His usual A's and B's turned into B's and C's, and a comment we had seen before popped up again: *Nick lacks self-control and does not pay attention in class.*

Mrs. Kelly welcomed parent volunteers to assist in her classroom; I had been in once or twice. Motivated to find out what was going on, I took more sub teaching jobs at school and signed up as a parent volunteer a few days a week. I saw that Nick had been moved to the last row in the class. The children in the front rows needed more help and garnered much of Mrs. Kelly's attention. Finally, she had a whisper-soft voice that reached to the middle row of seats. I couldn't hear her from my spot in the back of the room.

We made some efforts to transfer Nick to another class—perhaps with a more effective teacher. Then we fought to move his assigned seat from the back of the room to the front and talked to him about ways he could manage himself for success in the classroom. Halfway through the year, with the decline in performance accelerating, I investigated options to homeschool Nick. Given we were five months away from moving out of state, and with a few efforts promised by Mrs. Kelly, I decided to stay the course with the addition of dedicated tutoring by me and Ken at home. My sub position with the Hawaii Board of Education offered a myriad of school choices. But now, I would take job offerings only at Waikele, where ample opportunities abounded to intervene whenever possible in Nick's classroom. The hands-off approach was forever never to be trusted. Hands-on provided what my child needed to stay on course.

Lastly, I needed refreshing of my parenting skills, which had gone by the wayside with my own pursuits in Hawaii. Off to Barnes and Noble to hunt down the Gary Ezzo Wise series of books that I began when Nick was born. I snatched up Ezzo's next in the series, *On Becoming Pre-Teen Wise*. Row after row of self-help books were jammed back-to-back, offering stuck parents a plethora of answers to unfathomable questions which they didn't know to ask. I picked up Deepak Chopra's *Seven Spiritual Laws for Parents* and one aisle over, *The Seven Habits of Highly Effective People*, because this parenting thing to which I had dedicated this season of life was waning ineffective.

———————————————— **Nick's Perspective** ————————————————

*Here is the clearest thing I remember about Waikele: The church was in the cafeteria, where we would go on Sundays. Also, there was a tetherball on the playground—I loved that game and learned how to play at Waikele. Sadly, I don't remember anything about Ms. Fukumoto or Mrs. Kelly. The only teacher I recall was our Hawaiian Culture teacher, who taught us to speak Hawaiian. My mom mentioned she played the ukulele and we sang, but I only recall leaving our usual classroom to join her for lessons. We were taught how to say* humuhumunukunukuapua`a, *the name of the state fish. Outside of school, my memories are more clear. I regularly went to tae kwon do practice, earning my various belts. We spent a lot of time, in my recollection, at the local Sports Authority, and getting a shave ice after purchasing a new pair of cleats or some baseball equipment. I recall our open field across from our house and hitting a golf ball into a neighbor's window. Dad made me go over and apologize, and then I had to pay for the window. I had some really bad friends in the neighborhood; they encouraged me to hit the ball—said I couldn't hit that far! Melvin was older and knew how to take advantage of me, I guess. He had a Yu-Gi-Oh! card and managed to sell it to me for $100. I had some money from* *one of our garage sales saved in my piggy bank and gave it all to Melvin. When Dad found out he marched me over to Melvin's house to get my money back... I don't remember if he dropped the price, or if I gave the card back. Sorry Mom, we should have lived in all these fun places when I could remember more. But apparently, as I am told, I am a product of all the places I have lived and things I have done regardless of any clear recollection. Once again, I missed out, in a sense, on all the best places and experiences over my life. These early years which we can't recall shape us into who we are now. I think it must have mostly went great, because look at me now!*

In February, more than two years into our stay, accumulated red Hawaiian dirt had coated my running shoes and white picket fence. Millions of years prior to my run-in with the messy red gunk, tropical rains and winds beat the life out of the Pacific Ocean's spewed-up lava rock, pulverizing it into red dirt. There was a weather front I coined "The 90 Days of Rain" beating the life out of me and my house, slathering red up the roots of my hibiscus hedges and slippah-shod feet. We in Hawaii were not immune to nature; in fact, being outdoors in nature shapes daily activity in Hawaii, more so than most places on Earth.

But that February, the rains soaked us longer and harder than usual, nonstop for three weeks. News reports were already announcing flooding rivers and sewers bursting, spilling sludge into the ocean. Weather forecasters droned on about the atmospheric pressures, weak jet streams, and odd La Niña patterns creating the chaos. For locals in Hawaii accustomed to passing showers persisting for about ten minutes at a time, this incessant torrent was brutal. Our technically dead red dirt could only absorb small amounts of moisture before becoming saturated. Unable to hold another drop, water slid off the surface of this compacted clay. The constant flow of red-dirt water combined with the polluted waters pouring off chemical-laden golf courses and lawns.

This sludge joined forces with streams and rivers to eventually belch and heave the toxic roiling soup out into the ocean. Once Caribbean blue, the Hawaiian waters became a murky brown mess. For two straight months many beaches posted warnings of contaminated waters. Waikiki, a gathering spot for tourists and locals, was off-limits to all but the murk-loving sharks. As I was a scuba-dive-master-in-training, few spots on Oahu remained safe to explore with tourists who had long ago plunked down their hard-earned cash on a vacation in this most unfortunate two-month weather anomaly infiltrating the islands. But they came, and we found places to dive.

Mid-February, mid–scuba dive I grew light-headed. I struggled to breathe. I was leading four divers around a shallow reef, farther out to sea than usual, where the better visibility allowed for decent viewing of sea life. Motioning for the divemaster leading another team of four about twenty feet away to take my group, I deposited them and clumsily made my way to the safety line. Breathing rapidly sucks up the air in the tank, and in my hurry to not pass out underwater and find the line, I was running low on air. The dive boat was not in sight. Blinking hard to stay calm, heart racing, I found the coordinates on my dive watch. My legs pumping my swim fins harder than you should for five minutes, finally the shadow of the boat above was visible, and I knew the safety line was right below it. A year prior, my regulator responsible for the air coming into my mouthpiece from the air tank jammed, leaving me exchanging air with the divemaster while we worked our way up mandatory safety stops on the rope suspended from our dive boat. But I never panicked. I felt good and strong and handled the emergency well. This dive emergency was different and I was still woozy. My heart settled down enough for me to grab the line and inch my way up through a brief decompression ascent, necessary to avoid something called the bends.

Once safely out of the water on the dive boat, my vertigo abated, leaving only humiliation in its wake. I had panicked and dumped my dive group to scurry to safety. I had been diving for two years. I loved everything about the sport, short of when choppy seas left me nauseated. I found a tranquility beneath the surface of the ocean. But this panic episode would be the second-to-last dive I would ever experience.

Five weeks into the freakish deluge of rain and the dark clouds covering the sun, I woke up on a Monday to find my face was numb. I couldn't feel anything from my forehead to my neck on the left side. Or my arm. I panicked. It was like I was underwater fighting for air and trying to find my way to the surface and safety all over again.

Ken had already peddled off in the rain, training for another triathlon. Training did not stop when the weather refused to cooperate, so I was left to deal with the fright. Getting out of bed, I was overcome with vertigo, a massive headache, and nausea. After the diving incident, I made the rounds to various doctors, with no conclusive results. Twice, I was sent home from Tripler Army Medical Center, with a diagnosis of anxiety and depression and scripts to manage "island fever." I didn't buy that that was the problem. I had been living on islands for over five years. Could island fever be a legitimate affliction? I did consider that some psychological issue was possible. I managed to get the day going, then drop Nick off to school before picking up Ken at work and driving to Queens Medical Center, hoping for conclusive answers from a civilian hospital. None were forthcoming; all results were normal.

The remainder of The 90 Days I spent undergoing a battery of tests. Life slid to a halt. The treks to Tripler yielded two emerging health issues that I deal with still to this day. A kind, yet baffled,

Army doctor ordered a round of scans when test after inconclusive test returned no abnormalities. Then he called with news.

"Ma'am? This is Dr. Scary (my name for him—I don't remember his real name) from Tripler. I have the results of your brain scan," he said.

"Oh...thank you for calling so soon." My softened voice warbled into the phone.

Clearing his throat he continued. "You have a series of white calcifications in your brain."

He had my complete attention.

"While white spots can be found on more than half of all brain scans, it is the placement of yours that brings concern."

"Am I okay?!" I barked, holding back my complete fright with a quest for facts.

"You are now, we believe. There will be no need now for intervention, but I advise repeating the scan in three years, sooner if you develop symptoms."

"What symptoms?"

"Well, the calcifications we see on your scan are consistent with those found on the MRIs of MS patients."

*Crap...what the crap is he saying? I have MS?* Truly frightened, I let out the breath I had been holding.

"Are you saying I have the beginning stages of Multiple Sclerosis?"

"We don't know. This is a tough disease to diagnose on a scan early on. Your clinical exam showed no tell-tale signs of disease. That's the good news."

Relaxing only slightly that I was not going to need a wheelchair anytime soon I asked, "What is the bad news?"

"Not bad, per say...we don't know what the white spots are telling us—yet. Just repeat the brain scans every three years, and watch for clinical symptoms of tripping, dropping things, and dizzy spells. That type of thing." Dr. Really Scary said.

We wrapped up the call and I was left still not knowing what was wrong with me. The symptoms that brought me to Tripler had no link to these accidental findings. Why had my body suddenly crashed and gone numb, left me lethargic and twenty pounds thinner?

Health bomb number two was leveled after the additional tests brought me to the darkened office off of the cardiac ultra-sound room.

The ultrasound an hour prior to the consultation with the cardiologist went on and on; the darkened room's effort to lull my anxiety only caused panic, even though the technician had been patient.

Lying on my back on the exam table, I heard my heart, "Whish, schwa, whish, schwa." After the chaos of dealing with Nick's rocky start in Hawaii, I guess I was happy to hear my heart still beating strong.

"Flip on your side," said the tech. "Now lie on your back again."

"Whoosh, whoosh slosh, whoosh, slosh, slosh," my heart said then.

Dr. Love (I can't recall his name either) did not mince words in his office post-echocardiogram.

"You have a slight aortic regurgitation." He shuffled through some papers and then looked briefly in my direction.

"Have you had Rheumatic Fever?"

"What?? And no, never," I responded.

I was told that my aortic heart valve leaked, causing a whoosh of blood to reverse back into the heart. At the time, the leak was small. Should the leak progress, as they usually do, the heart would enlarge and be cause for concern. I would need to monitor this defect yearly and if it worsened, as they expected it would in ten years, they would saw my chest open and still my heart while the valve that had served me well since birth and ultimately failed to last a lifetime was replaced with a prosthetic valve. Lovely.

The doctor rushed me out of the office, suggesting I not worry about it, just avoid lifting anything more than forty pounds and keep my blood pressure and weight down! Staying trim was clearly not a problem as I was topping the scales at 110 pounds. The other two would be difficult. Typically, this heart valve defect in younger adults is from a childhood case of rheumatic fever, which I gleaned from the doctor's query. Until this past year, the medical community and I had no idea what had caused the valve to weaken.

The cause crystallized during Covid when I instantly understood the term *long hauler* in reference to people whose hearts and other organs were weakened after a nasty bout of Covid. I had experienced the coronavirus SARS, Severe Acute Respiratory Syndrome in 2003, but at the time thought it was a severe flu episode.

The rains moved on after ninety days, and the sun came out. Though I had stabilized, I still felt off, and wanted to focus on getting back my health. Nick and Ken, as player and coach, bonded over hours of golf, sports, and Boy Scouts. My calendar opened up after declining all sub teaching options and scuba diving trips, making space to pursue alternative therapies. Traditional doctors were clear that my heart valve and abnormal brain (ha!) were not to blame for losing my good health. I sought out energy healers, massage therapists, and naturopathic doctors. With Ken's full support I enrolled in a week-long retreat at The Chopra Center near San Diego, California. It was there I learned of Ayurveda, a fundamental natural wellness system that dates back thousands of years in India. With physical tools such as yoga and meditation I learned about managing stress before it manages you. Ayurvedic physicians and healers use a *dosha* test to help identify, customize, and prescribe lifestyle changes and remedies that will balance your body, prevent disease, and preserve health. Traditional medicine with its "wait until you are really bad" approach was really no approach at all. I was open to do doing something else—an about-face toward a new philosophy; I was desperate and open to alternatives.

We were given a simple test and guided to understand with a counselor the results of the test and how to achieve wellness by following prescribed lifestyle choices that support your dosha. Most people are a combination of one of the three doshas: pitta, vata, or kapha. Vata people, when unbalanced, are flighty and ungrounded. Pitta is fire (my husband is pitta), and they tend to be dominant and explosive leaders full of "piss and vinegar." Kapha trend physically toward sluggish, heavy bodies but are grounded and calm individuals. My results concluded I am the "wind" category, or vata type. Vata people are usually thin and prone to stress and anxiety, in need of perpetual movement. A diet of non-spicy foods and plenty of time grounding emotionally and physically in nature are the path to wellness. Adherence to this ancient medicinal structure leads to a balanced life. I had been living on stress, fun, and hamburgers and shakes from Teddy's Burgers, so it was no wonder my body crashed. The Ayurveda systems are a prescription designed to prevent rather than fix bodily issues, all tooled around your dosha.

Continually seeking insight into our guiding motivators, and understanding our innate personality offers less confusion and stumbles throughout life. I administered the dosha test to Nick and received shocking results. Though he scored as having a small percentage of vata, his dominant quality is the fiery pitta. This didn't compute. He is fun, easygoing, and playful. He loves games and adventure, not throwing himself into the fire to prove a point, or at least this was his personality growing up. If I bought into this very accurate and ancient health practice, this clue would explain to some extent how my sweet boy could morph from a calm child into a Pitta teen beast. It was a few years later, on another personality test, that I garnered the *key* motivator for Nick, a guiding force in stacking up errors toward his final meltdown. Nick literally comes from the country of Fun.

Ken and I discovered his new "nationality" at a marriage workshop we attended while living in Virginia. For three nights we braved Beltway rush hour traffic to the suburbs for the clinic called, "Laugh your way to a better marriage." Mark Gungor created a marriage course on the premise couples could laugh and have fun while resolving tough issues in their marriage. Sitting the first night in church pews with about one hundred other couples, tests were handed out to gauge our communication style—and determine to what "country" we belonged. Like the Myers-Briggs personality test from Katherine Cook Briggs and Isabel Myers, Gungor teaches that better communication and personal insight occur through understanding yourself and your mate. The Myers-Briggs classification tool helps you know how you process life, based on a combination of characteristics, and so does Gungor's. The Flag Pole is the guiding tool to identify what country you are from, and this leads to understanding what makes a person tick.

So lean in—I'll explain what Mr. Gungor posits. People are like countries. And each country has a specific language where only the citizens understand the colloquial words, customs, and attitudes. The countries to which one can belong are these: Control Country, Perfect Country, Peace Country, and Fun Country. Just as your dosha constitution and Myers-Briggs type are a combination of traits, most of us are also a combination of one or more countries. Though, similar to how our family roots often originate from many lands, we opt to identify closely with only one country of origin. Nick, hailing from the land of Fun with a sprinkle of Control, operates in a combo shared with the most successful people in the world. Mark Twain's Tom Sawyer, had he taken Gungor's test, would have had the same results as Nick, I feel sure. Tom was fun! He loved pranks and manipulated his peers to do his bidding, for his greater good. Shortcut, easy-way-out Nick, with a keen mind for a workaround to minimize effort and maximize conviviality, is Fun Country with a splash of control always driving his choices. I tested as from the country of Fun too. I was lucky that Perfect Ken swooped in with consistency, diligence, and routine to pick up where my lack began. For Nick, the innate sense of craving fun, shaped at birth, exploded with gusto into the teenage years. For over three years, Mr. Fun made some of his worst decisions. Hopping his borders, he consorted with people, in and around campus, from all sorts of struggling countries.

I was sidetracked during The Ninety Days of Rain by whatever health issue I had taking me away from the joy of parenting Nick. I wonder if our close bond suffered during that dark year of healing. I downshifted into selfishness again. His vibrant healthy mom disappeared for six months, both physically and mentally, and in the midst was a PCS back to the Mainland.

This bittersweet decision by the Air Force reached Ken's inbox in the midst of The Ninety Days of Rain. Our next assignment was mainland USA, Santa Monica, California, for a one-year fellowship at The RAND Corporation. Since that move from paradise in 2007, my yearn to return to Hawaii for vacation left me perplexed at my previous *anticipation* to leave Hawaii. Logically, I could conclude I anticipated change—change from the poor education for my son, my island fever, and finally the issues with my well-being brought on by the abusive deluge of rain. All this pushed forward the anticipation to bid a final *Aloha* to Hawaii. But the saying "Wherever you go, there you are" proved an incessant shifty stalker, peering in my windows and harassing my soul. What you escape, if unmanaged, will follow and fester to resurface at some other time. The last few months as we prepared to sell our home and relocate, and I worked to reclaim my good health, the sun came out. Hawaii wasn't the bad guy all along. I was my own bad guy. All the things we loved to do, and there were many, found an honored spot on our one-last-time checklist. An April trip to Maui and the Big Island were checked off. Rounding out the list of favorite farewell places, on the Island of Oahu, were Waimea Bay on The North Shore and of course, Waikiki. Waimea is famous for massive winter waves the size of small buildings, luring professional surfers from around the world to compete at not just Waimea, but in many choice winter spots on The North Shore. Summer was the chance for everyone who didn't surf to frolic in the placid, clear water. Summertime on Oahu, we would wake at sunup and pack our chairs, beach bags, and lunch to arrive early enough to secure a parking spot in the one tiny lot afforded to Waimea Bay Beach Park.

Speeding our way north, windows cranked down, allowed us to inhale the aloha fragrance blanketing Kamehameha Highway on a miles-long stretch of red-dirt pineapple fields. Three quarters of the way up from Waikele we would stop in the historic former plantation town of Hale'iwa. The last mile heading into it, peeking over the last rise before the ocean, the earth gave way to salty humid air, heavy with tropical dew. It was here, in this tiny historic town which still exuded a quiet stillness in 2006, where our quotidian selves transformed into vacationers. We teleported like Spock and Kirk from stressed locals into instant tourists for the day. Hale'iwa claims its Western settlement roots from the late 1800s with Hawaii's first destination hotel resort called Hale'iwa. Hale'iwa Joe's Seafood Grill occupied the real estate where the defunct hotel once stood. I pause to wonder if the boom in Waikiki brought fewer overnight tourists up North.

Still today, Turtle Bay is the only mega resort that calls the North Shore home.

Winding our way farther north on Kam Highway after breakfast, the attempt to nab an open parking spot began. If we didn't luck out after a few spins around the lot, we could park on Kam Highway and hump our gear a half mile to the beach. Wherever we parked, toting our load from the car and over the fifty-yard gauntlet of lava-hot summer sand to claim our beach real estate was mandatory. Often, we chose our spot for the day in the quiet alcove by the spitting cave of Waimea Beach. Finally, our lives on hold, we could recline in mesh beach chairs under the bright sun in the heat of another lovely Sunday morning in paradise. In summer, we spent hours in the placid clear waters, diving off the lowest point of Jumping Rock, snorkeling and playing in the gentle surf.

We could ride the crest of a small wave into the hollowed-out lava cave, then stand up in the brief reveals of shallow water before riding another wave back out. In winter, staying far away from the unpredictable giant swells to watch the talented surfers, our spot would be farther back, with only an occasional dabble in the pools of water left behind from fierce waves that dared to come closer into shore the night before. Winter or summer, we were always satiated from the salt air and sunshine, and always a bit sad come departure time. We would rinse off in the freezing outdoor shower, changing into dry clothing before packing up the car—quickly—to clear the way for one of the ten to fifteen circling cars waiting for our spot. Then on to Matsumoto for shave ice before heading home.

Our one last time as residents, in June of 2006, we moved more slowly, savoring each arduous step in the breakdown of our beach camp. Shake the towels, fold the chairs, pack the beach bag with half-empty sunscreen and still-sandy towels, shimmy slippahs on our feet, walk the gauntlet, shower, change, pack up the car, blast the air conditioning, and pull out to head back home. I shed a few tears that final time as we inched our way out of the Waimea Bay parking lot. We wound our way down the Kam to one last shave ice at Matsumoto, and one last picture at the colorful sign announcing the city of Hale'iwa. In that photo, Nick is flashing the typical Bangha shaka symbol: pinkies and thumbs extended, middle fingers tucked in flashing both knuckles, wrists crossed, squatting low with his tongue out. A classic Nick pose and fitting farewell photo.

Then, another one-last to Waikiki where we brought an inner tube to our favorite sandbar. When low tide pulls the used-up Waikiki Beach waters out to sea, an encouraged swath of buried sand one hundred yards out revels in its well-deserved rare glimpse of the sun. Preening for a few hours, Sandbar holds court with the tourists who typically make friends with the more popular main beach fronting the hotels. While not uncommon for underwater topography to shape-shift through storms and changing tides, this ocean spot in Waikiki stubbornly shrugs off change. For years, during low tide in front of the Pink Hotel, beachgoers could walk through waist-deep to knee- or ankle-deep water those one-hundred-plus yards to stand in the middle of the ocean on a sandbar the size of a football field.

Offsides of the squishy soft playground lay foot-shredding lava, making the inner tube a lifesaver should we have floated into the danger zone. Nick was taller three years after our arrival, and the tide took longer in rising back to meet his waist. This last day, we stayed offshore for two hours, until the ocean completely covered Sandbar. In due time, we glided back in with the sea, rinsed off, and made our way into Duke's for fish tacos and a Kona beer for me, and for Nick, the keiki fried shrimp and virgin mai tai. Nick and I would return for my birthday years later, where he ordered a real mai tai with Tradd's extra fake ID from Arkansas. Nick's last one had been apprehended months prior to that return trip.

Tradd's borrowed ID was confiscated by the server; she knew it was a fake. At that moment, I felt a whole lot like a fake responsible mother.

But that last visit as residents, with the dried sand clinging to our feet, we soaked up the serene scene. Tourists were baking in the sand, and in the gentle ocean surf a few novice surfers were falling off their boards in the mild waves. This all played out from our front-row lanai table. We lingered, then collected our gear for the trek back to the parking lot. As we approached the cash-only booth to pay, I found all the money I possessed to be about a dollar in quarters.

"Won't you take a credit card?" I asked the attendant.

"Nah...only cash here ma'am."

"Is there an ATM nearby?"

"The closet one is a mile up Kalakaua—inside the ABC store," he replied.

"Can't you let us leave? I promise to come back and give you the cash in a few minutes!" I said sweetly.

"Nah..." Two cars piled up impatiently behind me.

If I reparked the car and walked the two miles roundtrip to the ATM with Nick, that would put us smack dab in the middle of a ninety-minute drive home in rush hour traffic. I pulled out of the queue and back into a parking spot.

"Bud...what can we do here?" I asked Nick, who always had answers.

"You always hide money in the car!" He began digging in the usual places, behind the sun visor, in the glove compartment, but no luck.

"MOM! Can we sell something?!" Nick, ever the entrepreneur, was always scrambling to make a dollar the easy way by selling things. From lemonade to baseball trading cars to his own "store" at our yard sales, making money excited him.

"Yes! We have a used stack of CDs and some sunscreen!" We backed out of the space and began stalking people walking through the lot.

"Excuse me!" I said to the first prospective buyers. "We are leaving for the day and the parking lot only takes cash, which we don't have, and we have no time to get to the ATM. Will you buy one of our CDs, and bail us out of jail here?!" Nick was more animated than ever now, cheering my efforts.

"We have some good CDs, brand-new!" he chimed in, leaning over the console to close the deal with the client.

After a few firm "No, thank you's" we found a fun young couple who took pity on us.

"What do you have there?" the man asked.

"Garth Brooks, or Brooks and Dunn?"

"Umm, no. Not into country."

We had been listening to Shakira, *Laundry Service.*

"Yeah...we will take that one!" He happily peeled off a ten-dollar bill, and I let go of Shakira.

"Woo-hoo! Way to go, Mom!" Nick hugged me around the neck before bouncing back to his seat, buckling up as we circled around to the booth. We cheered and high-fived our way through the lifted plastic boom barrier, releasing us from parking-lot prison and into freedom. We celebrated our luck with one final and quick drive back home on the H-1 to Waikele.

The final weeks were a flurry of goodbyes with people we cared about and places we had grown to love, bookending our days up until the night we left. Coming full circle, our last two nights on Oahu brought us not back to The Hilton, but to the Hyatt in Waikiki. The symmetry of friends joining us poolside, dining at our favorite spots, trekking again to Honolulu Coffee Company, lingering at the Banyan Tree, allowed a closure befitting an impactful three years of life. I reflected back to that first day, landing in Honolulu, and my wondering if the verdant green below would mean verdant life for us. A resounding *yes* was the answer. The verdant Hawaiian life lessons we experienced run deep in all of us *because of* the rough waters we navigated during our three years of Aloha.

One week later we were on a plane to Los Angeles. Our house sold for double the price of our investment, and sold also was the Saab sedan we'd bought when we arrived. We had gained a dog, Maggie, and stuffed her in a too-small Sherpa carry case to fit under the airplane seat. During the overnight flight she escaped the bag while we slept, strutting up and down the aisles before the lovely flight attendant scooped her up to search for her family. The sun was just coming up as we landed at LAX. Ken's Chevy Blazer had been shipped six weeks prior and was ready at Long Beach dock for pickup.

## RUNNING OUT OF LAND

"KEN! A perfect apartment is available—just now listed! Where is my phone?!" I shouted to him across the small hotel room.

Two days of house-hunting with an end goal to secure our new place for the next year in a tight rental market brought not even a nibble—until now. Searching for a home in one of the most desired areas in Southern California proved a tall order. Priorities: first, excellent schools; and second, walking or biking distance to Ken's office. With reluctant hope our search of the seven-square-mile good-school zone began. Flying out in less than forty-eight hours to Minnesota for a family reunion negated my usual finicky criteria. We looked at every available unit in the desired zone, to no avail. We resigned ourselves, with eight hours until our upcoming departure, to leaving for vacation without signing a lease and our Hawaiian household goods heading directly from boat to storage. Once we returned from the Midwest it would be another hotel stay, this time with no tropical ocean view, sipping piña coladas poolside. We geared up for bed and packed for the morning flight. But I persisted, one last time. I hit refresh on the housing website I obsessively scanned, and *voila*!

As I was pounding the digits to the rental company on my phone, I rattled off the specs to Ken and Nick. Three bedroom, two bathroom, one-car garage, updated apartment, two blocks from Montana in Santa Monica. The nearby school ranked first in overall performance in the Los Angeles Unified School District. Several attempts ended with my call sent to voice mail. The fourth try, I finally reached a cranky guy, who we learned owned the entire apartment complex.

"I am sorry for calling so late. How are you?" After no response, and unable to care if I was disturbing him, I continued. "We just moved with the military from Hawaii and need to sign the lease on your apartment on Nineteenth Street, in Santa Monica. Now. Tonight," I pleaded.

"I am sorry, I can't help you tonight. Please call the leasing office in the morning; they can arrange to show you the apartment," he said almost patiently, like one would speak to a toddler up to no good.

"I know how odd this all seems," I said. "But can we please just come by and give you a check for the deposit? We are leaving town in the morning, and our household shipment is arriving in two weeks, when we return. The haulers need an address...now. We really need to get the lease signed tonight."

Accustomed to unsavory renters and LA oddities, he finally, with much reluctance, agreed to take a chance and meet us at the apartment. We grabbed our shoes and checkbook, threw on shorts, grabbed Maggie and Nick, and headed the three short blocks to 913 19th St.

We rolled up in minutes to a bland, well-cared-for building squeezed between two small single-family homes on a quiet street.

The owner had sent his apartment manager to escort us up a short flight of stairs and into the unit. We stepped into a bright and spacious remodeled flat, with a sunken living room and retro tiny kitchen. A small patio sat off the living room and a large picture window facing the street fronted the length of the upper level, next to a space roomy enough for the dining table and our leather recliner. What an amazing find! The rent was almost double our Hawaii mortgage, but we immediately signed the lease and handed over a check for $9,000.

Two weeks later, the family reunion complete and the fog of transition abating, we stood in the middle of our empty home to assess the fallout of the ninth-hour negotiations. The twelve-unit, 1960s-era building was well maintained and we had scored the best unit in the complex. Though the kitchen lacked size, it oozed charm, with black tile counters and a window overlooking the neighbor's palm tree. One of the two tiny, coveted garage spots was ours, saving us from fighting for two spots of on-street parking. RAND, in downtown Santa Monica, where Ken would commute daily, was less than four miles away. Montana Avenue, with its swanky shops and restaurants, was a walkable two blocks over. Most importantly, Franklin Elementary School—four blocks away—served up a fourth-grade teacher who had been awarded "Top 100 Teachers in America" recognition by Oprah Winfrey.

Ken's workday at RAND began at a jaw-dropping 9:00 a.m. Not since nine years prior had my early morning solo runs lacked the rush of pushing homeward in time to see Ken off to a 7:00 a.m. start to a busy workday. A long run would begin downhill, course through nineteen blocks to the Santa Monica Pier, then turn north up Ocean to Palisades Park at an easy jog to stop for a scan of the Pacific Ocean and a quick stretch. The turn back toward home was an uphill two-and-a-half miles. So gentle was the incline I hardly knew the reason for my short breath and sore legs. Walking the last hundred feet, I would hang left to Montana, to ferret out a go-to coffee shop. Toward the end of our year in Santa Monica, we would boast close to eight unique spots to grab a pastry, coffee, or breakfast.

In the first week, post-run, standing in a line snaking seven people long for their turn to order, I noticed a familiar-looking guy. Turning my head, looking politely out of the side of my eye, I thought, *Footloose*! Yes, Kevin Bacon, at only six degrees of separation! I liked his work, and he seemed like a decent human, but I cooled my excitement to give way to his privacy. My first-week Bacon sighting began a fun trend to tally up all the actors and celebrities we spotted over that year. Like finding Waldo in the mess of activity on the page of a book, we found stars in the mess of the environs of Southern California.

The Brentwood Country Mart evoked images of a remote farm store selling just-picked, mud-encrusted melons. But, this was LA, where fake things are made to look real. The Mart is a block-long, enclosed, upscale shopping and food spot with an exterior facade replicating a red-and-white barn. The "farm shop" carried French wine, James Perse T-shirts, jars of caviar and pate, and "homemade" treats. It was an easy drive from our house, and we enjoyed a weekend breakfast outing to partake of their gourmet offerings. Over the course of a year on different visits, we would spot Reese Witherspoon, Jerry Seinfeld, Harrison Ford, and Meg Ryan. It was fun to see them, but looking back I wonder why. Did I feel that rubbing elbows for a red-hot second would elevate me to star status? By touching fame, was I more worthy in some way? Or, there was this "perfect" caricature, an ideal person on the movie screen; by merely basking in their glow, was I validated and perfect too? It was the same with the "popular" crowd in high school or college. Rub elbows with the shiny and your sparkle increases?

While I'm not certain what the attraction was, Nick and I engaged in "I Spy" the celebrity. My favorite run-in was Owen Wilson at the Teahouse in Abbott Kinney near Santa Monica. Nick and I lingered at the outdoor table finishing up our tea and sandwiches when Nick spotted him.

"Mom! Isn't that the guy from Starsky and Hutch?"

Sitting al fresco, I had a good view of the porch on the tiny teahouse.

"Well, heck. It sure is, Nick. That is Owen Wilson," I whispered.

He stood on the small porch with his tea, one hand in his pocket, looking around at the scene with an eager expression. Honey blonde tresses and an open smile, he oozed Golden Retriever energy. I was always sincere to respect anyone's privacy, but his playful demeanor begged for attention, so I encouraged Nick to say hello. He looked approachable, ready to engage, but Nick held back as Owen bounced out onto Abbott Kinney and disappeared. A short time later we heard of a possible suicide attempt by Owen; some emotional issues the tabloid said. I thought, how many troubled, broken humans are strolling around in my midst every day, looking happy to engage? We never can know what might be simmering deep in a person's soul, ready to erupt after a timely provocation. Like Bobby.

Our world swirled around a rare, yet, stabilizing time for my little family. Ken enjoyed minimal stress, working easy days at RAND. Golfing, triathlon training, and mentoring Nick in Boy Scouts occupied most of his days. As an Eagle Scout himself, Ken set a goal for Nick (before he was born) to achieve the rank as well, beginning in Hawaii with Cub Scouts. Ken's gung-ho enthusiasm for Scouting singled him out—from day one with every troop Nick joined—from the other dads to be Scoutmaster parent. And of course there was the impressive school.

—————————————— **Nick's Perspective** ——————————————

*Boy Scouts. I can't believe I actually made it to Eagle Scout. If not for Dad pushing, and me knowing from an early age there was no way out, I would not have reached that rank. It was like school—you know you have to go and get your degree or your life will be a disaster. The difference between school and scouts, though, is that I enjoyed the social aspect of school and I truly never found "my tribe" in any Boy Scout troop. Moving around from place to place and troop to troop made it impossible to even find one consistent friend along the way. Getting the badges, what a process that was: so many badges to earn. But somehow, even as a kid, I knew that was good for me, to go after something I didn't quite enjoy to get to the prize at the end. And, doing it with Dad made it all bearable…until high school when I hid it from my friends. It was not what the "cool kids" were involved in.*

We found soon enough that the "public" school was heavily funded by "Hollywood" and LA business elites, many of whom lived on the wealthy side of Montana Avenue. My son received the largesse of these moonlighting Hollywood parents and their connections, who poured their skills and money into all the children. There was art class from an award-winning cartoonist, music class from the Los Angeles Philharmonic flautist, and theatre productions directed by a Hollywood director, who boasted projects with Meg Ryan and Robert DeNiro. All Franklin parents, even the plebes like us, procured invitations to the big gala of the year to raise money for all this hoopla.

The auction was organized by a director of the world-famous Bonhams Auction House. From all the buzz on the "poor" side of Montana Avenue, we gleaned that this was a first-class production. My sister zoomed down from Las Vegas to be my companion. Ken happily took the night off. My excitement loomed large with my intent to bid on surfing lessons with actor Simon Baker, a wine dinner with chef Josiah Citrin, and the one I was pinning all my hopes on, an intimate evening cocktail hour for eight with playwright David Mamet.

We popped into The Beverly Center in LA for a shopping excursion to select just the right outfit for the auction. It was a big deal, and my Hawaii togs would not be sufficient. Held at Shutters on The Beach, we were told by my fellow apartment-dweller neighbors, 1) they would most certainly be attending, and 2) the elementary school parents treat this event like a Hollywood movie premiere.

"I am definitely attending!" I proclaimed to the French mom next door who was always overwatering her plants, allowing the runoff to flood my teeny-tiny patio.

"Alors! You will be made to feel the outcast, no doubt Susanna!" As a longtime Francophile I always loved her pronunciation of my name. Even when I complained of the inconsiderate watering habit, her arguments sounded melodious.

"Susanna! The perimeter of our verandas are such that the runoff is, how you say? A done deal! There is little option, if we want the plants to live, d'accord?!" she said in her heavy French accent.

I chose a Theory white fitted suit with black silk blouse and paired it with black suede stilettos, purchased in Italy for one of our events at Lajes. I looked good, I thought. With my desired items circled in the parents pamphlet, Cindy and I set out for Shutters. The swanky event was nothing like our little fundraisers at Waikele, where the parents wore shorts and slippahs to the cafeteria to bid on homemade quilts and koa-wood keychains. Standing in the back of the room with my round auction paddle, I engaged for about four bids on the expensive items not offered for write-in bids. My comfort zone peaked as paddles raised and lowered—escalating quickly out of my price range. Once the elbow rubbing, sycophantizing, and inapporpriate pinching of random women by drunk male attendees amped up—I mean this literally—Cindy and

I were ready to go. The following week the evening's tally was announced: over $220,000 raised for Franklin Elementary School. The hefty haul more than funded another year of school programs helmed by Hollywood volunteers, allowing the moneyed parents bragging rights to a public school rather than the much-eschewed elite private school education; a private one reeked of having money, and lots of pretending you are not wealthy among the wealthy goes on in SoCal.

The Franklin administration informed me that parents secure their child's spot for kindergarten at least a year ahead of their matriculation. Entering Nick in fourth grade there was not a given, just because of a correct address. The principal relayed that some children zoned for this school stood a good chance of being shifted elsewhere. *What the what?* My understanding on the legality of this shifting eludes me still, but we lucked out and Nick was admitted to Franklin. We were considered a feather in the cap for FES, I later learned, with patriotism at an all-time high coming on the heels of 9/11. Ken, holding an officer rank in the Air Force, was a coup for a school district so far removed from a military presence and "normal" American struggles.

Shockingly, or perhaps not, come time for the picnic signaling the finish line of fourth grade, Nick was actually performing at a fourth-grade level. We participated in this anticipated picnic event with our response to the email from the elected room mom—a title earned in a heated contest over contributing the most to a year-end cash gift for the teacher. We reached deep for $25. Flummoxed almost explains my shock upon Ms. Barthol opening a fat envelope toward the end of the picnic. Her normally stoic demeanor departed, giving way to childlike excitement while tearing into the class gift. As she bounced up and down on her toes like a young girl at her first sleepover, I wondered how a gift card, or whatever, for $400 could evoke such glee. But, I soon saw the reason for her uncharacteristic exuberance.

Out from the envelope she pulled a wad of cash. No Hallmark card, just a wad of green bills. Her automatic decorum, and similar gifts from years past I am sure, helped her resist counting her fortune on site. I was about six feet away from her and could see her shuffling through the money. Most of the bills in her clutches, that I saw, were hundreds and a few fifties. She struggled to keep the haul in a neat pile. My guess at her windfall: over $10,000. Of that bonus payday, $25 was from us.

Ms. Barthol deserved every cent of that under-the-table windfall. This award-winning teacher, through skill and diligence, was solely responsible for Nick's educational turnaround. I was thrilled to have my son attend a free "private" school that indeed did have one of the best teachers in the country. Ms. Barthol attended posthaste to correcting the horrible habits Nick had developed in the Hawaii school system. Through persistent attention, skilled teaching, individual assignments for him alone, frequent "coaching" with Ken and me, and consistent accountability, she prevailed. For this and for all these generous and/ or accomplished Franklin parents with their benefits and special funds for additional education outside of the public budget, I am eternally grateful. Truly, this school was a godsend, a stopgap to three prior years building sloppy educational habits. We prevailed as parents in pressing into the nonnegotiable quest to secure our home in an area known for the "best" elementary school. We held strong in Nick's placement with the "best" fourth-grade teacher. These two priorities, combined with the ease of living in a walking community on the same continent as family and the comforts of being back in mainland North America plugged up the tiny cracks threatening my child's firm foundation.

---------------------- **Nick's Perspective** ----------------------

*Like Hawaii, I don't remember much about California. In fact, my first sturdy memories didn't happen until we moved back to Virginia, for fifth grade. If we had lived in Santa Monica when I was sixteen, when my memory had kicked in, that would have been amazing. My mom recently called me and wondered what I do recall about fourth grade and our time in California.*

*I distinctly remember a few things about Ms. Barthol. I understand what an excellent teacher she was—she had command of the classroom, she was creative in her curriculum, and she held kids—me—to task. The financial haul at the end of the year confirms the parents thought her excellent, too. People get asked who their favorite teachers were, and mine was Mrs. Harriet, from high school Honors Math. I bring her up because she and Ms. Barthol had the same way about them.*

*For recess, I enjoyed playing handball on the small court they had on the playground. Also, my dad and I used to bike up to Franklin, my school, and play on their court on the weekends. Fun stuff. I also recall a pool party at the end of the school year. All my classmates were playing at this kid's birthday party, around the pool. The house was amazing! But one of my favorite consistent memories was of Maggie, my Cavalier King Charles Spaniel.*

*We had a cool apartment close to the school, and Mom would park her car in our small garage space directly under our big window, facing the street. The space allowed just enough room for the car and about eight inches on one side to open the door and squeeze in. She would do just that when we took the car somewhere. I would wait on the sidewalk for her to back the car out of the garage, stopping for me to climb in. While I waited for her, Maggie would work her way in front of the curtains and sit staring at me, I guess waiting for us already to come back home! It was hard to leave! Then when we would open the garage door, coming home from wherever, she would hear us, and by the time Mom walked around to join me on the driveway, there she was! Sometimes, I wondered if she sat there all day, because after a walk to the store or library there she would be, sitting in front of that big window waiting for us!*

Only God was good enough to walk us through the lava fires of Hawaiian education to the calm Santa Monica waters with such grace in our clumsiness. In my past, customarily I ignored His divine hand at work. I see now that tangled up in that three years of sloppy scholarly habits forming were yet more layers of godly character being built. The balm of Santa Monica was a respite to all the previous tough lessons and a pause on the isolation and character building inherent in living in remote lands, working tough assignments, for six years. The tough produced abundant blessings. Living so far removed from family and the familiar with six years of rich experience defines us still. It shaped Nick in as many positive ways as negative. But Santa Monica and Franklin ES—and the meticulous Ms. Barthol—arrested for Nick an epic academic fail.

Watching a sane woman rightly salivate over a massive stash of cash at an elementary school picnic shocked me into full understanding. We had hit the Mega Jackpot with every single correct number on a California Pick-6 lottery.

It was summer PCS season. And after one year in Santa Monica, Ken was beckoned back to the Pentagon. Nick took a really tough hit this time, as a solid group of boys had had accepted him in only one year. He had to break ties and start all over once again. Nick didn't quite grasp the heft of returning back to "home base" after seven years, four homes, and three schools, all before fifth grade. But he sensed the change, and this time, it hit hard that he was leaving so much behind.

Ken flew back East in April 2007 for business at the RAND office in Arlington, Virginia. He was tasked with securing a rental home for the next two years and would spend Easter Sunday with his parents, then drive south to Virginia for the RAND meeting and house-hunting. My intense searches on Military By Owner and other websites produced three solid options for viewing. Ken would tour the homes, send back a few pictures, and plunk down a check for the deposit—unless they were terrible. There would be no more cold, moldy, isolated homes without proper heat. No more month long stays at over-the-top resort hotels in paradise (Ken's requirement, not Nick's and mine!). No more middle-of-the-night, last-minute sprints to beat our furniture to the front porch of a new home. And of course, no more "bad" schools. Essential was a stellar review on "rate-my-school" websites. Fairfax County had for years been lauded as one of the "best" school districts in the country. They had high graduation rates, low crime in schools, high test scores, and low numbers of free-lunch students—a well-known marker for a desirable school district. His Hawaiian school had a highly populated free-and reduced-lunch program, and I was avoiding *all* stats similar to Waikele ES.

The rental choice that drifted above the others was a simple ranch-style, circa 1970s home at the end of a quiet cul-de-sac set back off the bucolic, tree-lined George Washington Parkway. Just outside the Washington Beltway toward Mt. Vernon, home of our nation's first president, the rental prospect's location on Holiday Drive screamed, "Rent Me!" The four miles north to historic Old Town Alexandria or equal distance south to Washington's farm, Mt. Vernon, offered up a drive, bike, or rollerblade trip much like our first place in Arlington had. Importantly, the traffic flowed fairly pleasantly over the eight miles comprising Holiday Drive, which paralleled the bike trail to the Pentagon. Pictures of the house and property sent by Ken were impressive: they portrayed a three-thousand-square-foot house on an acre of land. With a wood-burning fireplace, spacious kitchen, and finished basement featuring a few recent updates, the place was move-in ready! The front yard sloped down to the cul-de-sac where a basketball hoop stood. A plaque I found months later, outside our fence in the space between our yard and the neighbors, read, "Once the boundary of George Washington's River Farm."

After Ken's trip to Virginia, there were the usual "one-last" activities to squeeze in before the move. One of those lasts—also a first—was a coastal sweep to Northern California. Yosemite held the top spot on our one-last list. When I think of places I want to live, I once ranked California number one. No other state boasts the variety of environments it does. Despite the tragedy of human interruption riddling the state, there is no mistaking the irrefutable fact of 1,100 miles of stunning Pacific Ocean coastline bordering the entire state. California is flanked to the east by the highest mountain peak in the contiguous US, Mt. Whitney, soaring to 14,505 feet high. It is here that 3,000-year-old bristlecone pines thrive. Their tenacious roots burrow deep into dolomitic rocky soil for a short growing season bookended by harsh winters. Roots of life can survive anywhere that tenacity and the right soil offer up a spot to thrive. But without this mix and some careful planning, you can quickly go the way of the Donner Party.

Caravanning covered wagons cresting into the Sierra Nevada after a trek through the arid plateau might initially have experienced that common relief offered by the cool mountains. The Donner Party of 1846, entering into the Sierra Nevada just north of Death Valley, offer a time-honored cautionary tale on bad planning and shortcuts. Breaking off from a larger group, the party troubled through the Wasatch Mountains to Salt Lake City. With ticking time and transitioning seasons their foe, in haste to make it over the Sierra before winter, they shunned waiting in SLC, instead choosing to depart for the final mountain crossing in late October. The following year, and four months later, forty-five of the original eighty-nine emigrants, most of them children, descended out of their hasty shortcut horror in the Sierra and toward the calm season in Northern California. Many survivors went on to be pillars in their communities. They rallied and prospered, with a resilience required to carry on after a horrific ordeal.

I learned much of the Donner history from the comfort of our sturdy SUV as it ferried us easily past varied topography and climates to our bed-and-breakfast. I had thought of shortcuts as an unconscious, yet lazy, mental rationalization to speed up a task or journey, believing the outcome would look the same as it would taking the long way around. The Donner disaster might even show us what happens when an impulse isn't accompanied by knowledge of the landscape you're going to claim. Knowledge and wisdom are what young people lack, today especially, in the pinnacle period of sifting through life's most crucial choices, all propelled from an undeveloped reasoning center in their brain. The Donner Party's faulty leadership guided gullible followers, but the hasty choices yielding devastating consequences made through impatience continue to guide all who will listen with crucial second-hand wisdom. If you misjudge the landscape and your abilities, it can consume you whole.

My son was his own little Donner party, and to this day, a hint of lazy hounds him as his Achilles heel. He fights it daily, knowing in the dawn of maturity, never to let it get the best of him.

In clarification, I don't suggest humans are going to *literally* eat others to survive. But, metaphorically, many of us enduring far less trauma and stress "consume" our loved ones in the quest for survival. Like the Menendez brothers of 1989, convicted of killing their parents in a fugue of greed and hate, would a teen take out their parents physically or emotionally if they stood in the way of their quest for "survival"?

There was no Donner Party drama or perilous hikes or even a broken-down vehicle on our one last sweep of California. As I recently sifted through the road trip photos, there were Nick and I, always with our arms wrapped around each other, him hanging like a monkey around my neck. In one, we perched happily on a fallen Redwood tree. Another showed Nick in his tattered Yankees T-shirt, throwing a baseball to me from the sunroof of our SUV. Ken captured another of us lunching and laughing, clinking glasses al fresco in Carmel at the Hog's Breath Inn. One more favorite: Nick was standing close in front of me, my arms around him while a gentle fog rolled in behind us. Perched on the outcrop in the background was the 250-year-old Lone Cypress on Pebble Beach's seventeen-mile drive. Cypress trees are native only to this stretch of California. They are tough, resilient trees, like the Bristlecone Pine, with complicated root structures that can penetrate into the coastal rock, clinging and thriving in treacherous conditions. This Lone Cypress, a Western icon, is a popular photo stop, a sentry guarding the posed tourists.

Coming from Yosemite, we wound through uncharacteristically fertile California vineyards and farmland to enter Highway 1, the Pacific Coast Highway, just north of Monterey and west of Mt. Whitney. Popping over to the loop around Pebble Beach Golf Course and the Lone Cypress brought flashbacks of the awful corkscrew road to Hana, in Maui. The loop was admittedly four times shorter and far straighter, but the same panicky sensation from Hana murmured in me throughout the seventeen-mile stretch. The murmur was a nice break from the urge to scream I had on the Hana loop, but nonetheless, each delivered the same message: "You can check in, but you can never leave! Keep on going!"

All too similar is this echo in parenting a rebellious child. The road ahead will eventually straighten out; just press the pedal down and steer around the curves. Parenting my son through the dark years was like these precipitous curves that never ended, only the exit was blocked by a landslide, and I was forced to loop back around and have another go at the twisty road again the next day, the next week, month, and year. But, there we were on the PCH, arguably the West Coast's most scenic oceanfront thoroughfare. We later heard on the national news of a massive landslide that took out a good chunk of the historic road. Any tourist or local lucky enough to travel the famous stretch can affirm that a landslide was a long time coming. A quote from California resident/geologist John Duffy speaks to the impermanence of shaping nature to meet the needs of man as it relates to HWY 1. "It's an emerging coastline geologically speaking, and it's in a constant state of trying to come to some stability." In the end, the road becomes safer after the fractured earth gives way to the sea, creating a possibility for more stable earth up above the road.

We initially loved the holiday house. The backyard, with its lovely gazebo, was one more reason we rented the place over other housing choices. The yard was lined with flowering bushes; the thick grass looked like a playground for Nick with many choice potty spots for Maggie. After a year in an apartment with no yard, this was a huge selling point. Its setting atop an entire acre of grass and trees, a backyard patio perfect for lingering on comfortable outdoor furniture, and five cul-de-sac neighbors with children Nick's age promised a continuation of his post-Hawaii upswing.

Sadly, the yard never worked out because of the ubiquitous mosquito swarms. The lovely gazebo saw our presence about one time in two years. We spent all our time in the cul-de-sac and surrounding neighborhood.

Our home was the twelve o'clock center of the Sac, and Mr. Easton lived next door. His modest home was set back at the two o'clock position, the highest cul-de-sac point. Nick and I were carrying in a piece of furniture we had bought at Ikea, and upon seeing our struggle Mr. Easton rushed over to help. At ninety-two, he had survived a stint overseas serving the US interests in World War II. And a few years ago, he survived the death of his wife. Our Waynewood neighborhood had sprung up as a response to the baby boom and postwar growth in the late 1950s. Nick's elementary school was built at the same time as our Sac in 1959. Mr. Easton, as the only original owner on

Holiday Drive, had seen George Washington's land plowed up to accommodate this subdivision in which he raised his family. He sent his children to the new school, and over forty years later my own child would walk those same sturdy halls. A servant to his country, to his church, he became a friend to yet another new family moving into a new home. For years, he had lived a vibrant life as a pillar in the community, and he was reminding me how to be a good neighbor.

"Hello! Can I give you a hand with your chair?" he offered.

He moved to Nick's side to assist him. However, his weathered, well-used body allowed mostly moral support to help move our chair up the stairs and into the house.

"Welcome to the cul-de-sac. Where are you all coming from?" he inquired.

I filled him in on the details and he responded, "Nick, you come over anytime. I am known to have a constant supply of homemade cookies on hand, thanks to my daughter."

Turning to me he added, "You come on by if you need some help with your boy."

Two months later I watched out the window, concerned, as he paused too long while pulling out of his driveway.

"Ken! Would you run over and see if Mr. Easton needs anything? He has been idling his car for ten minutes." Just as Ken was hustling into his shoes, Mr. Easton pulled away. A few days later, we saw his daughter in the driveway, packing up her car with boxes. I went over to chat.

The night we saw him pause in the driveway, she explained, had been his last moments in the cul-de-sac. A quiet heart attack had claimed his last breath as he knocked on the door of friends who were awaiting him for dinner. They answered only to find him unresponsive, in a heap on the steps, the dessert he brought still clutched in his hand.

When I think of the life humans are called to live, I think of Mr. Easton. He was a stellar American who served his country before he and his wife embedded deep roots for his family in this community. He branched out his reach to all as a faithful servant to what God had entrusted to him. In the very last minutes of his productive and worthy life, he backed out of his driveway, paused, and drove on to his intended destination. He walked unaided up his friends' steps for a meal, before quietly departing to join his wife in heaven. I don't recall who moved into Mr. Easton's house, but if memory serves me correctly (and I pray it does, as I am writing a *book* using said memory), it stayed vacant for over a year.

Our time in the Sac offered everything for which we had hoped. It was a two-year season of positive growth, doubling down on the good efforts of Ms. Barthol and the rebuilding season in Santa Monica. Most importantly, Waynewood fulfilled my intention for a sturdy education for Nick through both fifth and sixth grades. Though the roots of the curriculum established in the 1950s remained resistant to a sweeping new trend in the country to "teach to the test," subtle changes in public education took power away from the teachers, placing many decisions for children's well-being and growth with administrators at an office building somewhere in Fairfax County. The teachers were stressed and overworked with the pointy heel of the school board grinding into their backs, tearing into their love of teaching. But good education, though riddled with frustration, poured into my son yet again.

Summer was in full swing for the dwellers of the Waynewood neighborhood when we arrived on Holiday Drive, followed a day later by the moving truck we had just packed up in California. Sports camps, scout camps, and memberships at the local swimming pool were *full*. What were we to do for another six weeks, after the boxes were unpacked and Ken was fully ensconced in a tiny cubicle in the Pentagon's C Ring? I came up with a one-person camp for Nick, complete with an activity booklet for our week. It contained daily activities centered around historical sites, along with a brief synopsis of each, with pictures and maps. There were even badges he could earn for learning historical factoids about each place. Here was the lineup of Nick's Summer Camp: A Stroll Through America's Roots.

Day One: Fort McHenry in Baltimore, site of the battle in The War of 1812 that inspired Francis Scott Key to pen "The Star-Spangled Banner" following Britain's retreat in 1814.

Day Two: Bull Run Battlefield in Manassas. "Bull Run was the first full-scale battle of the Civil War. The fierce fight forced both the North and South to face the sobering reality that the war would be long and bloody."[2]

Day Three: Arlington National Cemetery and The National Mall in Washington, DC. We rode the now-defunct Tourmobile (horrible decision to eradicate this gem—wish they would bring it back), hopping on and off all day at all the various spots highlighted in the camp booklet.

Days Four and Five: A horseback tour through the battlefields and monuments of Gettysburg, VA, site of President Lincoln's Gettysburg Address. There, Nick and I planted our feet in the very spot where 130 years prior, during the height of the Civil War, Lincoln stood. For Nick, I hope a passion for his country transferred to him and runs through his own veins from not only being exposed to so much national history but from being born in our nation's capital.

─────────────────── **Nick's Perspective** ───────────────────

*I wish I knew at the time how cool it was to be around all that history! I am sure I complained...a lot. I remember the place, but the only clear memory is of Gettysburg. Sadly, the photos we took comprise most of my memory of these childhood events! When people ask me where I am from, I don't say Washington, DC. I say Sumter, SC.*

## Chapter 6

# Wayne-Would

*T*hrill and excitement won out over the stress of PCS-ing as we had globe-trotted to Portugal, Hawaii, and California over the previous six years. But a peace of mind to circle back to the DC Metro area surpassed all the adventure and its constant specter of the unknown. Northern Virginia was home—and promised a simple transition. Ken immediately enrolled Nick in the local Boy Scout troop, took the training to become a Scoutmaster, and signed up as a coach for Fort Hunt Youth Football. We had two years to thrive. Nick dug in and soared. For me, it was two years treading water in a dead calm waiting for the next milestone. Over the entirety of my life to date, I had claimed residence in nineteen geographic relocations.

But I claim Texas as my home country. Texas still runs through my veins. Nick claiming Sumter surprises me. I consider him from the DC Metro area. We lived there longer than anywhere else and he was born there. We have returned many times to visit friends and family. It still feels like home to me. It feels healing to go back to where you are from, to remind yourself of your old self and validate your life somehow.

But does revisiting old haunts really ground a person? Did I gain any insight after visiting Texas once on a long Dallas-airport layover? I felt some peace at the time, and a yearning nostalgia for the innocence of that joyful kid who lived in Dallas. I *know* the roots are still there in that place. The blood I shed on so many patches of concrete after falling off my bike melded forever my DNA with the neighborhood. I have no doubt that the blood of my son was sprinkled all over South Carolina. Still, with stories yet to be told of his last year of high school and first year of college, I know much of his blood blended into the soil and cement of Sumter and Clemson.

Long before all of our moves, enduring passions and significant seeds of interest had germinated in Nick. Once, as I fixed dinner in our tiny galley kitchen in the Crystal City apartment after a shift at my part-time position at Worldgate Athletic Club, I heard a commotion. My guys busted through the front door filled with excitement.

It was a perfect spring day in 1999, with Washington shining just across the Potomac from a peek-a-boo view off our fifth-floor balcony. The cherry blossoms were in full-blush bloom; the next day we'd get on our bikes and head in to catch them at their peak.

Leaving my boiling water to check on the excitement, then two-year-old Nick and Ken hurried into our apartment. Ken had a tight grip on a giant plastic Toys "R" Us bag.

"You WILL NOT believe what we found at the store! You WILL NOT believe this!" Ken's tone rang out a rare note of excitement. Nick's blond curls bounced up and down, thrilled to reveal what was in the bag.

Ken raised his arm to secure the big reveal, away from an eager Nick. "Do you remember that video on the golf channel last week? Tiger Woods...on *The Tonight Show*? He must have been about three years old?"

We had stumbled upon a nickname for Nick...Tiger.

Of course I remembered the video. "Pretty cute. He is destined for greatness."

Nick jumped up, grabbing the bottom of the bag.

Wa-La!! Out came a gigantic plastic golf set! A thrilled Nick took the prize from Ken and shoved it my way to open the package.

"MOMMY!" he shouted with a glee reserved for adventures like sledding and building snowmen.

"I'm gonna to be the next Tiger Woods! Open my golf clubs!! Will you?! Will you open them NOW?!" I ran to fetch the kitchen scissors to cut off the cardboard top.

That sweet, oversized, plastic set in bold colors presented to us the first clue to a natural athletic ability in Nick. Golf came easily. His passion layered up as he drove plastic balls across the fake turf on our automatic-return putting green or across the shag carpet into plastic drink tumblers. Many times we came up empty in the kitchen cupboard looking for a plastic cup. I would pause, and look instead behind the couch, in the toy chest, or in a corner on the balcony.

That Christmas Santa brought Nick a tot-sized golf bag, large enough to carry three-iron clubs. As he grew, so did the quality and size of his clubs. Under our first Hawaiian Christmas tree was a complete set of US Kids Golf clubs stuffed in a navy-blue golf bag. I took a picture of Nick and Ken walking side by side, golf bags slung across their backs, heading from the parking lot to golf eighteen holes at the Turtle Bay Golf Club. In the distance, the clubhouse and the driving range stood ready, shaded under massive palm-tree sentries guarding the perimeter. Epic photo. Nick went on to win several US Kids Golf championships at Turtle Bay in his age group. He would abandon his clubs in high school. Until his sophomore year in college, they gathered cobwebs in the corner of the garage. Then, stored in the back of his SUV at Clemson, they served as a hiding spot for his contraband.

Recognizing the genius athletic potential, as most parents deceptively do, we wasted no time registering Nick in all things peewee. Peewee baseball, soccer (a no-go!), basketball, and flag football were all passionately pursued.

From peewee through Little League, then high school, athletics and professional teams consumed him. Pro athletes are elevated to heroes for children, and their respective teams emerge as favorites. For Nick, it was the New York Yankees and the Indianapolis Colts. With their most notable athletes of A-Rod and Peyton Manning, these teams secured a spot in our hearts and under our Christmas tree in the form of game jerseys and hats, blankets and bedding, posters and trading cards, and tickets to attend games on home fields. One year, a trip to New York City and seats to Yankee Stadium joined the ever-growing stack of experiences shaping Nick's understanding of life's possibilities. The next year's birthday gift was a trip to Indianapolis.

The massive domed Lucas Oil Stadium, open for its first season of play in 2008, offered an eye-popping backdrop for an eleventh birthday gift. Softly woven into the folds of my brain and the cells in my heart are memories of a trip for just Nick and me. His youthful exuberance rolling downtown by day on his dual-function Heelys wheeled sneakers and dressing up in his blue striped button-down that night for our intimate dinner for two at McCormick and Schmick's mark my heart with love and memories. The snap-cracking, fresh-off-the-boat Alaskan King Crab, buttery and soft, ranks to this day as the finest meal I have ever tasted. This quiet intimacy inherent in a bucket-list getaway with adventure and fine dining nurtured our impenetrable bond. Even now, it is our friendship, more often than my mothering, that defines our relationship. I credit our enduring compatibility and preference for one another to these many opportunities for adventure we seized throughout his life. To this day, every celebration in my household includes a steaming plate of fresh (or previously frozen) crab legs.

A constant companion in the fight to help my son was my easily harnessed imagination. Through mental imagery and redundant, frequent prayer I envisioned God pulling a Moses out of his book of miracles, where he parted the sea to lead the Israelites out of slavery. But in my make-believe, I was leading Nick out of a sort of slavery. I scurried through the muddy earth of the parted waters with my son in tow. Our hands clasped firmly together, as in a million times before, we would scamper up to safety. Just as the mighty ocean sealed back up, drowning the demons in hot pursuit of my child's soul, we would arrive safely on the other side of it all. We were spent, but ready to be cleansed with heaps of blessings. It played out as a dramatic vision, yet it calmed me time and again, because deep down was a churning faith that all would be well.

A favorite pastor from Hawaii once said something in a sermon that stuck with me: A shallow root system for any living organism results in increased exposure to the elements. Sprinkled throughout nature and different climates, trees have varying depths of earth-grounding root systems to uniquely thrive in their given environment. Those with a deep, complicated root system like the white oak and walnut might indicate the tree has been weathered and strengthened through storms and deprivation, making it sturdier to withstand hardship and thrive. Storms can strengthen a root system, but so can human interference, with fertilizer, water, and frost prevention. For people, the transport system for fertilizing and nurturing a human life involves a varied approach. Through education, lessons, instilling emotional and spiritual health, and intentional parenting, one can raise a good human. Nick blossomed through the course of all our adventures. The trip to Indianapolis fed the roots of our relationship in a mighty way.

I found another guiding quote from author Lisa Bevere that speaks to root systems and parenting. "They are to be carefully aimed and propelled, for they will not easily miss their marks. We are promised that, by raising them in the way they should go, they will be more inclined to hit the target of their destiny in God when they are grown."[3]

Sports helped build Nick. It began with that plastic golf club and a complicated parent/coach relationship with Ken. Ken alone functioned in the triad role of coach, Boy Scout leader, and dad. One year, without a coaching job, Ken joined me in the bleachers for Pop Warner football. This was the first year to shed the flags from fourth grade for full-on pads and a helmet. Nick excelled and was awarded at an end-of-the-season party with a trophy for Most Valuable Player.

His first year in Fort Hunt Athletics made clear his natural ability to make a decision quickly, execute a complete pass, or run in a football play called the *triple option* to secure for two years his spot as starting quarterback. He guided his team to the championship trophy the second year as a Fort Hunt Federal, this time with Ken as assistant coach. Good stuff—resulting in a great foundation of connecting the dots between hard work and positive outcomes. Football, on game day as well as in practices, fed the roots of Nick's confidence, giving him courage to move toward a life of desired outcomes. School, however, was mostly a regress. The heroic instruction from Ms. Barthol in California devolved with the unlucky placement into the class of a burnt-out teacher.

Mrs. Doral had begun instructing at Waynewood ES about the time Mr. Easton's children were attending. With several complaints against her in what would be her next-to-last year before her retirement, her anemic efforts put her in the crosshairs of the principal. In between her rants about how "stupid" the students were, there were the occasional class drop-ins by administration. These unplanned visits and her ability to instruct on automatic pilot kept her productive enough, and the class remained grounded in learning. Mrs. Doral should have retired years before Nick arrived in her fifth-grade class. I wonder if teachers who began the profession in the era where the school system empowered them to teach a certain curriculum within their own framework—trusting they were skilled and equipped to advance their children well to the next grade level—might experience a sense of helplessness and loss in the current educational system. Waiting it out to get maximum retirement benefits, if this was the case for Mrs. Doral, proved less than ideal for my son and others in his class. Two children transferred to other classrooms, but by the time we requested a change of class, escaping her lair was not an option. The principal offered a compromise: a reasonable offer to be some of the only parents granted the choice of the four sixth-grade teachers the following year if we would gut it out with the sputtering efforts of Mrs. Doral. So Nick finished out fifth grade in her class, and I understand in hindsight that it was meant to be.

A month or so before the end of the year Nick had an activity-free day and agreed to join me early Saturday morning to shop yard sales. Our fourth stop was an older, well-maintained brick house already swarming with bargain shoppers sifting through items stacked on card tables in the driveway. Nick jumped out of the car and headed over to some dusty sports equipment, while I pawed around for treasures hiding among the castoffs. I turned at the sound of Nick's voice coming from inside the garage.

"Umm...hello—Mrs. Doral," Nick stammered.

"Well...hello, Nick! How nice to see you this morning!" she cooed.

"Yeah, sure. Umm...hello!"

Just as I was picking through some outdated slips and garter belts, I heard, "This is my yard sale, Nick! How nice you found some toys you like!"

Dropping the delicates like hot lava rocks, I turned to take a good look at the woman talking to Nick. Could it *be* Mrs. Doral, the hateful fifth-grade teacher, speaking so sweetly to Nick and whose garments I was running my fingers through?

To see her as a human selling off her belongings to strangers tugged at my hard heart developed over the many months that Nick suffered in her care. Here she was, acting decently. Nick was just flat-out embarrassed picking through her old toys, as was I with her underwear. But, I imagined her as a younger lady rooted in a desire to educate, beginning her career in the 1960s with excitement to impart goodness and to train young minds to think critically. Here she was now, a bitter holdover from a career to which she clearly had lost not only her passion, but her humanity. We said our farewells and squealed out of her street, racing the four blocks back to our house, excited to dig instead into some yard work.

The backyard at Holiday House required considerable maintenance. The first task upon moving in was to rent a power washer and blast off years of accumulated moss and gunk concealing the beauty of the brick-paver patio. I labored forth in a raincoat to deflect the messy splatters for the better part of three days. Cleaning up the red brick covering a third of the nearly half-acre backyard was fueled by the imagined weekend gatherings outside, barbecuing with the adults while children frolicked around the gazebo, playing croquet in the massive yard. But even with a moss-free patio, the resilient pests and rodents had no intention of ceding their territory to interlopers. These pests were of good stock—certainly descendants of George and Martha's bugs—and refused to leave the premises. Setting off a pre-party bug bomb offered us two hours of relief from the mosquitos and gnats before their return at sunset when we were forced to retreat indoors. All the backyard proved good for was a place for Maggie to relieve herself and a payday for Nick, who slathered on the bug spray to mow it weekly six months out of the year. One week after our first Thanksgiving, we noticed Maggie slathered from floppy ears to snout in a greasy substance, and toward the end of the week her matted fur took on a stench of sour milk. Concerned, I eventually carted her to the vet, thinking she had something wrong with her gallbladder. A clean bill of health later, it occurred to Ken that it just might be the grease from the Thanksgiving turkey pan he'd dumped in the back of the yard. Maggie had easily found the grease and lapped it up for almost a week before we latched onto her little snack spot in the bowels of the yard.

Two years later, with Nick four inches taller, he celebrated his graduation from sixth grade. A photo after the ceremony shows Nick and a few best friends, arms slung around one another, leaping off the brick wall in front of the school. These were the boys whom he played shoulder to shoulder with in all Little League sports. They bonded outside of sports and school, attending confirmation classes at our church, culminating in a weekend retreat. One of the boys named Alex was Nick's best friend. They were alike in personality, character, and the shared interests of gaming, sports, and making everything fun. Alex was one of the boys out of a circle of six we invited out on a laser-tag farewell event for Nick.

Ken had gone on ahead to our next assignment in Sumter, South Carolina, while Nick completed elementary school, a trend we repeated more than once. Nick and I were left to pack up the house, direct the professional movers, and deep-clean holiday house. The previous spring break, we had selected a home in Sumter. We followed up the house-hunting by playing tourist in Charleston, South Carolina, before driving seven hours back to

Virginia. Ken moved into that house in May, missing not only the graduation, but the farewell shindig.

Ken often missed the messy business of our military moves. His job would demand an early appearance, leaving me to deal with moving trucks and final utility bills. My cousin Karen often stepped up to help with finalizing our stays, taking over the role Ken would have filled. She not only assisted with move-out day, she was a fun backup adult for Nick's farewell laser-tag party. I noticed an add-on party option on the laser tag website: For a mere $100 more we could rent a Hummer Limo to pick us up and then cart us back home again after our party. This thing pulled up into the Sac slowly and carefully. It was so huge, I would guess about one hundred feet or more in length, that it backed up and forward twice to get its front end situated forward. The website boasted all the features: a maximum capacity of twenty-two passengers, a black leather interior with stargazer lights, and a 5,000-watt sound system. Karen and I claimed the back of the Hummer, in the "VIP Area," to "supervise" the boys, which is to say we parented very badly. I am ashamed, in retrospect, that I allowed the boys to be boys to the fullest extent of their desire. The subwoofers boomed and shook while the disco lighting and stargazer lights blazed, inviting the boys to alternate between a bounce and bash into one another on the bench seats, and rolling on the neon-lit floor screaming and shrieking as Karen and I took sips of wine out of our water bottles. I reined in the urge to stop the boys' rambunctious abuse and disrespect of the Hummer. One boy sat still on the bench, avoiding the revelry. I recall locking eyes with his beseeching look in our direction that pleaded: "Aren't you going to stop this?!" How could I bring an end to this unleashing of pent-up energy when I was ripping Nick away in a few short days from these strong bonds he had formed? Guilt and fear are powerful enemies to doing the right thing. After the limo dropped us off, one of the boys signed the journal memory book I brought along. "Nick. You are a great friend and I will miss you! Love ya dude!" I felt less bad about my permissiveness after reading that.

At Lajes, Nick shared a weepy farewell with his best friend and partner in crime. They had bonded firmly over all their shenanigans. Once, I opened the back door to our duplex to find dirt on their faces, hands, and clothes. They were digging for treasure in the neighbor's little flower bed. He loved Andrew. Then we left. Just like with Alex.

In Hawaii, Noah was the sleepover pal and go-to playmate. He and his mother had joined us for a stress-free day at the hotel pool after we had packed up our home. We had a full day before our flight back to the mainland. The boys splashed for hours that last full day on Oahu before a sad farewell dinner at a favorite spot, Teddy's Burgers.

In Santa Monica, after finding his groove with the boys at the pool party, Nick had forged a nice friendship with Josh. Josh's mother was the kindergarten teacher at Franklin and had written a series of books for Scholastic called Ready Freddy. She once told me she gleaned insight and stories for the Freddy character from her own children. They were good people of great character doing good things in the world. Nick and Josh went to Military Day at Los Angeles Air Force Base, dressing up in camo and face paint, climbing around the jeeps, being boys, and having fun building memories that didn't last. Then Nick moved.

Back in Virginia, these friends in this Hummer were on the way out of Nick's life. And unlike in Lajes and Hawaii, he had a pretty good idea this would be the last time he would see them. Knowledge is good. And knowledge can sting. Then, one day it is shaped into its better self called *wisdom*.

On the way back from tag a few hours later, our water bottles long since empty, with the neon lights glowing, I turned down the 5,000 watts in the Hummer so the boys could hear me.

"GUYS! Stay in YOUR seat all the way home!!" I hollered. The exhausted kids, perhaps craving some discipline, complied. Karen patted my knee in solidarity. *God, why was it so tough? Why couldn't we just stay, dig in, and build these friendships that could last and last?*

*Chapter 7*

# Sumter Part 1

$S$outh Carolina might have more dirt-covered back-road playgrounds than the average state. Listen to any country song and this impression becomes fact. They sure churned up visceral memories of my childhood Texas dirt roads and Southern roots. There would be chilled public libraries cooling a sweaty body after outdoor play and snacks of pimento cheese spread on ritz crackers after adventuring barefoot all day through the subdivision for Nick on this assignment. In Sumter, you could almost hear the parental shouts echoing in the fading light of day as they called children home for supper, while crickets sang in the backyard and fireflies ushered in the heat of summer. The red dirt of the Deep South, though, invited one to spin out on an off-road vehicle or circle up and drink around an upset fire pit, furious at being contained and controlled by drunk teenagers.

Scores of dirt road songs exist in the country genre. Songs I had loved since college and sang along to with Nick were about drinking, getting mud on your tires, and chilling on these roads. I suppose it all transferred to my son's subconscious. When we moved to South Carolina for this first time after our second Pentagon assignment as a military family, vague ideas of unpaved roads I had only heard about in those songs crystallized into something concrete. Red dirt roads were everywhere...and they felt familiar. Places where the blacktop road ends abound in Sumter, South Carolina.

We were already sold on the idea of exploring back roads, hunting, fishing, and four-wheeling—exciting and logical ways to spend Sumter weekends and free moments when sports and school didn't demand our attention. Nick was attending a small private school called Franklin Hills Prep. Down our narrow, blacktop street was another cul-de-sac. Like Holiday Drive, this one also backed up to forest, inviting us to come explore it on our Honda ATV. Nick would beg me to head out with him. I was enrolled in a Master of Public Health program an hour away in Columbia at the University of South Carolina, and if I arrived home in time, I would pick him up on the ATV at the entrance to our subdivision, around the corner from the school. We would drop his backpack off at the house and then double up on the seat to head right back out. I hung onto the steel rack behind the seat, as Nick expertly maneuvered the ruts and puddles as we wound through the trees on the miles and miles of red dirt, wooded trails. Writing now, I can feel the vibration and the jolts as we dodged the ruts at full speed. When I close my eyes and dig back I can still smell those last precious moments of youth with my son. The sting of leaving friends seven hours north of us in Virginia still fresh, my extrovert yet gun-shy Nick was slower this time to find a best friend, so he sought companionship in me.

The woodsy Carolina pines mixed with ATV exhaust are an odd combination that provoke a flood of memories. This is one of many happy scents that randomly waft into my olfactory memory offering a happy gift to relive time and again, precious moments. The sound of an ATV, the air redolent with dirt and fuel, and the chill of fall on my face embed in my brain the last moments of Nick's childhood...the last moments where my son was still mine and our connection was mostly untainted by the screams to conform in the world outside our bond. The sadness oozes into regret to realize the loudest screams to fit in emanated from his own mother. Guilt is a powerful behavior shaper. Along with the cousins of shame and denial, it anchors deep. It is an insidious and pervasive guide to the gallows when we fail to forgive ourselves for our greatest blunders. I heeded the "experts" too much and though that is often *good*—sometimes mama bear instinct is a *better* guide.

I succumbed to what I thought was "best" for Nick by having him repeat sixth grade. Three months after graduating sixth grade with close friends in Virginia, he was back in sixth grade at a new school—with strangers who didn't know the secret he chose to keep. He was ashamed. He felt stupid, like he was being *held back*.

Kindergarten back at Lajes had brought a hefty fork-in-the-road decision. Nick's fifth birthday was two days before the cutoff to qualify for school admittance, so he was four years old in August, on his first day of kindergarten. He was the youngest in the class and might have been the least focused and most immature. When we noticed he lacked the fine motor skills necessary to easily hold a pencil, we loosely decided to treat this year as a pre-school, and next PCS season we would push him back a grade. We never followed through on that plan. Just like his newborn Apgar score of 10, he scored a 10 in reading and arithmetic, and actually excelled in kindergarten. Logically, we enrolled him in first grade in Hawaii. He did fine, but his maturation was not equal to the peers in his class. Still, he was smart...and all seemed well.

After five years in public education Nick was doing fine in school. But when the chance came to matriculate him into his rightful grade in Sumter, we seized the opportunity. With the firm encouragement from the Franklin Prep headmaster (the same one who later offered us his great wisdom), we ended up enrolling him in a repeat of sixth grade. He stopped communicating with his best friend, Alex, who was now in seventh grade in Virginia. On our trips back to Virginia, he refused to visit old friends and those relationships ceased. I wonder if, like a painful splinter lodged under the skin, a sense of embedded shame festered for Nick over this decision called "holding him back." Despite agreeing with and understanding at some level the reasons behind our decision, the emotional component remained fuzzy for him. This setback, in his mind, checked the box called *failure*. And this sprouted big harmful secrets.

Despite all the hullabaloo with grade swapping, on the surface, life was good. At last, pursuit of my master's timed well with our move and I wedged in the two-year degree, just in the nick of time before relocating one week after graduation from the University of South Carolina. Occasionally, while commuting for my graduate degree, I would make the trip twice a day to be present for Nick and his life. Homework in between being a stay-at-home mom crowded out the friends and hobbies I usually enjoyed on our short Air Force stints. Ken latched onto a volunteer dad job of assistant coach. Nick thrived in B-team football at FHP for both sixth and seventh grades, where he once again earned the spot of starting quarterback. Having Ken advocate for Nick in a new town full of competitive boys was a key reason Nick managed to break into the local boys' already-well-established realm of middle school sports. Nick avoided by default having to advocate for himself not only in sports but hunting, scouts, and all things life when Ken was there with influence and a boot in Nick's butt encouraging him to break into an endeavor and go after whatever he was doing with intense focus. This seemed to me an unsavory aspect of being an only child of a military family who was required to reinvent himself every year or two, and a stolen opportunity to self-motivate. Thriving in life requires the trait to motivate oneself toward worthy goals. Nick would soon come to a crossroads to *thrive* or *fail*, and choosing the thrive option required him to incorporate this necessary skill the hard way.

Breaking into a crowd of about eighty hormonal preteens who had for the most part been doing school/life together since kindergarten at times seemed an impenetrable wall. Like moving to Hawaii and ridiculously expecting the locals to call you Ohana, assimilating takes time and diligence. The "secret" code at FHP could be cracked by interlopers—but only rarely and randomly, with luck and one alpha kid willing to vouch for you. More often, fitting in to this small, stellar private school had a code without a firm solution. But Nick found a friend whose mother took it seriously as a Christian to enfold everyone in the mix. Dee embraced Nick and me, inviting us to dinner and birthday parties, Bible retreats for me, and pool dates for Nick and her son. She even nominated me for entrance into the elite Junior League (turns out I was too old and her nomination was denied—welcome to the South!). I believe to this day that God laid it upon Dee's heart to mentor us and to lead Nick into the group of kids who were guided well to achieve academic success. Nick was on that path in sixth and seventh grades. Franklin cherished, within its walls, the dedicated teachers and staff. Coupled with Dee's pure intentions and Ken's ability to parent Nick well when not traveling, Nick thrived in Sumter. He was at the precipice of acceptance; he was one digit away from breaking the code. And then—we moved. Back to the Pentagon. The lingering shame had Nick pitching a fit not to return to our former school district. Instead of the familiar, we moved south of the Pentagon, to McLean, Virginia.

There are years in life, seasons perhaps, where we might not swing big at any goal, or worse, never step up to the plate. Instead, ticking off the days on a calendar full of essential tasks is enough—failing is not a possibility because you aren't really *in the game.* Moving back to Virginia, round three for another two years, was an awkward and stagnant time, with Ken plodding toward an unexpected retirement from the Air Force after only a year. Our search for housing thrummed like a washing machine on the delicate cycle: "stellar school, stellar school, stellar school." I respected Nick's fervent wish not to be near his former peers, who were all one grade ahead of him. Thus the choice of Longfellow Middle School. It was inside the Beltway, in McLean, where we found a rental home listed on Military By Owner near none of the wonderful connections we had made during round two in Waynewood.

Longfellow was a reputed feeder school to a world-class science and technology high school, Thomas Jefferson, or TJ. Green-card parents from around the world rented small homes or apartments, stuffing generations of family in small confines to matriculate their American children into the "best" free education available in the country. Longfellow specialized in Gifted and Talented curriculum, most specifically math and science in preparation for successful scores on TJ entrance exams. Nick had in eighth grade some of the nation's finest teachers. He tested well on math scores, landing him a coveted spot in Gifted Math. He almost held his own the first few weeks, where curving scores didn't exist in a class of striving students who consistently scored over 100 percent.

One class friend scored an A- and told Nick, "I am going to suffer tonight with this score. My family will keep me locked inside all weekend studying."

At the suggestion of Nick's teacher, we hired a math tutor recommended by the school, but the tutor taught the wrong math methods, causing Nick in three months' time to earn failing scores and a discreet bounce from GT to normal math class. The *ouch* of the bump coincided with the onset of a pattern of fierce headaches, and a speed bump interrupted the usual reliance on sports for integration.

Ken had a normal work schedule but no desire to figure out how to break into coaching football at a public middle school. Nick signed up, weighed in, and was ready to continue playing football. But the first week in practice, he ran full speed into a hole on the field and broke a metatarsal of his right foot. My child was bored out of his mind waiting for the bone to heal and the cast to be removed. With no practices or carpooling, a wealth of free time opened up. Liberating! At first. For me, with the winter mornings inching down toward freezing, I nixed the usual morning training runs and began running after picking Nick up from school. One late afternoon, just as I set out on a three-mile loop from our musty 1950s rental home, a line of trucks and cars one street over caught my attention. A few of the bystanders quickly included me in the excitement.

"Ben Affleck is filming a scene from a movie!" a neighbor I had not met relayed. "They have locations all around McLean...this is the filming of final scene of the movie."

"Fun! What is the movie?" I was intrigued. We had often bumped up against filming in Santa Monica and always found it a fun pastime.

"Some historic drama called *Argo*," he said.

Life in McLean had sucked worse than an old vacuum these past three months, so I eagerly gobbled up the distraction, abandoning the run and hunkering into the waning daylight to check it out. After about an hour, as the day was fading to dark, we heard a loud, "THAT'S A WRAP!" A small crowd of ten or so of us remained; the payoff for standing guard in the cold came our way when Ben came over and spoke to the devoted crowd.

"Hey everyone! Would anyone like to grab a picture?!" he asked sincerely. A few awkward seconds passed with no takers on his kind offer.

"Well, sure!" I popped out of the crowd in my running gear to stand alongside Ben. One other person moved forward, taking up the other side of Ben. I imagine he dug deep for this effort, operating certainly on his last gear of the day. He chatted with us though, and hung in there like sand stuck at the top of a timer that would never run out. Someone in the crowd fumbled with my phone camera, allowing what felt like a full minute or more of snuggle/chat time with Ben. I thought about his incredible work ethic and ability to shift into one more gear, despite any exhaustion he may have been experiencing. I would have been proud for my son to turn out to be this kind of man.

The winter marched wearily forward in McLean. Ken drove the George Washington Parkway to his Pentagon job daily to do battle with his one-star boss, The General. She was hungry like a bear out of hibernation for a second star. He and the others in her lair paid the price for her self-motivated aspirations over the course of that truncated year. One particular night, with battering ram persistence, she drove her fifteen-person desk job staff to a near breaking point to reach her insanely ambitious goals. On the table for weeks was version 37 of a bonus structure for pilot retention. Her myopic self-promotion in developing Air Force policy resulted in a lack of trust in her right-hand officer, and my husband, Ken—who knew the issue inside and out.

"You people have disappointed me, yet again! This policy will be completed TONIGHT! No one leaves until it is finished," she declared.

Several of the officers had young children at home—many lived thirty minutes away in Springfield, Virginia. Ken had realized early on, around version 10, that the policy was ready to send for approval to the three-star general. Holding steady through the twenty-seven reiterations, he had now reached the precipice where his duty as an officer was as a servant advocate for his airmen.

"Ma'am, our staff needs to get home," he declared. "Staying one more minute has them missing the last train out of the Pentagon, and juggling around for a ride home. It makes no sense to hammer this thing out to the wee hours."

"Colonel—I will tell you when it is time to go, and that time is not now," she shot back.

"Ma'am, this policy was buttoned up long ago," he persisted. "Certainly, if it was an urgent issue you would see us all sacrificing for the good of the mission. But I am releasing them from duty for the night. If you insist on staying, I alone will stay until it meets your insane level of satisfaction."

"You do that, Colonel, and I will make sure you suffer and wish you had made a different decision."

"Ma'am, I grew up with a dad who was raised by a father who served in the Cossack Czech Army. I know pain, ma'am, and I can take anything you dish out. Let's go," he proclaimed. That exchange was the beginning of the end of a twenty-six-year military career.

While the Pentagon saga unfolded for Ken, Nick and I were in a head-banging battle as well within our own four walls. Driving Nick, along with Maggie, the five miles to school became our special time. He shared with me music he was enjoying: hip-hop tunes and Taylor Swift. We chatted. This precious car time from home to queuing up for drop-off took twenty minutes. Sometime after his leg cast was removed and the tutoring was nose-diving, the car rides began turning into an about-face back home, as Nick would feel sick. Dizziness and nausea spiraled into his headaches. At one point he lay at home for ten days with on again/off again debilitating pain. His pediatrician found nothing wrong. An emergency room visit complete with CAT scan showed everything as "normal." The cranial chiropractor offered some relief as he manipulated Nick's neck and scalp. To this day we are clueless as to the reasons for those headaches; I assume either growing pains, an option offered by the chiropractor, or stress. His school load at this competitive school certainly created performance anxiety.

Nick shared with me during our ride home one day that a classmate was buying marijuana from a dealer who worked with the kids at Longfellow. I couldn't imagine an eighth-grader at a well-respected middle school buying illegal drugs. It crossed my mind for a brief moment that, in some way, Nick's headaches and desire to miss school were linked to peer pressure, not just academically, but socially. Coming back from the injured list in football had him bumped from starting quarterback to benchwarmer. He was too late and lacked the conditioning to compete for any spot on the team. So, he played more and more video games. Winter snow finally melting into springtime brought concern when he announced, "No more sports." Ken and I pushed back and listed three choices of spring activities: join the junior league golf team, play an instrument in a band, or the final option, attempt lacrosse. He chose lacrosse.

Nick excelled at lacrosse. The games were quick, with almost constant movement. Smacking opponents with your stick was not only allowed, but a strategic move in the game. He made a friend on the field. His grades were holding steady and the headaches abated. He put himself in the game; he risked this option and did well. Meanwhile, we were digging in for another year—with a tour of McLean High School and registration of classes—when Ken's unexpected dealings at the Pentagon would derail our trajectory.

Frustration with layers of policy ineptness over the years created a bed of frustration in him. When the complicated Pentagon crap was fertilized by the general's failure as a mentor and leader, the decision for Ken to retire was inevitable. The constant head-banging against the hallowed Pentagon corridor walls to improve and advance the mission of the Air Force, and coming up against impenetrable resistance, eroded his Air Force purpose. After four years at the Air Force Academy and twenty-six years of mission-centered focus, the wisdom to call it prevailed. The time had arrived to take his permanent leave from military life and walk away from the insanity unfolding not only in his department, but across the military in general. Twenty-six years of service—done. It was time to choose what came next.

Ken was shopping around for a new career. I was too. And Nick would be searching again as well. The year had not provided me with great traction for use of my shiny new master's degree. I quit the position with the American Society of Public Health in Washington, DC, after the juggling act with Nick's medical needs and, honestly, as the full-time schedule and mindless chores as the lowest entry-level employee brought clarity on my priorities. My hopes were high that once Ken retired and Nick proved self-sufficient in high school, my plate would clear to allow my career a chance to blossom. For all three of us, the year had been a miss. We stepped up to the plate here and there, but truly the year was closer to no hits, no runs, and a few annoying errors. I was antsy and primed to hit it out of the park.

After seven schools in nine years, preschool to eighth grade, and no firm next step for Ken in sight, we offered Nick a unique chance to help decide where he would like to attend his four years of high school. He gave us one option: Sumter—and Franklin Prep. Argh. I had not loved Sumter, but I did love the school. After visiting McLean High School and hearing of the massive class size and rampant drug use among students, we begrudgingly put a return to Sumter on the list.

Sticky notes began appearing in odd spots throughout our home. Above a doorway, a thumbnail-size note said, "Move to Sumter!" My bathroom mirror sported a tiny little note in the upper corner: "Franklin!!" Ken noticed a sticky note on his steering wheel: "You can find a great job in Sumter!" This went on for several weeks until news arrived that Ken's career transition was delayed, and still a few years in the offing. With this insight, and the amazing find of several options to utilize my MPH at Shaw Air Force Base back in South Carolina, Sumter chose us. Four glorious years digging in, rooting into a community, sounded promising, even if it was Sumter, population 40,000. Nick would begin and end high school on equal footing and with the same group of kids. What could go wrong? Cue the moving truck for another relocation.

# PART 2:

# JUST IN TIME

## Chapter 8

# Sumter Part 2

*S*umter, *the first time around, revolved around an ATV on dirt roads,* hunting, and sports. Now, with Nick ready to drive, and Ken's desire to own a pickup truck, we bought Nick a less-than-new Ford F-150.

I was fixing dinner one evening when I heard "Tony" roar into the driveway. I loved that sound. The rumble of his dual exhaust, the ground-shaking rap lyrics increasing in volume as Nick roared ever closer down the street, pulling up into our sloped driveway. Then, silence as he killed the engine. The thumping beat announced my son's safe arrival home from his day and evoked relief.

"Mom!" Nick slammed into the house, launching his book bag into the entry.

"Get your shoes on! Put your dinner making away and let's go four-wheeling. It's an epic mud day!"

I had loved going out on the ATV with him. Like previous ATV adventures, the truck adventures became another one of "our" things. But now that he was a sophomore, I yearned for him to find his "posse." At Franklin, students forged a group to do life with as early as elementary and middle school. Their circle tightened up in ninth grade and often persisted into college. Though interlopers were welcomed into an already existing posse, it was uncommon, and those not included, for a variety of reasons, were the fringe kids. They flitted about with only one or two friends, and a lack of automatic inclusion into each other's lives was the norm. Nick only came close to the unconditional support of a peer group during our military years and early on in Sumter. Since we were staying, I was committed to his inclusion into a productive group of friends. The young adult season, I knew, was a four-to-six-year stretch where kids experimented with stupid things, pinging off others to discover an identity.

"Hey Tiger!" I paused before replying. "What about your friends? Doesn't Tradd want to go out with you instead?"

"Naw...they all have basketball practice. Tradd is with his tutor and that leaves you." He grabbed a Clementine Izze from the refrigerator.

Our connection was fraught with bittersweetness since the "why we are mean to Nick" circle time in Hawaii, in that I was the person with whom he wanted to spend time. Fear guided me: the fear of his ending up friendless, or worse, stuffed in a locker, or eating alone at the lunch table—or ending up like Bobby. A nagging chorus of "Find friends, find friends!" devolved into a misguided and ungodly effort at parenting my child. Somehow, Nick having friends meant he was mentally sound, happy, and well-adjusted.

"Well, then I will put this stuff away and get my shoes on! Can Maggie come?"

Riding shotgun with our dog Maggie perched on my lap, it indeed was an epic mud day. A rainstorm had turned red dirt to rust puddles, and Nick's skilled grip on the wheel held us on course as we bumped and jostled our way down the backroads. Splashing through the shallowest part of the miles-long road, holding onto

Maggie, I lost all interest in "shoulding" all over myself. I was here with my kiddo and happy...normal. A half hour later the road turned to water as far as we could see. Putting the truck into park, Nick and I hopped out to assess the situation, letting Mags explore a dry patch of grass.

"This looks a bit hairy, Tiger."

"You wanna drive through it, Mom?" he said carefully, gazing at the road ahead.

"It's your truck, Bud. You know what you're doing. I'll stay shotgun for now. You think we will flood the truck?" This quagmire of slop refused to reveal the depth, leaving me concerned. We had two options: go forward, or turn back in the fading light for a sixty-minute, unappealing double-back solution home.

"Naw...but I will go fast to be sure we don't get stuck," he said, laughing.

Picking up Maggie, we returned to our spots in the truck. Nick geared into four-wheel drive as we readied to barrel ahead—fast—to avoid flooding or getting stuck. With no cell phone signal, getting stuck meant a mile walk to the main road for help, with certain darkness stalking our hike in search of a tow truck rescue.

I trusted my son. He was good at maneuvering these muddy country roads. I had confidence we would be home in twenty minutes, with light left to spare to wash down the truck and get dinner in the oven.

"You can't hesitate, Nick!" I said. He pressed on the accelerator and we lurched forward.

"Yep...yep...I got it..." he calmly responded.

"You're committed, you're committed, you're committed..." I needlessly repeated the only motivation I could think of. Red mud spit past my window, obscuring the view.

"Wahhhh!!!!!!" we shouted as we came roaring out of the muck, the windshield plastered in mud.

"You wanted to stop!!" he said, and I laughed.

"Didn't you?!!" I said as another motivating mantra oozed out of my mouth.

"ARRHHH! NO, I did not! That was FUN!" he roared with glee.

Windshield wipers slapping, opening up a glimpse of the stretch ahead of us, we were now able to view our path home. I no longer harbored worry or care about his fitting in during the rare and elusive gift of living in the moment with my boy.

Sophomore year at Franklin Hills continued to challenge Nick socially. Academically, he did well. Lingering echoes from the excellent education offered in California and then in Fairfax County had teed him up well. Earning entrance into the Junior Honor Society and subsequent placement in advanced classes ushered in a plethora of options to not only excel in school, but to settle in with a motivated friend group.

However, a reluctant Nick time and again did not latch on to this brass ring of opportunity. I pushed. He tried. I pushed more. One night, an invite came his way. He had little interest in accepting a movie night with classmates, but at my insistence he headed over to class president Beth Anne Mayberry's house. Returning only an hour later, a droopy Nick blamed the short stay on boredom. A few years later, it was Beth Anne who was the epicenter of fun and success at Clemson University. She and that same posse ran the Greek life at Clemson and graduated with honors in four years.

"All they do is sit on couches and watch Disney movies," Nick had said. He grabbed an Izze and joined us on our couches where we were doing pretty much the same thing, minus the Disney.

"That sounds like fun...to be with kids your own age over your equally boring parents?" I commented.

He scooped up Maggie with his free hand and plopped down on the couch.

"Well, they are boring. No one talks. They just sit there."

"You have to start somewhere, Nick," I badgered. "Eventually, you will be doing other, more fun, activities with them. Last week I heard Beth Anne's mom say they all went to the beach over the weekend!"

Another offer came from a school friend to meet him at the Young Life gathering held at school. Young Life is an organization partnering with Christian adult leaders to guide and grow children and teens into their Christian faith. Nick went once with an almost friend named Madeline and did not completely hate the meeting. But Nick said it lacked "fun" as he summed up the evening: "Everyone was on their phone, and then we had donuts and came home."

With no siblings to cling to in our constant flux, I was both Nick's mother and best friend. Because he was an only child, we avoided the usual parents vs. children dynamic. It was just us, a mighty trio with blurry boundaries between Nick as child and Nick the equal partner. Looking back, of course, I see my desire for Nick to fit in with the "right" crowd bordering on obsession. I was the mama sparrow nudging her chick out of the nest and off the roof to soar. But it was also more than that, and perhaps at the time I didn't understand, couldn't even articulate, the importance of rooting in with an encouraging community, where there is an onus of accountability from the peer group you revere. At some point we all must leave the nest and soar (or crash) on our own. But I had learned that birds with a safe nest settle in longer, giving the chicks more time to reach full development—these are the birds that stand a good shot of thriving into adulthood. When birds are pushed out early, due to an unstable environment or other factors, there is a low survival rate for the babies. Did Nick need longer in the nest—and it was a safe nest—to avoid being shoved out before he was ready?

Every school has cliques. At Franklin, there were athletes and farm boys, and sometimes they overlapped. There were boys that loved hunting and fishing and boys whose families had wealth, and those overlapped too. Any of these boys could have been ready for an epic fail. A lifted pickup truck was the price of entry to hang with these redneck boys at Franklin. Some were fringe, many were just country boys—living in rural areas on farms and plots of hand-me-down land. More than a few of these boys were pretending: the ones who lived in the suburbs with an in-ground swimming pool and white-collar parents. Whereas most Franklin students drove a forgettable Toyota sedan or utilitarian SUV—cars that fail in defining a person—the redneck truck made a statement and became part of your identity. Typically, if you drove a lifted or beat-up truck, a can of Skoal completed the redneck image. I learned too long after our truck purchase that if you drive a truck, you dip tobacco.

"Boh! Did you see Caleb got a new lift kit and tires? He's rollin' on some thirty-fives with a six-inch lift! F'in amazing!" one country boy would say.

When finding a vehicle for Nick, my decision hinged on several data points that declared young kids are usually terrible drivers. Even if they perform well behind the wheel, history tells us that only hours upon hours of practice and training at any task brings skill. Insurance companies understand the risk posed by the still-forming brain—most specifically young male brains—on the roadways, and this knowledge shows up in extremely high rates. Nick's frontal lobe, still years from full maturity, demanded I choose a vehicle that offered an excellent shot of both brain and body arriving alive. As I saw it, the bigger the car, the better. A truck was practical. It could haul stuff, tow stuff, and keep my child safer than any other affordable option out there. So we bought a two-tone Ford F-150 with over 100,000 miles on it. While not extravagant or indulgent, it provided safety and dependability.

Nick was okay with the choice. He hopped up into his truck for the drive to his first day of sophomore year, clad in the "uniform" of a blue Southern Tide oxford and khaki shorts. The two-tone truck modeled stability with its standard tires and sensible profile. Ken's excitement for the family having a pickup truck showed with the purchase of thirty-five-inch tires, fancy rims, and a six-inch lift kit. In the guise of a sixteenth-birthday gift for Nick, Ken enlisted an upholstery shop to stitch a Browning logo on the massive center console. It was with all this personalizing—at the hands of his father—that Nick would eventually find his posse.

One day I was shotgun rider bouncing around with my son on muddy roads. Then, a few short months later, the same truck ushered in a bleak winter where the right seat was occupied by new friends. We encouraged him into this identity of boys who rode in trucks, all the while clueless to the fringe element of those skulking around at a tailgate party with dip in their lips. A persistent buzz I ignored for years morphed into a shrill message: If your kids aren't rooted firmly in a strong faith outside their perceptions of themselves and their abilities, external validation will become ever more important. Chasing stuff rather than purpose creates a God-sized void which will eventually wear down your values and close off your soul to the stable peace only provided by toiling toward a worthy mission.

The truck heralded, for good or bad, a crystallization of the image Nick slowly began to embrace. Passionate pursuits began falling off, starting with Boy Scouts. Few "cool" kids were still into scouting, and one mother confirmed Nick's shame at his lingering involvement.

This parent of a friend once said loudly enough for me and Nick to hear: "No, Brad left scouting long ago. All the boys at

Franklin started Scouts together and moved on to more important things, like sports and academics. I don't know anyone who is still a Boy Scout."

Nick persisted with his attempts to beg out of Scout troop events, despite the push and pull to the finish line from Ken. There would be no dropping out. In a pinnacle moment of successful parenting, Ken made clear that no escape lever to evacuate from the program existed. He cattle-prodded Nick to the rank of Eagle Scout. To be sure, Nick securely owns ten years of continual effort to achieve this accomplishment under his own steam. His Eagle Scout project stands today at Poinsett State Park in the form of a brick-and-mortar fire pit, flagpole, and base for Boy Scouts and the public to enjoy. The honor of completing the long process to Eagle was not lost on college admissions boards and future employers. In spite of all manner of bad choices creating a tepid resume, Eagle Scout rank shouted down the dearth, painting an accurate image of a stellar, dedicated individual of character.

When Nick approached me during his sophomore year in high school—pre-truck—with an idea to have a campout in the woods behind our house with a few new friends, my gut shouted "No!" But my actual brain kicked in and reasoned that in his fifteen years of life our relationship had only been a close one of trust and honesty; our ironclad bond left no room for doubt about his maturity and good intentions. Logic, history, and an intense desire to see my child find new friends fueled my affirmative response.

"Whose land is that, Nick?"

"It belongs to Dustin's grandfather, and he just has it sitting there with nothing on it!" he said persuasively.

"I think I need to call this grandfather and clear it with him. Do you have a number I can call, maybe Dustin's mom?"

Sensing the deal was almost done, Nick doubled down, "We will be right around the corner from our backyard, in those woods you walk past every day with Maggie." Maggie walking by the proposed campsite evoked bucolic images of young boys telling ghost stories and farting around a campfire. Nick was a brand-new Eagle Scout! Campouts were second nature to our entire family! I could drive by several times during the night! Something within me whispered that this was a bad, a very bad, idea.

"Okay..." I declared.

The phone rang an hour after my reluctant approval.

"Suz-Anne?! Beth Anne here! How you doin ovah' tha' today?" It was Beth Anne Spatts, the town's bold and brash owner of three nail spas in town (not to be confused with Beth Anne the high school student).

"I hear you're hosting a sleepover in the woods out by your place?" she drawled in a thick country accent.

Hosting?? Not even close.

Barely a moment passed to respond intelligibly to this second-ever call from her. My first call from this busy gal had been an understandable misdial, as her best friend and I shared the same first name.

"Well, hey Beth Anne!"

"Whose land is this??"

"It belongs to one of the boys' grandfathers, I think!" I said in my too-loud reply. "There has been approval!"

"Well, I'm sure you called down to this grandfather and got a thumbs-up on this thang. What are yo' plans to check fo' beer and take cah keys?" I had no clue what she was talking about. Check for beer? What was the next step after this "beer check," and pray tell what was to be done should anything turn up?

"Oh sure, Beth Anne! Nick has assured me he got approval and that there will be no beer!" My stomach rumbled as I ended the call with certainty I was in way above my pay grade. In hindsight, the call from Beth Anne was a missed opportunity to peel back the layers of ways boys can run amok. Not only was she plugged into parenting boys, she might have written the handbook that never made its way to me. Glossing over and outright misleading her in my desire to save face and seem like a responsible parent eradicated the opportunity for admittance into the club that seemed to know how to parent teen boys. She would go on through the years to be a take-no-crap mom: and the Lord had offered up, to no avail, her presence, pre-truck, to walk through the tricky years with a human bull-crap detector on speed dial.

And perhaps a lurking truth whispered, *What did it matter?* I had a teen boy excited about meeting with new friends to roast hot dogs and tell stories around a campfire, and *perhaps* they would drink *a* beer. An alliance with Beth Anne as mentor might have prevented some of the misfortune heading our way faster than Hurricane Hugo barreling for the shores of Charleston.

A few months post campout, which ended without incident, came The Truck. Ken had long yearned to own a pickup truck for himself. The two-tone F-150 ferried Nick and Ken out to hunting land one day after its purchase. Father and son, from birth, shared a furious pursuit of many endeavors requiring study, practice, and an end goal. These passions had begun with golf. The long-ago plastic, oversized golf clubs built coordination through living room practice where Nick learned how to swing and hit. From around age two, Ken took Nick on his golf outings. He would patiently instruct him on the driving range, with real, metal clubs and a plan to someday get him his own. Certainly from watching Tiger Woods, Ken harbored goals of competition for Nick. And compete he did. The Hawaii State Junior Golf Association (HSJGA) offered Nick and his teammates nine-hole rounds of golf on courses throughout Oahu, where no parents were allowed to stalk their children and "coach." One adult supervised four boys as they prepared for tournament play. Nick went on to win the title of US Kids Hawaii

State Champion in his age group, which moved him on to the finals in Williamsburg, Virginia.

Simultaneously throughout the year, golf, Little League sports, and Scouts occupied the flowing seasons of father-son pursuits. Hunting swooped in once back on the mainland with Nick's first hunting rifle. In high school, with the purchase of the truck and a lease on a plot of hunting land, the goal was tending to the land to attract the best chance of shooting deer. Heads together, the two forged a plan on ways to nurture their food plots to attract deer for their hunts. It was a new goal—this time just the two of them culminating not in a tournament but in bagging a deer or turkey.

Hunting paraphernalia soon crowded out the dusty plastic sports trophies, once artfully arranged on my son's bedroom dresser. The stalwart icons of achievement and healthy competition made way for mounds of camouflage hats, green face paint, and turkey calls. Signed and framed pictures of Alex Rodriquez and Peyton Manning came to share wall space with his mounted eight-point buck. Later, the hunting stands on the borrowed property became a place for Nick to take his friends to smoke or dip tobacco. I always embraced and nurtured his passions, from Thomas The Tank to Pokémon to golf and sports, then hunting. But competing gave way to Nick's urge for fun, and for a partner in crime. The ill-advised campout in the woods fanned the flames of a union with Tradd Watson. Their first escapade at the sanctioned "beer bash" behind my house spiraled into a Minor in Possession (MIP) fiasco at Tradd's lake house. The relationship with Tradd incited future troubling lake trips post-MIP, and fanned out through eleventh and twelfth grade into college.

In sitting down to write, a familiar exhaustion resurfaces in reliving events that bring regret in the retelling. You know the ones. The flood of memory brings a belch of discomfort deep in the gut. A class in nutrition I selected toward completion of my master's in public health at the University of South Carolina introduced the concept that humans really think with the "gut." New science claims there are brain cells in our stomach. The study promoted in *Science* magazine reveals "a new set of pathways that use gut cells to rapidly communicate with...the brain stem," and "the gut has a much more direct connection to the brain through a neural circuit that allows it to transmit signals in mere seconds."[4] This confirms the adage, "I have a gut feeling about that."

Ignoring this intuition in the gut, combined with sputtering courage to put my foot down with a tough "No!" was the fork in the road. Teens muscling away from the protective nest of their family in favor of identifying with peers rarely fail to inhabit the values of those close relationships. "The people you surround yourself with influence your behaviors, so choose friends who have healthy habits," says healthy living expert and author Dan Buettner.[5] You *are* who you surround yourself with. Common sense and mothering intuition evaporated at my flawed reasoning that any peer group was better than none. Still, the hum of Bobby's suicide (oh no, what if Nick not having—fill in the blank—puts him over the edge like Bobby?), and the guilt of ripping him from friend group to friend group at the whims of the military, were guideposts navigating my crooked path of parenting Nick's teen years.

Ken bowed out as assistant football coach the summer before Nick's junior year, leaving Nick a rare chance to navigate all alone his spot on a team. Beginning in Portugal, continuing into Hawaii, and then to Pop Warner, with a brief pause in fourth and eighth grades, then resuming with ninth-grade assistant coaching, Ken's presence was vast and grounding in his son's athletic endeavors. Ripping off the Band-Aid that was Ken's involvement the summer prior to eleventh grade opened an opportunity to notice that Nick's usual grit and self-direction had evaporated somewhere over the Atlantic or Pacific Ocean.

I got a call from Coach Larson a few weeks into summer practice.

"Hello, ma'am! This here is Coach Larsen!" he boomed and drawled.

"Well hello, Coach. How are you?"

"I been tryin' to reach yo' husband to no avail. Wondering if Nick is aw-right?" he continued, quieter now.

"Well, yes. Did he have an issue at practice today?" He had my full attention.

"No ma'am. He started practice with us, doing a nice job, and we haven't seen him for a while now. We sure hope he's aw-right?"

*What the heck?* "I am sure there is a good reason he has missed practice. I will definitely talk to him. Thanks for the call." I hung up and went searching the house for Nick.

Opening the door at the steps leading up to his room I hollered, "Nick!"

No answer. Marching up the dark staircase, I spotted his sleeping form on the bed and turned my fuming self back down the stairs to await the end of his nap. An hour later, calm and sadness had replaced my anger when Nick made his way downstairs.

"Nick, your football coach called this morning," I said, looking at him intensely.

"Oh yeah?" he exhaled as though relieved the secret was out in the open.

"Coach says you have not been at practice all week. You have been getting up, dressed for workouts every day. What's up, Tiger?"

Silence.

"Well...I haven't been going—obviously. I don't want to play football anymore." We had convened in the breakfast area, off the kitchen where I had set up a coffee nook with two big leather Ikea chairs and a cocktail table. Nick heaved up out of his chair and headed to the refrigerator for a drink.

I was speechless. He had loved the game for six years. More, if you counted peewee flag football in Portugal.

"I am too tired. It's just too hard, Mom," he admitted.

"Where have you been going, Nick?" Because he sure left the house every day dressed for football practice, returning home for weeks after lunch.

"I have been hanging out at Chick-fil-A, and driving around sometimes," he confessed.

"Coach is concerned. He mentioned you were doing well. I'm sure you can step back in to practices," I said.

"Naw, I don't want to play anymore." He paused. "I don't like it, Mom."

We lobbed words back and forth in my futile attempt to drill down to the real reason he was abandoning a sport he loved and excelled in. It still makes little sense to me. He was just too tired during the workouts, and perhaps an apparent lack of confidence in his abilities compared to the other kids on the team drove his lies? The Sumter boys had been playing together since kindergarten. Nick, the persistent outsider, and never a fan of fighting for his spot in a group, might have thought it easier to just quit.

In hindsight now, six years removed from that summer, I realize that Nick being untethered from his father—the advocate for him as a coach—left him floundering. How does a child develop a new identity from a lifetime in a duo to instantly existing alone? Since birth the paternal mentoring and coaching had enmeshed father and son in a wonderful symmetry on the field and in the everyday. Nick was left treading water in a churning ocean while Ken paddled for the shore. I liken this uncoupling to a "divorce" from one another, with Ken suddenly ceasing to continue his role of coach-advocate on the varsity football team at Franklin. No longer did Nick bask in the buffered existence as a coach's son. Adding to this insult we learned a month into the school year of a probable *why* he was too tired to go to practice that summer.

Nick dozed often in school, sleeping away through pertinent class instruction. These naps did nothing to bring him rest and renewal, though. We eventually discovered a real diagnosis: mononucleosis.

I learned from a search of WebMD that most cases of mononucleosis are caused by infection with the Epstein-Barr virus (EBV). Once someone is infected with EBV, they carry the virus—usually in a dormant state—for the rest of their life. But sometimes the virus may reactivate.

Not commonly understood by your average medical doctor, EBV can show up as strep throat, which Nick had several times, and then eventually, mono. Standard treatment involves staying home and resting for a month, with an antibiotic often prescribed. Falling behind in school, specifically in an Advanced Placement math class at the start of his junior year, prior to the arduous path leading to college placement, dealt Nick a major setback. When we have no control over our energy levels and fall off course, one of two things can occur. We can develop the grit to drill down to some untapped strength, or we can pretend. Pretending not to care protects a person from owning failure, and in his case, owning failure when success seemed impossible appeared to him a pretty good plan.

The cessation of the consistency of sports in Nick's life—and the comfort of his truck as the getaway vehicle—define the turning point from focused and directed youth to floundering, wayward fun seeker, searching for a new identity. Was it unfair to singularly herald the headwaters of the decline to this untangling of Ken and Nick? Pre-dawn father-son hunting outings dwindled, making way for solo treks for Nick. Ken's intense focus shifted. He earned a rare opportunity to own and operate a Chick-fil-A store. Nick's frequent forays to "check the deer stands" in the evening, code to *find a secluded spot to smoke and drink*, began in earnest. Ken had taken the exit ramp from charting a course for his son. Nick unceremoniously slipped away from sports, academics—and me.

Gaining an identity as a "redneck" with a jacked-up pickup truck, with certain acceptance among his peers, must bear some of the weight for the course change for Nick. Avoiding the tough stuff in life means living in those shallows—never swimming in the deep end—where one can ease back on the incessant quest toward achievement. It must have been a gift for Nick to stop striving. So much instability as a military child, so much grieving of constant loss associated with starting over again and again might eat at one's soul. Earning Eagle Scout, check. Advanced Placement classes, check. Junior National Honor Society, check. Nick had literally been coached and directed since age three in a symbiotic partnership with his father toward achieving goals, playing sports, and, in short, crushing life. Dad as coach meant no force or bully tactics to engage with Nick in these pursuits. Nick was lockstep with his father. They were marching from state to state and goal to goal, excited always in their shining duo.

"Participation in school activities, especially athletics, leads to higher self-esteem and enhanced status among peers, which some argue is a deterrent to antisocial behavior. The most dangerous time for bad behavior is the time after school and before parents get home."[6] Nick sought a sense of belonging with "fun" kids rather than those purpose-oriented peers with high self-esteem. I hadn't noticed this as a negative thing with the buffer of Ken managing Nick and blocking my view from the bleacher seats.

The empty summer rolled on, resulting in Nick's feeble efforts to heed our insistence to find a replacement activity for football. Between running around in the F-150 with other rising juniors free of rigid schedules, mowing our massive lawn, and hunting animals, Nick found his new endeavor: a black Labrador Retriever puppy whom he named Casey. Nick had a friend whose elderly dog loved her freedom. She managed to break out of her kennel with her longtime partner, and before their roundup a day later, she was pregnant. Sadly, Casey's promiscuous mama had no interest in nurturing her offspring. (I understand that urge, and from time to time, after that summer, yearned at some base level to behave less devoted and misguided, more like Casey's mother.)

Only three puppies had survived, and Casey had almost perished as well. The owners raised up Labradors for hunting and kept them kenneled outside most of the year. Casey was kept in the kennel with her mother and two surviving siblings. Jack—the boy who was selling Casey and would later become Nick's college roommate—had a sister named Millicent who heeded an urge to check on the puppies before departing for school. Approaching the kennel, she heard faint whimpering sounds from the nearby ravine. Drawing closer, the whimpering intensified. Barreling down the muddy slope, she slipped to a halt at the edge of a tiny stream, scanning for the source of the sound. Pausing, holding her breath, Millicent cocked her ear toward the direction of the whimper. Hiding in plain sight five feet in front of her was a struggling Casey, camouflaged in mud. Slogging through the sucking muck, Millicent swooped in and rescued Casey, then scampered back up the hill. Cuddling the shivering pup, she rushed her to a warm bath, dried her off, and returned her to her indifferent mother. Casey was safe, at least for the moment.

A few weeks later she was rescued once more by Nick and brought home to live with us and Maggie. The last month of summer prior to his junior year, instead of early morning practice, Nick trudged out with Casey several times a night for potty breaks. He stuck close to home for four weeks, training and caring for Casey. That month was a respite; with Nick detached from his peer group, he returned to his best self. Much like the boy who ran circles with Maggie in the yard in Hawaii, there was that same spirit, teaching Casey how to fetch. We took her for car rides in the truck—to the vet, to the pet store—and often stopped somewhere for lunch. I did not expect nor desire my son to never inhabit his maturing body or to stay my little boy. I *did* desire he find out who he was in healthy and productive ways—like raising this dog or achieving a worthy goal, like the Eagle rank. I expected him to stay grounded in the sturdy foundation which Ken and I diligently and patiently tried to develop over sixteen years. It was my last "normal" month with my son. I was grateful that, in a way, Nick and Casey trained each other that month—in dedication, love, and discipline—for the road ahead would require these essential traits to endure the arduous journeys to come.

Louie Giglio in his book *Goliath Must Fall* recounts a story about a pet tiger mauling to death his master, who had raised him since birth.[7] A giant, and seemingly gentle, Bengal Tiger raised from a cub in captivity went from enjoying a symbiotic performance partnership with his caregiver/trainer to mauling and killing him one random day during rehearsal. From tussling and playtime in the early years, a relationship was formed—on the part of the human. I imagine the tiger, who lays claim to the Panthera genus could never tell he was adopted into a Homo sapiens world, leaving the master to assume their relationship was one of familiar trust and love. Perhaps it was. More than likely, the innate nature of a wild animal toward wild behavior was overlooked during the unwavering bond the human forms in the early years. The playful and harmless tiger cub easily forges what seems to be a loving relationship as its master feeds and guides the cub in the way of the world, instilling in him manners and etiquette on all the ways of operating in the human world. But the tiger can't change his stripes. He is, and will always be, a wild animal. The master remained unguarded during that fateful day, when natural instinct prevailed in what must have seemed a shocking ultimate betrayal from his friend and partner.

Raising up my own Tiger from the cub stage followed the typical caregiver arc. From snuggles and feedings to potty training and manners; then morals and skills; and always direction on avoiding the pitfalls of drugs, drinking, and intimate relationships. My young cub soaked in the lessons with a mostly eager and grateful attitude, evidenced by consistent behavioral and verbal feedback from Nick that seemed to say: "We are on the same page in this thing called *family*. I am a contributing and engaged member, and I will do my part and not shred to bits the lessons I learn from your loving efforts and sacrifice."

My husband, son, and I together formed a triangle forged in steel. Unable to produce more than one offspring, Ken and I poured all our devotion and energy into Nick. Resting on this well-placed trust, we directed our worries for Nick toward external factors, such as school bullies, academic challenges, and pesky allergy issues.

Nick's formative years on the island of Oahu from grades one to three permanently shaped his habits and character. The circle time with Mrs. Fukumoto set him up to feel self-conscious—and to lie. After the circle times, he felt physically awful a lot. A few of the pediatric doctors at Tripler Army Hospital blamed it on Mt. Kīlauea on the Big Island. The oft-active volcano spewed its angry lava out and into the sea. The atmosphere absorbed the earth's molten innards, turning them to ash and toxic vapor. A miasma of bad air wafted over to Oahu on the tropical winds, depositing the evidence of Kīlauea's mighty force into our yard and air ducts.

One of Nick's physicians explained, "We have done several respiratory tests on Nicholas, and nothing comes back definitive for asthma."

That seemed like good news.

"Many kids experience these symptoms when the vog is heavy," he explained.

My eyebrows scrunched together as I was about to call bullshit on this diagnosis of allergic reaction to...*vog*.

The crusty Army doctor continued. "The volcanic ash spewing from the Big Island blows over to Oahu—mix that with our marine environment and it creates a type of volcanic fog, or vog, that can wreak havoc on lungs."

He was making a bit of sense now. My eyebrows retreated.

"Hmm...Nick's throat closing, black under-eye circles, and stomach pain are all fallout from the vog?" These symptoms spurred our diversion from normal to trudge up the hill to the massive pink medical complex, just outside of Waikiki, to receive this diagnosis. It brought some relief. I felt sure once we left Hawaii and/or the volcano calmed down, the situation would resolve.

Revisiting, yet again, those exploratory quests into "what's wrong with my son?" seems simple in the rearview. Ten years later, my family faced off at three corners of a disconnected triangle, and I wondered again, "What's wrong with my son?" This time my Tiger Cub turned on me—and I failed, and facilitated the attack. Worse, my husband remained unconcerned, floating in denial that his boy could do anything awful. I was floundering around in this betrayal all alone.

────────────── **Nick's Perspective** ──────────────

*I remember I went a few times to practice. Then, I didn't want to go anymore. It boils down to the fact that I just didn't love it enough. I would go to Bojangles, Chick-fil-A, or the house where I was dog-sitting and hang out and dip (tobacco), until practice ended. I didn't want to tell Dad. I felt like I didn't want to, so I didn't. I didn't enjoy waking up at six in the morning to go work out for five hours. If I had loved it, maybe it would have been worth the effort. I didn't think at the time I was falling out of love with football. But looking back, that was exactly what was happening. I did not enjoy playing anymore. Therefore, one morning I just said, "I am not going to go to practice." So, I went to CFA and then to pet sit, and just never went to practice. I dipped...drove around...and thought it was more fun. You know that song, "Write a Letter to Me" by Brad Paisley? Well, I wish I would have kept going...to get in a routine of working out, weightlifting, and doing it properly, every day. The discipline of it. Now, I am late to the game doing it on my own, working out and gaining the discipline to keep in shape.*

*I read what Mom wrote and she put some science behind me not wanting to go to practice. She could be right, but I think I just didn't like it anymore. And I guess I didn't want to tell my parents; maybe it was a fear of disappointing Dad.*

*To be honest, I learned a lot more not being in sports. I explored different avenues of life. I got all my badness—my rebellion—out of the way by the time I was nineteen. I got it over with. Well, that was fun. Now it's time to get internships and get serious about life after college. So, not having sports led me to hang out, drive around, smoke weed, and drink. If I had stayed in football, I would not have had that time to venture into rebellion. Now, I have no interest in that lifestyle.*

## A LOSING BET

Bellagio Resort Hotel & Casino on The Strip transforms seasonally their 14,000-square-foot indoor botanical garden into a showcase of inspiring sights, sounds, and colors. When the seasons change, so do the displays. It is very elaborate and fancy. Visitors the world over come to Las Vegas and meander around the majestic space, marveling at the use of flowers and greenery to create the massive flower sculptures. Mimicking the talent of Pasadena's Rose Parade geniuses, these artists at Bellagio go well beyond the float theme. It is full-throttle talent in winter creating Christmas villages, bridges, frolicking carnation flower polar bears, and a plethora of glitzy Christmas trees.

The mega resort barely existed in 1990, when I attended UNLV. We frequented Caesars Palace, The Sands, The Dunes (I often confused the two, referring to both as The Sand Dunes), and the new resort biggie—The Mirage. Fronting the resort, a lifelike rock volcano with a waterfall exterior spewed flames on the hour, high into the blowtorch heat of a summer sky. Buffet meals still cost $2.99 at Circus Circus. And, in the waning vestiges of mafia-run Las Vegas, one could still stuff the slot machines with quarters at Slots a Fun before crossing the street to the dark and smoky rendezvous lounge, The Peppermill. The casino showrooms were old school: tip the showroom captain (at Bally's it was tennis star Andre Agassi's father palming the cash) for a better seat, order a drink from the waiter, buy a light-up yo-yo from the cigarette girl, and...take a picture. That was me behind the clunky black camera. Taking artful pictures and selling them paid my apartment rent and UNLV tuition. Lucrative jobs—jobs you could tell your family about—abounded in Las Vegas prior to the influx of the mega resorts. Mine allowed ample time to complete my senior internship in broadcasting at KLAS-TV Channel 8 and graduate with a bachelor's degree that I ultimately determined was not a good fit for me. So with degree in hand, I relocated to Northern Virginia in 1994 to pursue my true passion in health and wellness.

My sister, Cindy, the reason I chose to attend UNLV, had left with her husband, Dan, to circumnavigate the globe. They returned years later giving Nick and me the chance for the occasional visit. Dan and Nick would rise before dawn to hike the hills around Hoover Dam. Afterward, they would head to the flea market to find "treasures" Nick didn't need and would eventually sell for profit at our yard sales. Always a return to Vegas was sweet nostalgia—I loved scooting around town, trying to find the Vegas I had come to know during my four years as a resident. Oddly, I still enjoyed tuning into Channel 8 news with Gary Waddell and Paula Francis.

The December of Nick's junior year, he agreed to fly with me from Sumter to Vegas to visit my sister and her husband. The early bonds strengthened through those hikes, science experiments, and shopping faded after Nick found his new peer group—and his truck. He didn't want to leave his newfound identity. And he had zero desire to be my traveling buddy. In a sulky act asserting his independence, he wore camouflage throughout the trip. His identity was rooted firmly in camo, trucks, and friends. Pictures taken that day show a man/child, committed to the identity he was forging. Looking back now at those photos evokes in me a respect for him not selling out to fit in—to wear nice clothes to a fancy exhibit. He chose to remain *him*. I also laugh at my camo kid standing taller than me as we pose alongside the marble paths in Bellagio's Christmas wonderland, with giant silver stars reaching down for us.

The MIP firmly behind him, life was good—mostly. My career in public health was taking off. I'd procured the aforementioned job at Shaw Air Force Base along with a regular schedule leading classes at Southern Bliss Yoga in Sumter. Ken was busy working in Columbia and immersed in final interviews for his new career. I lost track of Nick, assuming he was more mature at sixteen, in a great school, and part of what I thought was a great friend group. He reluctantly participated on the track team, but the lack of zeal proved he barely cared.

Then his grades started slipping, and falling asleep in class accelerated. He couldn't be bothered to invest in schoolwork; projects assigned were hastily completed the night before. With my busy schedule, Nick began eating at Tradd's one or two times a week. Our ritual evening meal around the table waned as Nick ate the excellent Southern food cooked by Tradd's father more often. Several times a month he would spend the night with them. After our winter-break ski trip with Tradd's family and two other best friends, Nick doubled down with Tradd for a kerosene surge in the slow burn toward a runaway, out-of-control blaze.

## MIP

Nick's Minor in Possession was that first, really-loud God whisper dripping with opportunity for intervention. But instead of awakening to the need for a course correction for my son, I hit the snooze button. The chance to parent courageously really began with the MIP. My response instead was one of rationalizing, denial, and plain cowardly avoidance of a hard choice. Time and again I puffed up my chest to level tough consequences—only to retreat, submitting to the burden of a subconscious fear that had run roughshod on my limbic system.

The early years we spent in Europe had left me with the notion that we could normalize alcohol with an end goal of demystifying it for Nick, avoiding the thrill of sneaky drinking and getting drunk in the teen years. Stopping short of an Italian custom to water down wine for a kid, I did offer ten-year-old Nick sips of my wine. Ken did the same with his beer in Nick's elementary years. I wanted to create transparency with my child, shaping him to turn to his parents as mentors in all things life. Get your kid's drinking under your watchful gaze early in life and *Voila!* There will be no wild party years in his future! In hindsight, the alcohol demystifying process could have included years of insistent encouragement to pursue a healthy endorphin rush through his athletics and instruction on how to structure himself with habits that excluded excessive downtime filled with video games and TV. I was proud of my personal example to Nick of how to care for your own life. But instead, there we were, not in Europe, dealing with an abuse of alcohol despite my best attempts to avoid such a scenario.

MIP should stand for Mama is perturbed; or Mom in Panic; or the ever-appropriate Meltdown Imminent, Pause. But alas, I learned firsthand it stands for Minor in Possession of alcohol. This possessing alone doesn't seem reason to believe my child was ready to sink. Didn't we all "possess" alcohol while underage?

The blazing fireworks of the Fourth of July had just concluded, and my siblings and mother and I wandered back in, ears still ringing, to the coolness of Mom's house. Gathered around heaping plates of homemade apple pie, the trill of my cell phone raised the hair on my arms. It sounded like trouble. That hot summer holiday, once festive and celebratory, was the day my sweet baby turned goofy adolescent and surly teen, introducing me to the really dark side of parenting. I stood with phone in hand in the doorway to the guest room at my mother's house in Missouri, some seven hundred miles away from Sumter; my life as I had known it for sixteen years shifted as I learned the meaning of a Minor in Possession. No one tells you the hardest part of parenting is when your kids grow up...and face a near arrest. The wrong kind of growth showed my son struggling to define himself in a way he never had before.

In that moment, on the phone, unable to lay eyes on my child, the rationalization began. Perhaps this MIP charge with its subsequent consequence of a "Do Not Drink Anymore" scare course, along with a day of community service at a food bank, would wipe the slate clean for Nick. After all, everyone to include me and my entire family drank before the age of twenty-one. Unscathed, each of the underage drinkers in my life arrived to legal status fully intact. Did it seem normal to me then? Was it merely a problem because Nick got caught? Moving into the bedroom, keeping this upsetting event from spilling into the festive atmosphere in the living room, I held onto the phone and braced myself as my husband, back at home, laid out the facts. Nick was driving somewhat drunk after a July Fourth weekend celebration. His jacked-up Ford F-150 truck all but shouted, "Stupid redneck underage person sure to be drunk with a cooler of beer IN THE BACK SEAT is driving this truck!"

I chose to spend the Fourth in Missouri with my mother and siblings without Nick and Ken, and came to regret the fractious fork taken. Ken wanted to hunt and Nick was excited to accept an unusual inclusion to celebrate the Fourth with Tradd's parents, Mary Kate and Tripp, and his sister, Lila. Mary Kate and Tripp would come to love Nick, include him in all family activities, and be the second family that guided and nurtured him unconditionally. They trekked yearly to their lakeside vacation home on a backed-up swamp turned lake for a fireworks bash with a side of boating, paddle boarding, and turns on the jet skis. Many of Nick's private-school peers would be at various homes sprinkled around the lake, seeking each other out to do what teens do at the lake— tan and get to bed early, I naively thought. I really did. It seemed wise to get up early, well-rested, and launch the boat before the crowds thickened up and the alligators lurked around, looking for a late lunch.

I grabbed my Blackberry and retreated into the guest room at Mom's, naively thinking that a Fourth of July celebration consisted of just waterskiing and fireworks. Perhaps. But my son rarely, until this point, gave me cause to believe he could go rogue.

"What happened? What does this all mean?" I sank to the bed in the guest room, scrambling to absorb the news of the MIP.

"He's fine," Ken said. "Tripp said he will take a court-appointed class and, given this is his first offense, the MIP will be expunged— like it never happened." It sounded like Ken was eating some potato chips.

"I hear you," I replied, seething, "but he was out at the lake with two respected adults! For crap's sake, one of them is a DOCTOR! A freaking HEART SURGEON!"

"I spoke to Tripp," Ken explained. "He says his son was pretty tanked. Nick seemed fine...told them he had only a few beers hours ago and was steady on his feet. They had gotten as far as the end of the dirt road from the lake house. Tripp says he was following Nick to make sure he didn't weave or anything..."

"WHAT?! I thought Nick was 'steady on his feet!' Why was Tripp concerned about WEAVING. Why on earth did they let him drive?!"

"Let me finish!" Ken shouted, then calmly continued.

"Tripp was sure he was okay to drive. He's a doctor! He should know! He followed Nick past a checkpoint—and Nick was randomly pulled over. I guess they saw the cooler in the back and smelled alcohol on Nick, which gave them a reason to search the cooler."

I glanced around the bedroom, helpless, shaking my head now. "Wait wait *wait*... How did Tripp and Mary Kate NOT SEE A YETI COOLER in the backseat?!"

"Well, they did. But they didn't check to see what was in it."

"Their son was TANKED! And they didn't check the cooler..." I mumbled, standing up and beginning to pace the small room.

"The cops checked the cooler and it was literally full of beer. Apparently the boys had already gone through one cooler full of that cruddy Bud Light. I can't believe they got drunk on that crap," Ken said, still crunching food as he spoke, in a less-than-stellar moment.

I uploaded the facts: Best Friend is taking a snooze in the car with his father while my son is getting pulled over and ARRESTED!! My trust in Tripp and Mary Kate Watson, whom I barely knew at that point, was misplaced. How could a family gathering at the lake with a group of sixteen-year-old boys devolve into my son getting arrested?

The prevalent "boys will be boys until they are men" paradigm permeated the minds of my son's friends and my own husband. *60 Minutes* and *Dateline* had covered the issue of a prolific and prevalent disregard for the law in supplying underage teens with alcohol. People who don't directly supply it tend to look the other way while the drinking rages on. I know this, because after the MIP, after the fear and thrashing about on ways to produce logical consequences to the MIP, after judging Tripp and Mary Kate so harshly, I too looked the other way. I bought the beer, and I sat complacent time after time.

The majority of underage drinkers of alcohol, and I have known many, scoot through the under-twenty-one years happily breaking the law with nary a consequence. I know I did. Tucked into the farthest recesses of my wallet as a teen was a second identification card—a fake ID courtesy of my oldest sister. She was a full six years my senior, and at eighteen I convinced her without a show-down to "lose" her Missouri driver's license and let me foot the cost at the DMV for a replacement.

I discovered alcohol my senior year in high school. My quest for fun coincided with earning a spot on the varsity cheerleading squad, which garnered an invite to every peer-thrown party in a thirty-mile radius of my house. There was once a time in history when police officers, pulling over the driver under the influence, might have searched the car, confiscated contraband, and sent the tipsy motorists on their way. The most sober one in the car was deputized to take the wheel, with instructions to go immediately home. This protocol was my high school experience in the 1980s—driving drunk was often tolerated if you could hold the car between the lines. But the DUI was a different beast now.

Nick got somewhat lucky on this first driving-while-buzzed incident with no mug shot or trip to the county jail. With a wide circle of influence in that small lake town, Tripp's intervention during the roadblock stop resulted in a thirty-minute chill-out in the rear seat of a county cop car. With a soon-to-be-expunged MIP citation, Nick would emerge none the worse for wear.

He was not fazed. His best friend, alert and almost sober after the brief snooze, was probably texting him from the safety of his father's SUV during the bust. This debacle cemented the thrill of living on the edge for them: with parents close by, certainly a faux bravado fed the excitement. What it also forged was an unbreakable kinship with Tradd. After bouncing around, losing best friends for the entirety of his childhood, Nick was hungry for this mutual, unconditional acceptance of a best friend. There was time to grow and nurture this connection, versus in the past, where we would relocate with the Air Force every year or two and snuff out the sparks, for better or worse, of any developing friendship. Fun and extreme bouts of daring one another at any cost would be the fuel that would set the two of them on fire over the course of the next four years.

The tsunami was churning as my world was shaking apart, the stress of it all eroding my rational thought processes responsible for managing fear and stress. The MIP was just the first ripple of huge waves heading our way. The ocean and swamp analogy used to understand this tumultuous time perfectly describes my sense of being sucked into hurricane waters, paddling for dear life while the storm grew ever fiercer. Over the years after that MIP, respites from the craziness existed. I stumbled upon friendships, grace, and glimpses of hope. There was always hope in the midst of the nonsense and crap that was in our life.

With the MIP, my son could relate to his rap music "heroes" and feel included in their dubious ranks of quasi- and full-on criminals. Did Nick conflate this episode with the crimes of the myriad of criminal millionaires sporting giant gold dollar-sign necklaces with their matching Gucci watches rapping about their high dolla' lives? In fact, his group began sporting gold-link chains on their hairless chests, with the top two buttons open to prove their maturity. If anything, this "arrest" transported him from smooth-faced, scrawny teen to a revered place in an exclusive club of truants whose images he truly admired. My child did not see the imminent and epic meltdown barreling toward him and saw no need to press pause. All the years of parental modeling of success and good morals seemed for naught. Lost and forgotten. All we had taught for sixteen years evaporated in the thrill of acceptance and union with a peer group desperately attempting to live on the edge in their upper-middle-class lives. My tepid responses early on in the fight to keep my son afloat are understandable to me now. The warrior mom in me had grown dormant. I hadn't been to battle for my son's well-being in several years. It was time to dig deep and activate that Mama Bear Crazy born on that ski hill in Austria.

---

### Nick's Perspective

*That Friday, Tradd, Phil, and I went to the lake. Mr. Tripp would be heading up soon. So we went fishing. We had about a case of beer and six mini bottles of liquor between the three of us. We were catching fish—one of the biggest I have caught there; it was fun.*

*Riding around in the boat (yes, while we were drinking) seemed normal. Around dinnertime, the rest of Tradd's family arrived. We were all three drunk, me less so than Phil or Tradd, who was way hammered. We sat down to the dinner that Mr. Tripp had made, steaks I think, when Tradd bounced away from the table to go throw up in the shower. He clogged it up.*

*Pretty much from there, Mr. Tripp had had enough. He said, "We can't stay here; we are leaving!"*

*Mr. Tripp asked me, "Do you have any contraband in your car?"*

*We said, "No sir, no sir, there is nothing in the car."*

*"There is a checkpoint—are you sure you are okay?" Mr. Tripp asked. We didn't think we would get caught, so we said, "No, it's all good!"*

*"Do you have anything alcoholic in the car in case there is a checkpoint?" he asked more pointedly that time around.*

*We looked at each other and back at Mr. Tripp and said, "No, no sir!!"*

*So we saw the checkpoint, and we drove through, thinking they would not search us. They search everyone, it turns out, and saw the cooler with all the beers in it. Mr. Tripp was sober of course, with plans to take Tradd home to Sumter.*

*The cops searched the cooler, found the beer, and took it all.*

*I clearly remember Mr. Tripp yelling and screaming. He lost it. I sat in the back of the cop car while Phil was getting questioned. That was scary. If you really want me to be honest, I was like, "I don't care, screw this. I am sixteen. I can have a beer. Bite me."*

*It was scary, but at the same time I was thinking,* Whatever, who cares. *I was a punk. I guess I knew it didn't matter.*

*If I had gone to jail, maybe that would have affected me. If, someday, my own child at age fifteen walks in the house a little drunk, I am going to say, "At least you Ubered." I personally don't feel that having a beer is a big deal. I might change my mind though. Heck, right now I am only twenty-two. It's about how much you consume.*

*The cops let us go with just that MIP and a date to appear in court. Once we were sprung from the backseat of the cop car, Mr. Tripp had a friend come to the checkpoint to get us. We actually turned around and went back to the lake, like it never happened. We succeeded in sneaking out to have another beer at the dock. Yes, I had a few beers AFTER my MIP. The court saw fit to have Phil and me enroll in "alcohol classes." The unscathed Tradd's parents signed him up, too, in a show of support, I guess.*

Ken was absent most of the summer—training for his venture into owning/operating a Chick-fil-A and preparing for an impending move to New Mexico in September. I would be a "single" mom the entirety of our child's senior year—a role that played out often in our military life. I needed some structure for my son, what with no sport, no puppy to train, and full-on defiance settling over my home. I insisted Nick find a summer job. I scrounged up an opportunity for a week of crewing on his aunt Karen's sailboat. This would interrupt his trajectory and perhaps plant some seeds of interest outside of being a redneck.

He did find a job, with the help of Tradd's father. An opening appeared for a tuxedo fitter at John's Formal Wear, an odd little shop downtown that never let go of the dated window mannequins donning ill-fitting tuxes. These mannequins were infamous in town for their gray skin tone and scraggy black straw wigs. I often asked Nick to liberate the window of those zombies. "No, Mr. John changes nothing in that store. I can't touch a thing."

The summer went like this for Nick: Sleep in and not eat breakfast on the days he wasn't sleeping at Tradd's. Next, get up and play video games or watch TV if the lawn did not need mowing. Three days a week, and Saturday, he would roll into an easy four-hour workday. Unless there was a wedding party to measure, he just sat in the back watching TV. At dinnertime, he would eat with me if I insisted. Then he would always head out to "the movies" or to Tradd's for "video games." Once, it was the circle-up bonfire on someone's farm on the outskirts of town.

My son and his friends drove twenty miles to the boondocks to gather in a field, circling up trucks to drink and socialize the night away—I was told it was to play music and make s'mores. They would "camp" overnight and drive home in time to stumble into their respective churches with their families the next morning. We had sampled most of the churches in town, and connected with none of them. It was easy to avoid, subconsciously, the commitment to our spiritual growth by declaring no Sumter church was as great as our one true church in Hawaii. So, we went on holidays to the Baptist church down the road. Nick was not one of the boys who stumbled into church every Sunday, and thus celebrated his Sabbath by sleeping in and either hunting or golfing with his father when Ken was home.

Like a nocturnal lion hunting prey in Botswana, I stalked my son. The first roots in an absurd, years-long stint as paranoid detective to discover the truth consisted of setting off under cloak of darkness to make sure he was alive. I crawled out of bed at 5 a.m. after a sleepless Saturday night, still worried, to investigate the remains of one of those red-dirt-road field parties. One rule

I strictly enforced was Nick's iPhone Finder must remain on—always. If it wasn't, I would track him down via his friends or the parents of friends until he was located. This iPhone stalking was another stressful constant I inflicted upon myself in that summer before Nick's senior year—and three years to follow. After only one enforced threat, Nick felt forever humiliated, and mostly left it on. Unless the battery would "die" for an hour. During one episode, after multiple tracking attempts and right before I sent out the hounds, I waited wide awake for him to respond.

"Nick! Answer me...now!" my text said.

No response. No *Read* below my screaming bubble.

"NICK! RESPOND NOW! WHERE ARE U?" in shouty caps.

"ANSWER ME!"

"I AM CALLING TRADD'S FATHER!" I texted rapid-fire, with no response. Then, just in the nick of time:

"Hey Mom! Sorry! My phone died! I am almost home! We had to stop for gas!"

His little face icon would pop up again on the GPS map confirming his location. This was how I found the red-dirt-road party. I tracked his icon on my phone while I traveled south on the quiet predawn highway. Following the innocent face, I arrived to a silent field off a country road about thirty miles from our house. Creeping as close as I could without looking like the crazed mother I was, I looked for his truck among the ones circling the smoldering bonfire in the center. Something close to peace of mind settled over me when the icon indicated his presence in the quiet field rather than crashed in some ditch or holed up in a nearby crack house. Reflecting back on my passive-aggressive, do-little/worry-often strategy, I have deep regrets in my lack of courageous parenting. Had my pervasive faults, my misguided morals and norms come to rest in the behavior and character of my son?

The "deck hand" gig turned out to be a bust. Nick drove his truck, alone, to meet up with Karen, her husband, and two retired Navy officers—the official captains. They would sail from Ft. Lauderdale to the Florida Keys. Ken and I would meet them for dinner in Key West. We drove down a day after Nick had departed. Karen's disappointment was apparent as we texted midway through their trip.

"Hey Karen! How's it going?" I texted.

"Hey! Smooth waters, heading into Key Largo now."

"Is Nick learning a lot?"

"Well...we can't get him out of the front trampoline—a large mesh lounging area in the front of a catamaran—for more than a few duties. He is on his phone pretty much nonstop—or sleeping."

Another text a day later:

"Hey! Wanted to check: Max (the Navy captain) is offering Nick some alcohol. Is that okay?" she texted.

"Heck no! We sent him out there to work and get away from all that!"

This was confirmation that adults ply kids with alcohol. I had done it with my niece when she was fifteen. I was part of the problem. Obviously, I did not see anything wrong with kids drinking. Did I?

When the boat docked at the completion of the sail, Nick roared home, making an eight-and-a-half-hour drive in seven hours, just in time to take a girl he had just started "talking to" to a party at the lake. Nick later confided he surpassed 100 mph most of the way home. He had learned nothing, and in fact spent a week tanning and texting on a fancy Catamaran.

––––––––––––––––––– **Nick's Perspective** –––––––––––––––––––

*I didn't pay much attention to speed limits. When I was happy, the sun was out, and good music was on it was more fun to drive fast. I had an app that detected*

*police cars with radar and avoided getting caught. It was only when I forgot to*
*use the app that I was pulled over and ticketed.*

*Now, I don't like going fast. I guess you could say I am a rigid rule follower.*
*But, back then we did not drink and drive much in high school. In college we*
*did. Mom is not going to like this...and I know it was wrong. When I moved*
*from my freshman dorm to my U Center downtown apartment, and I was close*
*to everything, I did not drink and drive much. Honestly, after freshman year my*
*parents encouraged me to Uber. It wasn't a big thing then, but they were paying,*
*and I thought it was a better option. Of course, that is all stupid stuff we did to*
*flirt with our immortality. I am shocked I survived it all.*

This was also the onset of regular summer weekends at Tradd's
lake house. Tradd's father, Tripp, worried less about his son
than Ken did Nick. No need to interfere in the trajectory of his
child's life.

"Boys will be boys!" he would say. "The thing that settles them
down is findin' the right woman! They just blowing off steam now,
sowin' theh' oats till they meet her!"

After the MIP and one other episode where "someone" vomited
on the curtains, I found Nick's time at the lake unsettling. Stories
every summer speckled local news of yet another drunk teen slam-
ming a boat into a bridge. Driving to and from the lake involved
back roads and byways, prone also to the same drunk teens who
made it off their boats intact and were heading back home. One
story in the news unfurled a horrific tale of a boy from a prom-
inent South Carolina family who slammed his boat into a dock,
killing one of the passengers. Paul Murdaugh, in a highly intoxi-
cated state, piloted his small boat on a cold, dark night back to his
house. His friends, helpless to stop the fate of the speeding boat,
paid the price for his drunken joyride. Why did they agree to allow
him to pilot the boat moments after stepping out of a dockside bar
for the return to his family lake house? The tragic tale took an

even uglier turn when Paul and his mother were found slain at their home. After months of investigation, Paul's father, Alex, was tried, found guilty, and sentenced to life in prison.

*Chapter 9*

# Screengate
# and Conditional
# Parenting

Nick's window screen was missing. *Summer days where temperatures* *exceeded* 90 degrees with 95 percent humidity were windows-closed, stay-inside-with-the-air-on days. Mowing the lawn one morning, I happened to glance up at his bonus bedroom above the garage and noticed something odd. I shut off the mower to investigate. Entering the cool house, I pulled open the door and marched up the carpeted staircase. As I paused to scan the room, his misstep peeked out from behind his baseball bag, perched alongside the window—the missing window screen. I slid behind the corner chair and sure enough, it was a poor attempt to hide this massive thing behind the chair. But why? Maggie was at my heels, but remained silent...she wasn't outing her master.

That night, I heard his truck roar up just before curfew, rap music belting out a jarring rhythm, and then silence. Five minutes later, the mudroom door banged closed. He was home. But the screen—off the window—sparked crazy thoughts. Would he be sneaking out later? Come home at curfew, and then slither out thinking I would not stalk his phone again? One sleepless hour later that gut feeling roused me out of bed and out into the dark, humid night, using my phone flashlight to aid my desperate forage through the bushes to see if he was attempting another getaway. Tradd was spending the night, so if any sneaking out was in the plans, it could have gone down that night. The stubborn bushes revealed not a single cigarette butt, belay rope, or bottle of booze. What was I trying to find? Nick and Tradd had slipped in right at curfew. Were they up in his room? Or had they snuck back out, as Nick confessed to doing when staying at Tradd's house? Absent in this craziness was any semblance of my usual rational thought. I surrendered the moonlight hunt and headed back inside. Still, something was off.

I couldn't rest until I knew Nick was safe at home—in bed for the night. His icon showed him home, but still, he once had let slip that kids get burner phones to take with them while they sneak out, leaving their primary phones in their bedroom. It was not an easy option to creep up the stairs to his bedroom. The only entrance was the door at the bottom of the stairs. Straight up for six steps and then turn...up six more into his space. Giving it one last shot to assuage my paranoia, I opened the door of the silent loft. After a moment, sanity returned with the bleat of a large fart, affirming they were indeed asleep and safe under my roof. The whole missing-screen insanity paired well with all the stalking I allowed to occupy my life, merging in a mix that made me feel certifiably crazy.

I earned my own education in pulling off screens and sneaking out windows as a high school senior, when a friend and I slipped out on more than one occasion for late-night ballyhooing. I would kill the engine on my yellow Ford Pinto and roll silently to the curb at her highly parented, darkened home. Inside, she was fashioning a pillow into human form, topping it with a wig before climbing out the window. Off we would roll, howling with glee toward the drive-thru liquor store. Josie looked older, so she would sit in the driver's seat despite her inability to drive a stick shift. Squeezing her modest chest into a hint of cleavage, she would stick a cigarette in her vibrant red lips and cruise up in first gear, full of flirt and sass, to the window.

"Hey Cowboy! Can you get me a bottle of Stormy Nights and a fifth of Sloe Gin?" she drawled in her Hispanic accent.

"Hey pretty lady, you don't look old enough to be out so late." He was onto us as he leaned his little body on the drive-up window sill.

"Awww, of course we are. The kids are asleep and it's time for mama to have some fun!" she cooed, threatening our credibility.

I reached around to the floor of the backseat for our tin coffee bank full of cash. Clad in matching cheerleader shorts and skimpy tops, we would beg money from travelers on the intersection of Rio Bravo and Isleta Boulevards in Albuquerque to earn funds for our cheerleader uniforms. We kept the leftover money for ourselves, somehow justifying the unethical act as earned income. Counting out change and dollar bills, we paid for our booze and off we went, changing drivers around the corner as we hurriedly unscrewed the bottle tops before screeching off to a nearby party with our open containers.

I felt unsure and timid; my own former antics helped create an elusive rationalization, blocking out my essential bravery to confront head-on errant behavior brewing under my own roof. For years I would do this sneaky dodge and weave into the storm, creeping around the periphery like my Screengate night in the bushes with the prickly pine needles underfoot. Perhaps the normalcy of expressing my own independence through drinking and sneaking initially jammed the radar on detecting and deflecting Nick's own stupid journey. A less-seasoned mother would have attributed the relocated screen to an innocent desire for better airflow. And a braver me should have known better than to give him a pass.

------ **Nick's Perspective** ------

*You see, there is really not much of a story to it. The night before she found the screen was off, I did sneak out. (The accuracy of her instincts to this day surprises me.) I am sure Mom told me I could not go to a party or hang out with friends. I said to myself, No! So, I found a way to do it. I took the sheets off my bed—the fitted sheet, normal sheet, and the comforter. I tied them all together, then affixed the "rope" to the bottom of my bed frame. I took the screen off. Thankfully, I knew how to climb, so I used my Eagle Scout skills to rappel down the brick house. I was young and stupid, and I did not care about falling or getting back up...I just wanted to go to the party. I was never nervous that Mom would come and check on me. I just didn't care.*

*I didn't drive, so I guess Tradd picked me up. The Sumter "screw-ups" held these boring parties—usually that was where we went. Occasionally, we hung with the good kids, like Brad and Spat. Always after 1:00 a.m., I walked back into the house through the side door. Once back to my room, I hauled the sheet rope up, made the bed, and went to sleep content. It begs the question, Why did I shimmy down the bedsheets rather than just sneaking through the door? Well, sober, I thought I would get caught; coming home drunk I cared even less about Mom finding out. I think that was the first and last time sneaking out of our house—if I wanted to go somewhere Mom wouldn't allow, I spent the night with Tradd.*

*Tradd had snuck out also, the same night of my sheet-rappel adventure. It was really easy to sneak out of his house—we did it all the time. His dad had one of those CPAP machines, and we knew his parents would never hear us. And their bedroom was downstairs, far from his window. Sometimes, when I was over there, we would sneak out and just dip, and stroll the neighborhood. It was the act of doing something you knew you shouldn't. The parties were never that much fun. It was the thrill of getting away with something. Did I just upset you, Mom? That was the younger me! It was a long time ago! But, I'm sorry if I hurt your feelings!*

I felt that my child, who I thought never kept secrets and adhered to the rules, could always be trusted. He came home with stories about how this boy was smoking pot or another kid was taking Adderall for fun. I felt relieved at hearing these stories, thinking that my child was wise to avoid drugs and alcohol. At this point, I suspected he had the occasional drink but had no idea how much he enjoyed getting buzzed. But the truth had been building since the MIP a year ago. Screengate layered on facts that my son was not the innocent one surrounded by punks. My child who never kept secrets was lying. As a teen, I had parked my bottle of Sloe Gin under my megaphone. Was my son so much like me that I lacked the distance to see clearly?

The first of many of Nick's contraband hiding spots was found by accident under the Ikea chair cushion. It fessed up his stash during my snooping, outing a can of Skoal mint-flavored dip. When I confronted Nick, Tradd claimed it was his while Nick swore he didn't dip. I believed him—*Tradd* was the "bad kid"—and early on, dipping Skoal seemed horrendous. Finding chewing gum in the bushes outside near the Ford F-150 offered another chance to rationalize the purity of my child. I knew the gum couldn't be Nick's. He had since kindergarten despised the feel of swirling the slobbery glob in his mouth. With only a hint of doubt, I attributed, for a full year, these habits to the friends Nick brought over.

The Childwise series I had relied upon for guidance declared the preteen years as the season to construct your child's character. Failure to do this equates to failure to stack up the foundation on your little construction project, which leads to eventual epic fails, cracks, shifts, and collapse. I had tallied more wins than losses in the parenting game, leaving me to spin around blindfolded in unaccustomed helplessness while my child slid out of control. Was there a festering of sores underneath the seemingly healthy skin of all the "excellent" parenting I had witnessed in the schools, on sports fields, and in our churches? I don't buy that teens "all of a sudden" pop up in the wrong friend group or suddenly "go off the rails." I believe it happens in tiny stages. Through the years thousands of often-imperceptible chances existed for me to exhibit the bold courage required to embed in my child the seeds to bloom into a person who makes wise choices autonomously. And I took advantage of many of those opportunities. I did a great job in the early years guiding my son into a person of character—I'm sure of it.

I taught Nick to be thankful. Every gift received was met with a mailed thank-you note. I taught him to speak kindly. When his harsh words were leveled toward me or someone else, he would write a hundred times, "I will be respectful." My actions became ones to model. I always took the shopping cart back to the rack rather than leave it in an adjacent spot. I did what I knew to do to raise a responsible and morally-centered human. I read books too.

The "Wise" series by Gary Ezzo began with Baby Wise, moving next to Toddler Wise, and all the way through to Teen Wise. Ezzo lays out the necessity to instill morals and self-control from the earliest years, first through parental instruction and consequence, before gradually releasing control to your maturing child for them to self-correct and manage choices on their own. By the time the hormones kick in and the quests for independence inevitably surface, your child will ideally be prepared to choose well without your intervention.

Should instilling basic moral traits and essential self-control fail from the toddler years and forward, there is little chance to recoup the opportunity to assist your child in the teen years. The Ezzo series advice was my guidepost—I did hold Nick accountable in those early years, which helped build character. How could his rock-solid character tank, in light of all our good work early on, in this short span of a year?

Shivering, unsteady on my feet I was ready to vomit on the admitting nurse at Palmetto Hospital in Columbia. She noted my rising temperature and the massive gray blister on my toe. With no ER bay to assign, she ordered up a gurney. Rolling it into the hallway in front of the storage closet while directing me to lie down, she explained that a room would open up "soon." A few hours later, in my own room, the doctor whipped out a Sharpie marker to circle the red rash creeping steadily up my leg from the blister.

"You have a nasty staph infection, it seems. We can't rule out a worse infection, so I am ordering lab work while we admit you for observation."

*WHAT...what the heck?!*

"What is worse than a staph infection?!" I recalled reading about an athlete with staph who wound up with an amputated body part. I guess cancer would be worse. But the doctor had noted that we caught it early, and they were on top of whatever it was. I hoped he was right as I asked for more details.

"Well, we can't rule out necrotizing fasciitis," he explained calmly. Flesh-eating bacteria?!! I'd heard stories of kids in comas after wading in bacteria-tainted water with an open cut. I had just had a pedicure a few days prior, but no wading was involved. Could soaking a bare foot in a dirty pedicure tub equate to wading in filthy water?

Still shivering as Ken and I waited out the arduous admittance process, I began vomiting. What started as a cut from a nail salon technician five days earlier had morphed into a blister and a fight to save my toe (life?). The doctor assured me that regardless of the type of infection, I had caught it early. We would need to be aggressive with an IV antibiotic and observation. I should make it out alive with all my limbs, I assumed in my fevered state.

Meanwhile, Ken had a loaded U-Haul in our driveway, ready for the move to New Mexico where the open interviews to hire his new Chick-fil-A crew were scheduled one week hence. For the next year we would be a family divided between two households. He was taking basic items: a bed, couch, desk, and kitchen items to hold him over until I, Casey, and the bulk of our goods moved to New Mexico the following year. I would join Ken in our New Mexico foothills home once Nick graduated high school—when the following summer gave way to his move to Clemson. It would be a simple enough. I was looking forward to ending the almost two-year struggle—the last year as a single parent. But first, the infection appeared to be the launch pad for the year ahead.

Initially, compassion eluded Ken. I insisted on heading to the hospital to get antibiotics for what I knew was a raging infection. "You just need to suck it up and ride out the infection at home," he said. This would allow for his scheduled departure the following day. His patience improved once he realized I had a chance, albeit remote, of losing a limb. At best, I was contending with the real possibility of a systemic infection requiring serious intervention. Hooked up to the IV antibiotic after a fitful, fevered night, my wakeup call the next morning was from Ken, announcing he was on his way over with a title company agent. There were papers for me to sign to seal the purchase of the new home in New Mexico.

My overnight in the hospital, hooked up to IVs and monitors, offered an unexpected respite from worry for the first time all summer. Overcome with illness and nervous the infection would spread, I had left me little time to care about Nick's shenanigans. I. did. not. care. The nasty blister on my foot had silently festered undetected for days before spawning the infection in my veins. Intruding like Pac-Man into my body, the pathogens traveled up my leg searching to destroy my blood and good health. In a way, Nick was acting like this festering, puss-filled blister infiltrating my perfect toe. Like the infection, I felt as if Nick was trying to seek and destroy my very existence with his selfish agenda. Lying awake that night in the quiet, darkened room, I briefly surrendered to my challenging season. I mourned the loss of the kind, considerate, honest, funny person I had raised. Some goblin had reached inside of him, snatching away all his goodness seemingly overnight. I had no tears, just a soulful sadness and acceptance that my "buddy," my "Tiger," was on hiatus. Acceptance is where peace awaits. I found it while supine, and surrendered to it in a hospital bed.

Two days later, I was out of the woods and back home. Ken buoyantly set out at last with the U-Haul and the exhilarating future awaiting him. For me, it was recovery from the wallop of the infection and the toxic meds that made me well, a son who couldn't be bothered to care about me, and the looming tsunami rolling our way. I was left behind to grapple with the dizzy frenzy of a messy spill left from everyone else moving on. The next year would require me to get a grip, despite navigating all on my own with a broken compass.

A few years later, Nick's girlfriend, in a sort of divine clarity, said, "You know Nick, all your trouble started when your mom was left alone to parent you. She was a single mom. You are a statistic."

The US Department of Health and Human Services states, "Fatherless children are at a dramatically greater risk of drug and alcohol abuse." Also, "There is significantly more drug use among children who do not live with their mother and father. A study of 1,977 children...living with a residential father or father figure found that children living with married biological parents had significantly fewer externalizing and internalizing behavioral problems than children living with at least one non-biological parent."[8]

A month into Nick's last year of high school, I left my full-time position at Shaw Air Force Base. Many single moms work full time and run a household, and I stand in awe of those that manage it well. But I had a choice. Nick was eating most nights at Tradd's, contributing to the drift away from me and his family. Just as important, this was my last year to live under one roof with my son—to be his hands-on mother. God had blessed us well, financially, giving me space to be present for Nick. I would still teach yoga two nights a week and on the occasional weekend. With my days free, I would return to substitute teaching at Franklin and volunteer as the Landscape Manager appointed by the PTA. I would stay busy and engaged. And close to Nick's world.

I never thought Nick would do anything illegal other than drinking underage, and he certainly wouldn't do drugs. Up until that summer, he had resisted even the tiniest over-the-counter headache medicine. An acceptable solution to end the pain of his headaches was cutting the small caplet in two with a knife and chasing it back with pudding. I was stunned when he woke up one morning with a headache and swallowed two Motrins at one time, snapping back his head to assist the pills' journey down the gullet with a splash of juice. I stood next to him, speechless, gobsmacked all at once in a revelation. After he left for school, I marched up the stairs to search his bedroom.

I stripped his bed, taking off the sheets to launder them, and lifted the mattress looking for...something. I searched the adjacent, unfinished attic storage closet, full of boxes and loose items. Fluffy pink insulation pulled back easily throughout the cramped space. I pulled open drawers, looking under layers of outdated clothing. I opened Band-Aid boxes under the sink, peered through the folds of stacked towels, lifted the tank on the toilet with dread and poked around inside the shallow water. Crime movies show drugs taped to the sides of toilet tanks, so relief flooded me to discover only toilet parts. The next morning before he left for school, I crept out to his Toyota 4Runner, purchased after selling his truck. He had reasons out the wazoo for getting rid of his truck: I still am not clear on the *why*. I suspect it had to do with his huge new speakers that covered the entire back of the SUV. Gone was the passion for hunting and all things camouflage. His good ol' boy redneck friends gave way to unseen faces who gathered in urban parking lots and back-road fields.

The 4Runner glove box gave up a sleeve of mint-flavored dip. Looking closely now for the first time, I saw the threads of tobacco worn into the carpet near the driver's seat.

The next morning, I knocked at his stairway door before marching up to confront him. Nick was showered and dressed, back in bed with his stocking hat covering his wet head. Five years ago Nick and I discovered a solution to taming his curly blond hair. We tried the blow dryer; it frizzed and puffed up his hair. I burnt him twice with the curling iron. After these failures, hanging his head out the window of the car served throughout elementary school as a flattening blow dry. The real fixer was washing his hair, combing it, and carefully arranging his black knit ski hat over the wet curls. After a half hour he had some semblance of a hairstyle. Before that last summer, Nick would shower and come down in his khaki shorts, tucked in Southern Tide polo shirt, and the "hair flattener" to join me for breakfast. Now he skipped breakfast in favor of thirty more minutes of sleep while his hair styled itself.

"Nick...hey bud. Look what I found in your glove box?" I held the sleeve over his prone figure.

Opening his eyes, he said with a blank expression, "That belongs to Tradd. He keeps that in my glove box. Give it back please."

"Nick. Are you dipping?" I demanded.

"Nooo...Mom. Now give that back. I am going back to sleep."

The evidence raining down from the ever-present dark cloud circling over my head became a deluge I continued to mostly ignore. My kiddo was a habitual truth teller. He outed his friends, revealing it was THEM drinking alcohol and taking Vyvanse for fun, driving their cars 100 mph while drunk, cheating at school. He was the little Boy Scout in a pack of wolves. I placed the cans of tobacco on his nightstand and left.

Two weeks later, while vacuuming under the Ikea chair cushion, I found a single can of Skoal. Nick was in the kitchen with Tradd when I waved the can at them. Tradd claimed it.

"Ms. Suzanne. That's mine. I can't keep it at my house; my parents don't know I dip," he said innocently. I didn't believe him.

After they left, the niggling gut instinct demanded attention— another sweep of his bedroom loft. Nothing turned up in the attic. His dresser drawers held nothing but clothes. Then, later that day, I found threads of tobacco spattered behind Nick's toilet while cleaning his bathroom.

"Damn!" No doubt he was dipping, but that now seemed minor compared to what unprescribed pill he might be swallowing. Nick was lying to me. Faith held me in its grip for years. Faith that my child was honest. Faith that the bedrock of our relationship had room only for trust. My faith in him evaporated in that instant, morphing quickly to disgust.

Tragic possibilities usually lurked in the front of my thought processes, just beyond my common sense. The MIP, the cessation of involvement in sports, slipping grades, and a declining attitude should have had me reeling toward all sorts of horrific scenarios for my son. He had sold his beloved truck, and now his pile of lies had entered my sightline. My lingering denial smashed to bits with the sucker-punch lethal dose of reality. My anger demanded action. He was dipping tobacco, and more upsetting, had been lying for a long time. I charged downstairs and into the garage, and returned with a hammer, screwdriver, and determination. My anger fueled the strength to pound up the bolts of his bathroom door from the frame. I eased the door off the hinges, parked it up against the wall, and rushed down to hide the bolts in my bedroom. He lied to me. He had been lying to me.

He didn't rage and wail at me in hothead anger about the door. In fact, he never brought it up. Sadly, neither did I. I waited...yes, I waited him out. Did he just stop dipping in the bathroom, not caring much whether he had any privacy? Did he wonder why the door was off the hinges? Lest he think the door was off for repairs, I told him a few days later that he broke the rules and lost his privacy as a result.

*NICK: Yeah—that was not going to change anything. Again, I was unfazed.*

Looking back, my shock and outrage seem sanguine and silly. Where is the precipice when teenage shenanigans devolve into habitual, long-term behaviors spiraling in to an epic fail? Teens drink, experiment, pull away from their parents to identify with their peers. Normal. Is it unique for teens to attend parties and experiment with weed and alcohol? Moving into college, many who did walk a straight line in high school catch up to their wild peers at frat parties and college bars. Normal. Greek life is sanctioned by the governance on college campuses despite a tacit agreement to massive amounts of alcohol in pledging and frat parties. Nick was taking a dark path, fueled by the easy access to a banquet of behavior-altering substances. Gary Ezzo had warned me: If I didn't properly direct him *under my own roof,* then once out in the world, what was to stop him from a reckless self-pre-scribed path?

I woke up to the ping of a midnight text. My heart didn't leap because I knew my son was in his room. I insisted he stay home several nights after my staph infection. I had just dozed off, having returned to bed after peering out the window to see that his truck was in the driveway. Just in case, I checked and his iPhone icon confirmed our location was under the same roof.

It was from Mary Kate, Tradd's mother; she had become my good friend. "Have you heard from Nick tonight?"

"He's upstairs—he's been home all night." I exhaled a huge sigh. "What's up?"

She called in response, instead of rapid texting.

"Tradd just called. He sounded out of his mind. He couldn't tell me where he was—he wasn't making any sense. Worse yet, he was driving," she said, remaining composed.

We went back and forth on possible scenarios for Tradd's whereabouts.

"Let me go check with Nick. I'll text you in a minute."

I knocked on Nick's door, and with music to my ears, he responded.

"Come on in! I'm up," he replied.

He was sitting on the Ikea chair, toggling the joystick on his PlayStation.

"Tiger—Tradd's mom is worried about him. He called her—he sounded drunk, lost—and driving his car," I said. "Have you heard from him?"

"Yeah—he was at a party with John and some dudes from Sumter High. I think he was heading home." Nick picked up his phone to text Tradd.

*Ping!* Tradd texted back. "He's on his way to John's house. He doesn't know where he is though."

"Can you tell him to call his mother, please?" I asked.

I texted Mary Kate that he was okay and would be calling her. Twenty minutes later, at 1:00 a.m., she phoned in an update.

Tradd had left the party in his own car, John ahead of him, leading the way in his new Chevy Silverado. After getting separated by a red light, Tradd, clearly well over the .08 threshold, had driven aimlessly for an hour. Too drunk and stupid to register his precarious situation, he answered his cell midway through the drunk driving when his mother called, speaking gibberish and sending her into fright mode. She had implored him to return home. Then he hung up, and she texted me. And there we were. Tradd had dropped the ball on our request for a follow-up call to his mom, but knowing he was on his way to John's, she spoke to his mother, Georgia. For once—for one night only—I sat secure and at peace. My child was home, where he belonged.

Georgia's Southern roots ran deep. Her ancestors were hoteliers dating back to when Atlanta still had dirt roads. Fire had ravaged their establishment at the hands of the victorious North during the burning of Atlanta. I suspect their resilience to prosper in the face of that aggression resided still in the DNA of each generation, reaching Georgia herself who feared nothing, embraced everything, and always had a room available to road-weary stragglers.

"Mary Kate. How are y'all over there tonight?" she inquired at one in the morning like it was an afternoon call inviting her to a garden party.

"Hello, Georgia. We are actually concerned about Tradd. Have you seen him tonight?" Mary Kate replied.

"Yaaas! He is sittin' right here on the couch with John. They are fiiinnnee! Just out celebratin' a little earlier. He is fixin' to head on up foh the night after the movie ends! We will sure send him on home in the mornin'!" she trilled, using her best concierge manners.

Years later, one of the Sumter High kids who was part of Nick's party crowd was out celebratin' at a concert in Columbia. His drive home had him within a few miles of his mother's house, near the stadium, but he chose to continue on to Sumter, drunk. He ran off the road four miles from his destination, killing the passenger, his best friend. Celebratin' and driving are a toxic mix; and my son and his crowd, and many stupid people, thought it a fine idea.

# Chapter 10

# Angels All
# Around Us

Nick, Casey, and I approached the agent at Hartsfield-Jackson Atlanta International Airport.

"We need to check in for our flight, with our puppy," I explained, handing her the necessary documents required to travel with a pet.

"This is her first time traveling on an airplane! I hear it's as safe under the plane as in the cabin?" I asked, knowing the answer but seeking reassurance.

"Wellll, actually—we have lost some pets. So many that Delta is phasing out allowing pets under the plane. We will be moving to service animals in the cabin of the aircraft only," she stated matter-of-factly.

My eyes grew as big as saucers. "Excuse me? What do you mean, you've *lost* pets? Like, they got out of the kennel and roamed the tarmac?" I asked.

"No, no. When the plane lands, we find the pet has sadly expired." She showed no remorse.

Shocked, I mentally reviewed all proactive and meticulously executed steps in preparation for a smooth flight for one-year-old

Casey's three weeks in Albuquerque. First was a visit to our trusted vet, Dr. Wiley. He recommended zero medication, as sedating a pup often compromises their breathing, especially if they are nervous fliers. We gathered facts on gradually introducing her to the plastic travel crate with small cutouts and a metal latch door. He also advised putting her name on the crate, for all airport handlers to see when necessary. Taking that tip a step further, the printout I created had family photos and said, "Hi! I am Casey! I am one year old and very friendly! My family loves me very much, so please take good care of me!" After receiving all good news from her health examination and executing the many suggestions, we were confident the flight would go well.

Then, at the counter, I'm told flying is risky business for my dog? We had driven four hours to Atlanta for the only direct flight to Albuquerque. Leaving the house at 4 a.m. and arriving three hours before departure left us ample wiggle room for hiccups. But I did not plan on this mental hiccup. The option to back out of the flight, take Casey back home, arrange for pet sitters, and then rebook a flight was nonsense. Fact: careful planning to build a foundation for her comfort and safety was implemented—that had not changed. The only thing that had changed was a snarky gate agent with an alarming opinion. We would push forward.

Three remarkable encounters prior to dropping Casey off in Oversize Baggage and boarding the plane restored my confidence and infused peace into the process. First, as I waited outside the airport restroom for Nick, Casey still with us and on her leash, a man and woman approached to gush over Casey.

"Oh! She is gorgeous! Where are you traveling to?" They knelt down to Casey's level, rubbing her smooth back as she nuzzled and wiggled in delight.

"We are heading to Albuquerque. This is her first flight!!" I blurted out.

"Ahhh...she will be fine," the woman said calmly. "We had a black lab who lived to be fourteen. We traveled with her all the time, never a worry! She will be okay."

Nick was starving. I sent him to The Pancake House, and Casey and I wandered into the gift shop to grab a magazine. A lovely woman with Irish Setter red hair, porcelain skin, and emerald-green eyes approached Casey. She knelt in front of the pup, held her muzzle in her hands, and spoke to her softly.

"What's your pup's name?" She stood up and gazed at me.

I told her, and gave her our travel details.

"My pup traveled with me often. She was a golden lab. The airlines took good care of her—always. She lived to be fourteen," she explained.

As she continued to talk about her dog and all the places they had traveled, an odd thing happened. I became calm—and happy. I can't explain it. And what was completely beyond reason or earthly explanation during this five-minute exchange was this: The glen-green surrounding her pupils seemed to reflect the image of a gold cross. Yes, lots of secular reasons exist to explain this, but no matter the angle I moved my head, or how I shifted my weight to confirm this, the crosses remained, in the center of her pupils. Jaded by skeptical people with whom I've shared this story, I doubted the truth about real-world encounters with the divine. Despite my superficial relationship with God, I came to believe these whispers of comfort were offered from a spiritual realm to bring me peace.

Lastly, upon boarding the aircraft and requesting a heads-up when Casey was loaded, the flight attendant assured me I would be notified.

"Oh...what breed is your puppy?" he asked. "My lab mix lived to be fourteen. Your girl will be just fine—I will let you know when she is boarded. They load the animals last!"

I understand that God will send angels in the form of faithful followers—and I am open to actual angels among us. He knew my diligence—understood the enemy at play in the form of the gate agent creating chaos with her comment—and sought to strengthen me in a full display of His grace. It came to light a few years after these divine encounters that God had intended to strengthen my wobbly faith.

On that journey west my son and I partnered together in a rusty yet familiar symmetry in managing dog needs, juggling bags and kennel, and making our way to meet Ken. Nick waltzed out his calm-in-the-storm personality. The three weeks we were in New Mexico I was treated to his natural compassion, kindness, and wit. Ten months later, he would be completely lost to me. My recall of these three encounters—mostly, the angelic red-haired woman—would bring a calm in the coming tsunami. The seas *could* turn placid within the storm. Always right in front of me and within me, and when I fail to allow for grace, God will insist on presenting me with assistance along the journey.

Life resumed in January 2016 with an acceleration of my "mama crazy" as Nick and Tradd dropped figurative matches and gasoline everywhere they went. They shared not only a love of hunting for fun in town and for ducks in the predawn swamps, but sports too. Waterskiing, Tradd outbalanced Nick on one ski behind their boat, while Nick excelled on snow skis, waiting at the bottom of the runs for Tradd. They'd played B-team football together before the spark of the friendship. So, when sign-ups for varsity baseball rolled around in January, before graduation, Tradd suggested they try out and Nick was all-in.

As I sat in the darkened cool of the Beacon cinema, my phone vibrated with a text from Nick. He was on his way home from baseball practice after catching a fly ball with his forehead. One of the other players had volunteered to drive him home on orders from a concerned coach. The kid had dropped him off in our driveway and sped back to practice. I hustled out of my movie seat to criminally surpass the speed limit back to our house. I found a sweaty Nick slumped inside, on the couch, in a red dirt-stained uniform, holding an ice pack to his head. His eyes glanced my way, reminding me of his eleven-year-old self, begging me to fix a broken toy or make his awful headaches go away. He looked woozy and disoriented yet relieved to see me. Beneath the ice pack was a bloody and swollen forehead, and beneath that, a possible concussion. I drove him to the Urgent Care around the corner. After all the interminable waiting and testing—they confirmed that Nick had a concussion. With a slight fracture above his eye socket, he would require further treatment from a specialist. In the meantime, Nick was to follow the concussion protocol of no reading, watching TV, or playing video games. And that night I was charged with waking him up every few hours.

The specialist we saw the next day suggested an operation to repair the slight fracture; or we could just watch and see how it fused without intervention. Neither option held certain hope for a perfect recovery, so we chose to wait. Nick missed another week of school, and two weeks of baseball practice. With the exception of a halfhearted effort in track, his first love, baseball, had lured him back into sports. And there was this untimely setback. Another pause in his momentum both academically and physically proved a catalyst for Nick to double down on his erratic path. Instead of knocking some sense into him and developing grit and a course correction, three days post-smack in the head with a baseball, he had his car keys in hand and was heading out the door to a party.

"Tiger! What the heck?!" I said. "You have missed school all week, and are still recovering from a CONCUSSION!"

To have him home at night, lying on one couch, me on the other in the living room, watching old favorite shows on TV, teased me with comfort and peace. Our etched-in-stone bond, though chipped and cracked, seemed under repair over the past three days of recovery. But wasn't our closeness the source of his pulling away from me? Establishing himself as a man couldn't happen in this idyllic mother/son bubble. Like an iceberg calving from the terminus of its glacier to float away and exist under the mercy of wind, water, and sun, he too chose to float away, drifting wherever the ocean of his "screwed-up" friends took him.

"Nick, give me your keys!" I demanded. "You have been told by two doctors, no driving for a week."

"No, madre. I am fine!" he declared, lacing up the white sneakers his good buddy, John, had bought for him from a Chinese website. "I will be home early."

"No way! You can't drive and you definitely cannot drink alcohol—and I know that is what is going down at this party."

"Mother. I am going. I am leaving now. It is ten miles away. I will be home early," he said slowly and emphatically as he moved toward the garage.

"Nick! NO! You have a CONCUSSION!" Just that morning he'd complained of blurry vision and headaches.

"Bye!" He scooted past me and out the door. I heard his truck gunning up, the thump of his subwoofers booming out rap music down the driveway, and then finally, silence.

Courage. Courage to make a bold move when my child was at risk. I knew it was lurking somewhere in me—I had been mama-bear crazy on his behalf many times. I had been mama-bear insistent as he grew—brush your teeth, wear your seatbelt, do your homework. Now, I summoned mama-bear crazy when my wisdom was in direct opposition to what my teen thought was best.

I phoned Tradd's father, Tripp. Tripp had stepped up often and been a role model for Nick. The family included us often in their lives, and supported me, the "single mom." While Tradd defied his own father, Nick would heed Tripp's advice.

"I will phone him now and get him to head back home, Suzanne," he promised. "That is just not right. I will drive out to that house party if I have to."

Ten minutes later, an enraged Nick squealed back up the driveway, bolted into the house, and slammed the door on his way up to his room, shouting at me with words I don't remember. Did I push it too far—embarrassing him to a man he respected? Still the thought of Bobby and what that last straw was for him, that pushed him too far, resurfaced. Recently, I read a book by Jon Acuff called *Soundtracks*. He explains the well-worn loop in our brains, a soundtrack, resulting from a conditioned pattern of thoughts so familiar that we remain unaware they have outgrown their usefulness. Instead, the sound we hear is out of tune and off-key, informing the way we think and respond to new situations. I knew my own "Bobby soundtrack" existed, that it informed my parenting (or lack thereof), but I remained unaware that the outdated track needed to be replaced with a new tune more appropriate for my rebellious son, who needed a courageous mom to make tough choices for his well-being.

This was Nick's second diagnosed concussion, with two significant head bashes in between the major blows. The first was at nine months old, when Ken lost the grip on Nick's chubby leg as he sat perched atop his shoulders while we were preparing to board a flight at BWI. Like a missile crashing to the terminal's thinly carpeted cement, his head caught the fall. The horrible sound of a baby skull connecting with an unforgiving surface, as his cries cut through the airport din, cause my face *right now* to scrunch in anguish as I cringe at the memory. My baby's forehead instantly swelled to the size of a baseball. Paramedics stabilized him on the stretcher, loaded us into the ambulance, and raced across the tarmac to whisk him to Johns Hopkins in Baltimore. Awaiting our arrival was a gowned and gloved ten-person pediatric medical team. Other than a slight concussion (diagnosed only through a practical exam to spare his growing brain from CT radiation) and the massive lump on his forehead, he was fine. An hour later we were on our way home. We returned to the very same gate at BWI the following day, commencing our journey to Boston.

Years of harmless bumps, knocks, and bruises gave way to fifth grade and roughhousing with friends, where getting thrown on his head up against a wall provoked dizziness and another swell on his frontal lobe. I always wondered how many tough hits the frontal lobe—the center for rational thought and self-control—can take before a person loses the ability to manage their own behavior.

Nick moved past his concussion and returned to benchwarming on the varsity baseball team. I went to all the games, in a cloak of pretense that my kid was a star player. He liked the dugout over getting called to the field after the fly ball encounter, I suspected. But, there is a picture of Nick and me beaming for the camera during the final home game, which was parent/senior night, in a sort of farewell homage to his lower-ed sports career. It felt normal and right to support him in sports in any capacity, and that moment, with us on the field and him in uniform, was another lily-pad, respite of calm between frantic traffic dodging in our ongoing game of Frogger.

Despite all the concussions and frontal lobe impacts over his lifetime, Nick excelled on the ACT and SAT college-entrance tests. A computer-generated recommendation based on his scores shockingly suggested a course of study in engineering. The college counselor at Franklin, Mrs. Palmer, disagreed. At the start of each school year, this counselor actively pursued a personal relationship with all seventy seniors in order to better guide them into their futures. For Nick's appointment, which included an invitation to his parents to discuss his options, she ignored Nick while she told me, "There is no possible way Nick will be accepted into a college of engineering. And he has only applied to TWO schools—USC and Clemson. With his GPA hovering at 3.0, he needs a third, safety school application submitted." Nick refused. He also refused to assent to the head-master's recommendation of the University of Arizona, and, not knowing his own career aspirations, acknowledged the wisdom of the SAT score and applied to the school of engineering at Clemson. Mrs. Palmer was beside herself. In her attempt to "help" Nick, she relied on his shaky reputation around the school to form her opinion of his abilities.

Months later, Nick received mail validation for acting on gut instinct and his innate confidence in his intelligence in the form of an envelope from USC exclaiming "YES!" printed atop a giant Gamecock image. This was his second choice, but relief flooded me. Nick was going to college.

Despite all the tomfoolery, he had a future that looked bright enough. But still, I had gone to USC for my master's degree and preferred he go elsewhere. Checking the mail with bated breath daily for more good news rewarded us on February 16, 2016, this time with an envelope covered in orange Tiger paw prints that shouted, "You are Tigertown Bound!" Nick was accepted to Clemson and was Tigertown bound for the engineering program. His Eagle Scout achievement and a few extracurricular efforts, combined with the phenomenal SAT score had pulled him out of truancy and into respectability. This easy win for Nick was a shock to many of the "good" students who had been wait-listed for Clemson, destined to spend one year at the community college in a bridge program before matriculating to the gloried institution up the road. To the chagrin of many, Nick would follow the Orange Tiger Paws emblazoned on the local roads into the esteemed

Clemson University. He was not surprised. Mrs. Palmer seemed miffed in her wrong assessment of a student.

The year ended in a whirlwind of senior events—an awards ceremony, pictures, and prom. Franklin Prep rolled out a prom night rivaling any $1,000-a-plate extravaganza. It all started with a time-honored tradition which insisted random parents, in assorted groups based on who was dating whom, meet at someone's house to take pre-prom photos. Twenty or so kids dressed in tuxes and long gowns coupled up in bunches across the sweeping brick entry stairs, then next to the Magnolia tree or the tractor parked in the yard. Nick's date was a last-minute ask, someone who was available, whom he had little to no interest in. Toward the end of the photo session, Nick snubbed his date in favor of making it a boys' night out. He and Tradd took off, dashing up the stairs two at a time to dart into the house to the privacy of the bathroom. Nick came out with wild eyes and red cheeks, with Tradd asking, "Are you good? Are you okay?" With bile rising in my throat, my shock at his earlier ease swallowing Motrin confirmed he had taken something. Should I have yanked him out in his tux, dragging him away to CVS for a drug-test kit? Probably. In my defense, my one great flaw as a mother in this season was relentless evidence developed in previous seasons of his moral goodness. It surely prevented me from holding Nick fully accountable for his actions. Instead I chose to hound him about whether he took something, with both of us tacitly understanding his "No, Mom" was a lie.

After pictures, the kids piled into cars to relocate to someone's large home for a fancy sit-down, pre-prom dinner, served by parent volunteers. Then, back into the cars they went to the school gym, with parents in hot pursuit, for a senior introduction into the prom. Like A-list actors walking the red carpet, the gussied-up pre-adults swaggered into the festive gym, Noah's-ark style, as the headmaster on a loudspeaker shouted out their names. Niiiccck

Roragen! Nick hurried in with his date, fidgety and unsmiling, seemingly eager to get on with the night. Senior parents once again hovered around after this walk-in. Lined and stacked like eager paparazzi, we flocked at the edge of the dance floor, snapping photos. Once Nick passed through the introduction and awaited the last few seniors through the gauntlet, he abandoned his date for Flo-Rida booming from the speakers, singing with gusto about popping a cork on a bottle of champagne and the onset of a fun night of revelry.

With wild eyes and savage energy Nick bounced up and down to the rhythm, chest-bumping Tradd and John. I straggled out of the gym with a friend, over to my next stop to prepare for the senior breakfast.

After prom, the senior parents planned and *served* another massive meal at another large home. The kids changed from formal wear to khaki pants for the boys and Lily Pulitzer dresses for the girls, for "breakfast." I was acting like a groupie, trying to grab a sighting of my son while tending the post-prom beverage station. But Nick avoided me entirely. He and his friends managed to stay at the breakfast for an hour before roaring off in their trucks. I wrapped up my volunteer duties and returned home to sit and wait for Nick. I tracked him at 1 a.m. to a home in Dalzell, ten miles outside of town. At some point in a nod to excellent parenting, I had bought Nick a breathalyzer to put in his glove box in the event he or one of his friends flirted with drunk driving. I still worried as I lay awake clutching my iPhone.

I was a "single mother" from September 2015 to August 2016. As a military spouse, solo parenting was nothing new for me. During the several months leading to Ken's departure to New Mexico, with him absorbed in the overwhelming process of earning a Chick-fil-A restaurant, I had weaned off his paternal support. Though there was nothing new about his absences from co-parenting, it was tougher then. This time, through the vacuums created by Ken's job, my teammate was AWOL. He had written me off. Nick left as often as possible to join up with Tradd's family and the new friends walking a crooked path. The constant, day-to-day concerns of reining him in toward a decent future, keeping him safe and pointed toward a godly path, began a teardown of my sturdy soul. Your child careening down a slippery slope, away from the nest into a bold and healthy life is expected, alas, encouraged. But this unplanned and unsafe departure I found offensive and unwelcome.

Once, during a middle school vacation skiing in Colorado, we had driven the short distance to a snow-tubing center. The day was cold and cloudy, and the sun was considering setting for the day. We picked up the tubes, plopped into them, and grabbed for the tow rope to ferry us up the long, steep hill to the launch point. *Wowza.* This hill was far steeper than ones we had enjoyed on the East Coast. Hanging on to the plastic tow hook presented a strength challenge; I looked back at Nick and Ken, who looked comfortable with the ascension. We reached the launch point, released the tow hook and toppled out of our tubes. We took our place in the queue for the three separate lanes, to race down together. Then, it was our turn! Nick put his tube down at the precipice of the drop into his icy lane. The tube shot out from his grip, dragging him behind the black, tractor-size inner tube. He flew down the steep slope on his belly, headfirst! An instant, fierce instinct to launch myself after him—to save him—was squashed by the employee, who cautioned the danger in both of us flying down together. Nick would be fine, he assured me. Helpless, I stood watching him zip down the lane, flailing to figure out a self-arrest. I launched into my tube for my turn, willing the thing to go faster, tailing behind to witness his frantic efforts. The hill flattened out at the bottom, and he slowed with plenty of time to ease to a safe stop. He stood up, encrusted in ice and hooted, "WHOAAA!!! Can I do it that way again?!"

Now, here I was years later, watching the slide from the top of the cliff as he careened down an icy slope. The grappling hooks I shoved his way for a self-arrest remained unused as the momentum for thrill ramped up. The option for me to *do something* insisted I take action. Like the single option to wait out his headlong slide in Colorado, I was forced once again to follow behind in my own tube to assess his well-being once he arrived at the bottom.

Ken missed not only prom night but also the parent/student banquet, a highlight of Senior Week, but showed up in time for graduation festivities. Nick's three aunts and one of his cousins flew in to celebrate with us, as well as my mother and Ken's parents. My gift to Nick, other than the post-graduation party, was a movie of his life I had created on my laptop. At the end of winter, I started collecting words of love and wisdom from friends and family. I searched my photo files for videos from his childhood and scoured hundreds of photos from our spiral-bound photo albums. Creating and editing Nick's iMovie on my computer literally dragged into graduation day. The completed video was ready to premiere during the post-graduation party. It's shocking to watch the video now. The love for my son—unconditional and profound—soared out from within me, clearing the miasma of my angst, allowing my heart to tackle an arduous and time-consuming project that had a fifty-fifty shot of being appreciated. The tribute/intro I created, rolling like a *Star Wars* opening, states, "This is a tribute to you, our sweet Nicholas." And, "We are proud of the young man you are becoming." Did I really feel that when I crafted the graduation video? I am certain I did. I am certain documenting snapshots from the past pulsed forth reminders of the person I *knew* my son to be. Parental love in its purest form is unconditional and forgiving, full of never-ending hope and devotion.

Ken departed, back to the thrill of running his new venture, the moment after I swept the graduation confetti from the patio. I was left solo to tackle the leftover food crowding the refrigerator and an "adult" eighteen-year-old son feasting on long, bucolic summer days that he would turn into hazardous memories.

I found a bottle of vodka in my freezer. I don't drink vodka. We were wine and beer drinkers back then.

"Nick! Why is there vodka in my freezer!" He was on his way to a Luke Bryan farm concert, outside of Columbia. After high school graduation, Nick and his friends found a source online to forge fake IDs that were actually made on the equipment used by the DMV—in Arkansas. All these boys had IDs with their REAL NAME and a random Arkansas address. He, Tradd, and John had ordered two each; if one was confiscated or lost, they could still run around engaging in underage drinking. He eagerly showed off his new purchase, and I harkened back to the days he called me over to show me a cool baseball card he had bought at the swap meet. How bad was this? I did, after all, convince my sister out of her driver's license for use as my own fake ID. He was on his way to Clemson! *Everyone drank in college!* I stared down that ID and raced through my options. One, I could take it away and scissor it up, whereby he would order another set. Two, I could counsel him on drinking responsibly and how to choose his (limited) wisdom every time over stupidity. I chose option two.

"Oh, yeah. That belongs to Brandon!" he fibbed. "I bought it for him with my fake ID! We are just drinking beer, Mom! He is a nut—drinks that stuff down!" This was also the kid that Nick mentioned a year ago, at the tail end of his innocence. The reckless boy drank like a fish while ingesting Xanax. My routine searches of Nick's bedroom ferreted out only the tobacco—and months ago I had come to terms with his dipping with the replacement of the door to his bathroom. Gradually, a desensitization toward ever-increasing unsavory habits and actions had me accepting bad things as "normal." He'd shared with me during freshman year in high school all manner of tidbits on his life. One story was how he and a group of guys spent the night in a friend's treehouse. They drank beer and rode bikes around town in the middle of the night. My concern drifted from stressing about those types of shenanigans to wishing he was *only* doing that rather than drinking beer around a campfire in the woods. A campfire with beer I would choose all day long over an MIP, the incessant lying to me, and the skipping of school. At least he wasn't smoking weed and taking Xanax like those *bad* kids.

The bottle of vodka belonged to a friend? Though largely skeptical of late, I bought what he was presenting to me as the truth. It wasn't his; he only drank beer and dipped tobacco. Buying beer with a fake ID and drinking it on the tailgate while watching a concert was about to be A-OK.

"Bud, you can't drink at a concert and then drive! *No way!*" He was walking out to his car with a brown grocery bag.

"Mom. We won't drink much, and I have the breathalyzer! It takes an hour to get out of the parking lot and there is no chance anyone will be drunk once we get on the road."

"NICK! You can*not* carry beer in your car! Did you not learn from the MIP?" That was the issue—another MIP? Not that what he was doing was wrong and dangerous, flirting with an epic fail.

"Mom, I have hiding spots!" He had been sharing those things lately. What was the point, since he was headed to college, in covering up his illegal and immoral activities? I was helpless, or so I perceived myself as a victim (enabler!), and knew I could no longer demand he stay home. *How* would I have made that happen—take his car keys? He was six feet tall to my five-nine, and a legal adult. I could change all the locks on the house and forbid him entrance unless he followed my rules. I had tried that a few times and instead of staying home, grounded, he ended up sneaking out of the house (Screengate) to his friend waiting in his car down the street. Or, I could help Nick be as safe as possible in his terrible behavior, as long as it wasn't *toooo* bad. I had my shot at building in him an earthquake-proof foundation. But the cement truck had pulled out of the construction site too early, and I was left managing alone all the cracks and shifting morals. The bottom line: Nick's dad was 1,500 miles away. Without his father returning home each night after work, golfing and hunting with him on the weekends, and without his desire that had developed over seventeen years to "be like" Ken, Nick had let loose those paternal constraints that had kept him honest and in control of his inner rebel.

Like all the times we had worked as a team building Thomas The Tank Engine tracks, erecting sand castles, maneuvering the canals of Venice, and discovering the best path through the trees skiing Deer Valley, a bittersweet team effort fraught with dysfunction ensued as I stepped in to help stash his beer.

"What if we pull the plastic cover off the back of your taillights? No one would look for beer way back here," I said. We spread out a full twelve-pack of Bud in all sorts of hiding spots in his Toyota. As he drove away, worry and sadness remained, keeping me company like the naive parent that I was.

"Music can change the world, because it can change people," Bono from the band U2 once said.[9] I believe music *can* change people, gradually. It can shape a belief system, subconsciously. Music inspires us with ideas to implement into our lives. Music can infuse people with a desire for goodness, or the opposite. I loved country music, the genre I see as endemic to America. Ken and a four-year-old Nick bonded as father and son over "Watching You," belting out the Rodney Atkins lyrics of a boy in a booster seat eating chicken nuggets and saying, "Dad, I want to be like you." Lee Greenwood's "God Bless the USA" played loudly on every patriotic holiday in our home. "Dirt Road Diary" is a song by Luke Bryan that somehow normalizes the country-boy life, what I deemed a good theme to live by, and one I endorsed for Nick.

I had cranked many other dirt-road party songs and sang along with Nick while we rode around dirt roads in his truck, setting up trail cameras to track the movement of deer and stopping to look for antler sheds. Country music carried in its notes memories of idyllic and innocent seasons of our life as a family, not a prescription for a dangerous lifestyle.

My Nick stalker-app confirmed it took an hour and a half to exit the Luke Bryan concert. It was close to three in the morning when he boomed back into the driveway.

The summer swiftly unfurled, with a sort of understanding that Nick would do what he wanted, and I would pretend he was making good choices. Like when he sliced his foot open on a broken bottle buried in the sand at Three Stumps, an unofficial party cove in the backed-up swamp called Lake Marion. With alligators lurking in the shallow banks, young people would park boats side by side, attaching one dock line to the other, building a bobbing aquatic redneck subdivision. They'd hop from one boat or jet ski to another, or when shallow enough, walk in the hip-deep water near the jagged tree stumps jutting up from the swampy mush—the murky water intimidated none of the party crowd.

Nick and I accepted an invite to overnight at Tradd's lake house for the annual July Fourth celebration. I spent most of the day on the dock while Nick, Tradd, Jack, and a handful of others took Jack's family boat out on the crowded lake. It was hot. We all knew the boys would be drinking, but again, we pretended they were making good choices. An hour late for dinnertime, they finally pulled back into the dock, drunk, sunburnt, and banged up. Jack had punched the boat in a fit of anger, breaking his hand, and Nick had sliced that deep gash in his foot. Hours passed between reaching shore and the mishap at Three Stumps. The toxic brew of Lake Marion seized on the ample time it took to reach medical care, free-flowing its seepage into the tender heel tissue. I drug a reluctant Nick into the bathroom to tend the wound with limited first aid supplies. Since my staph infection, I understood the persistent nature of bacteria. The germs most certainly were traveling through his tissue in search of his blood supply as I carted him to the urgent-care clinic after dinner. After an hour in a packed waiting room, away from the fun, with no imminent sign of care, he demanded we leave. He stormed out of the facility without me, and back to the car.

More negotiation. Nick agreed to visit our own doctor the next afternoon to treat the festering wound. Once back at the lake house, I changed the bloody foot dressing before he hurried down to the dock to join his friends. I went to bed, waking to the sounds booming from the dock around 2 a.m.

Common sense and wisdom inform us that no good happens after midnight. Especially when drunk, underage, plus stupid is a formula for disaster at that hour. I lay in the guest room, wide awake, and texted Nick, "Hey!" No answer. I texted and texted with no response. Eventually, when they were ready to call it a night, he drifted in. The lack of peace I inflicted upon myself was a passive and preventable dance away from courage, laden with a lack of confidence to *do something.* His anger when I pressed him hard to do the right thing and his defiance when I insisted (disconnected from his reasoning center), had me treading with caution. Bobby, when pushed to the brink, had killed himself. Boys on the verge of manhood with wandering souls look for outlets for their energy and burgeoning testosterone.

One friend in the group that night would hang himself, two years later, on the very tree blowing in the summer breeze outside my lakefront window. Spurts of volatile anger, born out of an all-thrust, no-vector frustration within churning hormones, are one recipe for an epic fail. Horrors played on repeat in the soundtrack of my mind: drink too much and die on your own bile, drive 80 miles per hour over the speed limit into a tree, or dive headfirst into the shallows. My child was worse than most and not as bad as many in his actions. Underneath his mandatory transformation in to a man was my sweet child.

The next day, after incessant bursts of scary information from me on ways he could lose his leg to infection, Nick acquiesced to the earlier agreement on intervention for his still-meaty gash. An agonizing sterilization of the wound and twelve stitches later, we drove to CVS for a heavy antibiotic. "Never let up when the life and livelihood of my child and his future are threatened" was, and remains, my mom description from day one.

The summer went on like this, with me silently obsessing about his impending epic fail, and him pretending he was an adult making his own choices. Once in a while we met for a normal evening watching a favorite TV show, and for Mother's Day he took me to dinner in Charleston. Like a parched Bedouin in the Arabian desert, I soaked up these last months, then weeks, he would be under my roof until the bittersweet wait was over.

When we loaded up Nick's Toyota 4Runner and my SUV to caravan the three-hour drive from the home we shared for *four* years to Nick's first day in college, there was a fidgety nervousness from Nick. Ken, home to help with the drive, was ready to ride shotgun with Nick. In a week's time, the clothes now hanging across the backseat would be replaced with idiot freshman boys on their way to a frat party. Midnight phone calls became common beginning one month into his time at Clemson. Eventually, I answered each small whisper for help with fear and dread, praying to hear my child's voice on the other end, not one of a stranger using his phone to call his mother. I was dozing when, one night, my cell phone trilled beside me.

Close to tears and raging in anger, Nick was walking down the highway after his "friend" John, from Franklin, drove off in his truck. Something had sparked a fight, Nick punched him, and John roared off, leaving Nick stranded on a dark road. Helpless. Scared. Drunk. I wanted to hang up on him and wake up when he was twenty-five. Instead, I did what I always do and walked him through the options. He had just enough battery left in his phone to call an Uber. Midway through stalking his iPhone back to his dorm room, his face icon stopped moving—his phone had died. I lay in a tight ball, wide awake for two hours, until he responded to my frantic texts. He was in bed—safe. All that fear was waiting for me while we bonded a final time packing up and pretending all was normal.

# Chapter 11

# Unsettled

*O*ne brilliant summer day in Sumter, with the household goods on their way to New Mexico, I lounged poolside, reading a summer novel while texting my son to join me for dinner on The Hampton restaurant's chic outdoor patio. The Hampton's bar had morphed that night into a stage for several spontaneous farewells. The first friends we made in Sumter, with whom we had drifted from contact, came by for photos and hugs. Nick's good friend Leigh from school showed up. Another family whom I knew well popped in too. It was bittersweet, both normal—my duo of me and Nick, enjoying time together over a good meal—and strained in understanding that all future meals would host Nick as a visitor in a home in which he never lived. I know it's not healthy to look back too often, as our focus and joy waver from the present—but I miss that dinner and what it represented: the community and living in a rare moment of realization that this was the most precious time in my life with the person who forced me on a maternal path ordained by God alone. It's dramatic but necessary to effuse over moments like this, demarcations in our life from one season to the next, that become forks in the road to a path of ease or hardship.

It was necessary to capture a family photo in front of our last home together and to bookend our first Christmas card photo, where we mugged happily with Maggie on those same steps. I yearned to freeze this point in time. Done were our eighteen years living life in lockstep. The sun behind us, our forced smiles belied our vastly different emotions. Sweet Maggie was gone. She had finally died a year before we had moved and was reduced to ashes in a box packed up in a tote in my car while Casey took her place. My upturned lips strained with the effort to hold back tears and fear. Fear for my son, whom I suspected even then was not ready to launch. In that last photo of us in front of our last house as a trio was a phony smile, my Bozo smirk a front for the pain of a season both magical and painful. There would be familiar routines in the years to come, holidays and vacations grounding us in the familiar, but none of them included the daily presence of my son.

"Grab the garbage! It's trash day!" I would like to remind him a hundred more times.

Taking place a few miles south of us was a scene much like our own, but in some ways the polar opposite. Nick's partner in past and future crime, Tradd, with packed-up car, was ready to leave home for Clemson as well. Tripp and Mary Kate would see Tradd off and go back into the house they had lived in all of Tradd's life. They would have breakfast, or mow the lawn, or maybe head to dinner with friends to talk about their new empty nest. The next day they would get up, go to work, and get on with their very same lives, only with one less plate at the dinner table. Two weekends later they would welcome Tradd back home for a few days to celebrate his grandmother's eightieth birthday. Mary Kate would bury her nose into his dirty clothes as she readied them for the washing machine. She would pick up his shoes he had left at the bottom of the stairs...yet again. She would lay eyes on her son, and assess his wellness or lack thereof.

No gradual letting-go blessing awaited us. We were being ripped apart all at once, the Band-Aid yanked off in one swift ouch, taking the scab with it and revealing a fleshy new sore. Ken, Casey, and I piled in to my SUV, and Nick into the Toyota, alone, along with everything he owned. All his new bedding, his ostrich bowtie given to him by John, his new twin sheets, the orange initialed towels from Tradd's mom, and the first-aid kit I had painstakingly prepared for him. Among its potentially lifesaving contents were bandages, antibiotic ointments, and tweezers. I added charcoal capsules for ingestion in the event he ate a spoiled pizza slice or rancid lunch meat, multivitamins, and several lip ointments (his bedside mainstay). A year later, when he moved into his new apartment downtown at U-Center, I found the kit in his drawer, intact and unused.

We set out as a tiny caravan, only slightly behind the moving truck ferrying our household goods to New Mexico. We would spend one night together, then the next day unpack Nick and overnight in the Clemson rental home before resuming the trek west.

These rearview glimpses appear larger in real time, weighty with indelible memories. When completing a marathon or sailing around the globe, the permanence of that experience etches remembrance forever upon your soul. So, there I was, backing down the driveway one last time, taking with me my baggage, Nick's black Lab in the backseat, and many bittersweet memories. We had pulled into this driveway four years earlier with ironclad certainty that Franklin Prep would shape our son in a wholesome environment, with small class sizes, skilled teachers, and under eighty kids per grade. This small town, this small stellar school was different—there would be no metal detectors screening kids for weapons, like in Virginia. There would be no drugs floating the hallways like at McLean High. We would dodge all the coming-of-age pitfalls that lured bright kids off course to epic fails. That was the vision.

I was uneasy. I knew Nick wasn't ready for the world. Should I have insisted on one more year living with us and working until he grew a brain? My once shiny hope sputtered out like a car on its last fumes of gas. My soul was dinged up from unsavory moments and loss that made me ready to move on or jump off a cliff. Parents had for years been launching kids to college and then out into the world for a transition to a promising new season of life. But Nick didn't care much about his future. His reckless streak, hot temper, and disinterest in academics made for a toxic start to a college career. Combining all the change with the loss of a familiar place to come back to on holidays, the usual college chance at reset and staying grounded with family did not exist. How was this a good idea to bustle him and his stuff out of the car and book on down the freeway to live so far away? I pulled onto Windrow Drive to caravan behind Nick to Clemson. One last glance at the house—at his screenless window—before I looked forward at the road ahead. We would overnight at an Airbnb and arrive for move-in at our appointed time the next morning.

Move-in day at Clemson is an organized process honed over years of drop-offs. Scores of non-freshman students and various volunteers abound, coached to jerk the fledgling collegian out of parental clutches and into their new 150-square-foot dorm room... quickly, quickly. Just *let go* and move on out.

I watched the well-orchestrated process taking place in the cars ahead of us, and waited our turn with my air conditioner losing the fight with the heat of the day. Still leading the way was Nick, with window open to the midday heat, as he waited in the queue on Fort Hill Street.

Fort Hill Street held onto a slice of the Old South, as mandated by the antebellum farmer and owner of Fort Hill House, Thomas

Green Clemson. One could tune in closely to hear the secrets of a storied history ruffling its sturdy magnolia leaves. Their fragrant white flowers helped anchor the past to an abundant present, weaving together one perfumed century after another to arrive at the season of my son's collegiate entrance, and the chance for him, too, to leave his mark on those hallowed grounds.

There exists, in the South, a centuries-old and still thriving tradition of debutante balls. Parents present in grand fashion their nineteen-year-old young lady into society, bedecked like a bride in white gown and gloves. The gala event that once ushered the lady into the arms of a husband is now more about tradition and partying and less about finding a man. Men get no such fanfare in their promotion to adulthood. So there, in some awkward handing off of the baton in a race, was my son crossing over and away from us into a sort of independence in front of Fort Hill House. It sat only yards away from the action at Holmes Hall, as though in watchful judgment and witness to the arrival of this batch of eighteen-year-olds. I suppose, though, the kids transitioning into Holmes were a beacon of hope, honoring and preserving dreams, cultivated over the years, of their parents. Me included. Despite all the muck of late, Nick was still a beacon of hope.

As we inched up to the pluck-off zone, soaking up the scents and sights, it is mercy, I see now, that most humans lack the vision to peer into the future. If granted that prophetic gift, would I have had the courage to halt this move-in, to demand Nick get his butt back into his SUV and follow me and his dad the 1,500 miles to New Mexico, away from the imminent implosion on the near horizon? Instead, my unforeseen future became one of ridiculous iPhone stalkings at two in the morning and logging on to the Clemson website in a feeble attempt to spot my child on the live webcam conveniently mounted on Fort Hill House, exposing all of Holmes Hall.

During one unplanned trip to Clemson, I drove down Fort Hill Street to its dead end at Death Valley Stadium and back up again and again when Nick refused to answer my goodnight text. I always lodged close by, at the Courtyard Marriott a few miles from campus. Despite the reason for my visits, they always offered a tiny respite from the constant worry gnawing away at me in New Mexico. Yet, being with and near Nick magnified our fractured relationship and intensified the pain of watching his downward spiral up close. This. Was. Not. My. Son. My son was generous, thoughtful, and careful with the feelings of others.

Much earlier in his life, on one of our trips to Tyson's Corner Mall for Christmas shopping—Nick was in sixth grade—we had wandered into a favorite cooking supply store, Williams-Sonoma. So many items held purchase appeal, to the point where I could not choose and made a decision to buy nothing. Nick then asked if I needed to go and get a coffee.

"Mom! You need to go get a coffee at the Nordstrom coffee stand. I will be okay in here, waiting for you!" Hmm...I realized his plan.

"Umm, okay, bud," I replied before honoring his request for my credit card. On the way out I asked the sales clerk to take care of him with an imminent purchase of a Christmas gift for me. I waited around the corner, averting my gaze from his sweet transaction. It was a common characteristic of Nick to put his generous nature into action. I remember opening that gift on Christmas morning, not caring in the least what the package held, with a profound understanding that the love and thoughtfulness *were* the gift. Beneath the wrapping paper and ribbon, cradled in a nest of tissue paper sat the item I'd pointed out in the store, a mortar and pestle made of lava rock. Sadly, months later a mouse trespassed on my beloved gift in the cloak of night, leaving urine and droppings for me to find in the morning. The toxic rodent flow had permeated the entire pestle and rendered it unsafe for future use. I cried throwing it out.

Many days on the Clemson campus awaited me. I would soon sit on the steps of Fort Hill House or walk the grounds in wait until my son's classes let out, and read the story of the house and of its former occupants. Peering into the windows in the early morning, I would grow to know it well.

But at the time, we were directed to pull into a freshly vacated spot on the courtyard. Nick was first as we pulled in side by side and opened the hatches on our SUVs. Descending upon us, eight students in matching orange Clemson Tiger T-shirts shouted, "What room?!" Nick replied, "Holmes, 502!" The plastic totes were snatched from my SUV and lugged off. I was careful to make sure they avoided taking the ones packed for New Mexico, and then I closed the hatch, aware of the pressure to make space for the car behind me.

We pulled out, found two empty parking spots a block away, and headed up to Nick's dorm to meet his roommate and snoop around. Attempting to make his space somewhat familiar to me, I lingered too long within the minimal square footage of cinder block walls. I made his bed with the new Bed in a Bag from Nautica, set up his wardrobe, then chatted with his roommate, John, and his parents who drove the short two hours up from Atlanta. They lingered too. It was crowded and jovial, almost festive in the tiny space. Nick's day was full. The engineering majors were hosting a gathering for incoming freshman, friends from Franklin were getting together, and that night, a whole campus-wide party was scheduled. Ken and I had one day and one more night in the Airbnb. Four years in South Carolina counted as the longest time we spent in one state over our eighteen years as a military family. This was the final and toughest PCS—Permanent Change of Station—because I was leaving behind my child. I once read a quote attributed to Miriam

Adeney: "You will never be completely at home again, because part of your heart always will be elsewhere. That is the price you pay for the richness of loving and knowing people in more than one place."[10] I understand at a cellular level this tough truth and wonder now how many parents feel this bittersweet consequence of raising kids.

We got a call from Nick as we were settling in to watch the Olympics at the house four miles from campus. I was struggling to get the cable to function, eager to watch the gymnastics slated for the night, when my cell phone rang. Nick was lonely and wondered if he could come over. He stayed for only an hour and was off again. Another call from him—two hours later. He was not feeling well. The move for him was different than for most of his peers. Absent from his reality was a familiar home to return to next weekend or the weekend after. Nowhere close was the safety of his family offering space to regroup and feel like the "old Nick." No grounding routines for him before heading back into the fray of college life. *Roots.* His roots were being dredged up and replanted, once again. This time he was alone in the process.

"Mom, my stomach is tight. I feel like throwing up," he groaned.

"Did you take some charcoal, bud?"—my panacea to every stomach gurgle.

"Naww...I don't know where it is."

"I put it in your medicine cabinet. Check and see," I responded, validated for my lingering and fussing earlier that day.

"Hey, let's meet for breakfast before you head out. I can see Casey one last time," he offered. We would see him again at Parents Weekend in six weeks, but Casey would be left behind.

The next morning, Nick had stories from his first night on campus. There were parties on his floor, he met his neighbors, had some drinks, and he felt excited to get back to campus, and get rid of us, as evidenced by his fidgeting and distant behavior.

He rushed us through that short farewell. Ken and I received brief hugs. But Casey was different. Whatever emotions Nick was processing and all the love in his heart and tears he couldn't shed for us, he poured into his dog. The dog he had adopted and raised up from a pup. She returned his love in equal measure with slobbery licks and body blows. Then finally, it was time to load her into my car.

Standing in front of the diner in the gathering heat of the morning, I paused. How could I do this? *This* was the hardest thing I had ever done. How could I just leave my heart on the sidewalk? I climbed into the passenger seat with care, my skin crawling and uneasy, leaving me to shiver off the discomfort as I closed the car door. Turning to look behind me for one dramatic final glimpse of my son as we drive toward the main road, I was granted only the wet nose of Casey and our household crap stacked to the roof, obscuring my view.

The sun was shining two weeks after the drop-off as my husband and I sat in the Whole Foods parking lot, sharing a Bluetooth call with Nick. We were on our way to our vacation property in Red River, New Mexico, three hours away. Our first visit to our ski townhome—without my son—as residents of New Mexico held a rare lack of agenda or expectation. On our call, Nick was excited: thrilled at the options to pledge fraternities, stunned at the plethora of parties to attend that night, and sharing a rare excitement for academics. He was happy, adjusting. Do all parents release long-held breaths when learning their children are adjusting well to life? I felt happiness. Relief that I had launched my child well, that my worries were all for naught, and that the empty nest made space for reconnecting with my own goals and dreams, constantly interrupted over the past nineteen years. I buckled up for our short journey, buoyed by the prospect of early fall spent in the mountains and reuniting with Nick in two short weeks. The future looked hopeful and exciting, despite an expected grief and sadness that comes with transitions. In two weeks I would lay eyes on him at Parents Weekend—assuring myself he was well and thriving.

Clemson, the town and the campus, is swamped during Parents and Family weekend. Restaurants and cafes overflow, traffic is heavy, truck bumper to SUV bumper, and throughout the campus small breakouts of various school organizations host mixers for students and parents. The ultimate draw and the pinnacle of the weekend festivities is the Saturday night football game—and tailgating. A massive effort is heaved into a Clemson tailgate. The university leases, at a hefty price, a spot big enough for a pop-up canopy and a bar festooned in purple, orange, and tiger paws. Row upon row in field after field and parking lots over the entirety of campus bear witness to love for the Clemson Tigers. The consumption of all manner of alcohol is standard practice. Orange-and-purple-clad super fans host elaborate feasts in their tiny rental spots. The air is thick with the heat of late summer and grilled food, buffets of Tiger-themed treats and Yeti coolers filled with ice chilling up lots and lots and lots of alcohol. Pillars of the communities mutate into bartenders come football season—they are complicit in supplying underage kids, or anyone who asks, with a beer or a mixed drink. The first tailgate I attended was in a choice spot on a field near Death Valley Stadium. I saw my son invited by the host to pop open the Yeti housed under the orange Clemson Tigers awning. He reached deep down into the ice, grabbing two dripping Bud Light cans. Shoving one in the pocket of his wrinkled khaki shorts, he popped the top on the other and gulped down half the can.

"You enjoy that beer, Nick. Here's a Koozie—keep what's left in that can covered up, ya hear! Go Tigers!" exclaimed the parent of a friend from high school, clad in Barney purple. Gazing at the parent and his over-the-top tailgate effort, I didn't judge him. I knew I too would push alcohol on minors. Heck, I'd even hidden it in Nick's car before the concert in Columbia. Other events for the Parents Weekend slated to start on Friday were all ones Nick vehemently opposed. He had changed his major from electrical engineering (not my people, Mom!) to business. The business school was hosting an informal, Friday evening dinner for all students and their parents—but he knew no other business students and refused to attend. Parents of the Greek-life students dug into the weekend, guided by a structured schedule. But Nick had chosen not to join a fraternity—a big mistake, in hindsight. Pledging discussions occupied most of our first month on excited phone calls with Nick. In the end, the process intimidated him; he opted out. Months later, his roommate offered him a vacated spot in a fraternity without the mandatory pledging ritual. Nick declined. Navigating the first year of college free of a tether to a structured group or activity was the setup for stupid actions and relationships with other kids unwilling or unable to bond in healthy ways. Nick spent most of his spare time at the apartment of his two best friends who attended the community college down the road, studying in a program to gain entrance to Clemson for their sophomore year. He chose them and that extension of high school, over fully investing his energy at Clemson.

No one tells you that the hardest part of raising your children is letting them go. On a cellular level, I knew this. I understood my son enough to believe his increasing emotional distance was necessary to define himself outside of the child he would always be to me. He needed to surround himself with peers who validated him as this carefree and fun nonconformist. Fun was centric to his personality. I happily witnessed and fed his God-given nature through innocent and innocuous play and learning. Then, the stakes for fun seeking grew past the bounds of harmlessness into dangerous pursuits. Take a bored fun seeker, add some newfound freedom, and normalize the plethora of drugs and alcohol on a college campus—and wait for consequences to roll in like massive waves in a hurricane. Self-control and well-developed morality are the trustiest brake you have in life. The brief glimpses in high school of the party side of my fun son were nothing compared to the front-row seats, viewing up close a perfect storm of the toxic ingredients needed for an epic fail. This was parents weekend.

My child, completely devoid of a sober mind, shocked me. We parted ways at gametime after winding up together in the stadium. We sat with friends at the fifty-yard line on the visitor side while Nick joined Tradd in the student section. When we met up after Clemson took the win, Nick stumbled over to us in the parking lot where we sat waiting out traffic. He had clearly been celebrating... all day.

"Bud! Let's wrap up here and head to dinner in town," I said.

After exchanging small talk with us, he began weaving back to a friend's car.

"I am headed to meet up with Tradd! I shall see you mañana!" he slurred.

My attempts to arrest this binge day of drinking were as feeble as using a wad of chewing gum to plug a hole in Hoover Dam. Efforts to shift him from his trajectory and into my rental car backfired. He quickly hopped into the passenger side of a friend's car, smacking the back of his head on the doorframe. He would stop when he wore out, and then call to notify me of the crash.

He had toed the line, been an ideal son, for sixteen years. This catastrophic eruption brewing at his fun-centric core was leading him toward a messy spill in a dark place; a place where I was not invited or welcome, but dragged into to watch from the sidelines. Many times during the writing of *all that comes next*, a silent and awful howl vomited out from the marrow of my soul. In a dizzy hurl of emotion I ask, "Why did my son not just let me let go?" Why would he drag me time and again into his descent? The person in the world who I love more than myself, whose well-being has always come before my own, would only *almost* let go. The majority of the teen years he spent in a push-and-pull of "Leave me alone!" "Help! I need you," "No, leave me alone!" This only amped up in college. A black hole is an area in space where the gravitational pull is so strong, so fierce, that once held in its grip, nothing can escape the force. The black hole's gravitational pull reduces everything to nothing.

I had lived in a black hole for three years, with no light and limited hope. An allusion of certain catastrophe sucked the possibility from my once familiar, visceral connection to hope. Hope, as I have come to know, is an essential component for a joyful life. Hope is the third leg for a sturdy table—stable enough to sustain the weight placed on it by burdens. Grit and faith, along with hope, create a foundation to maintain momentum to serve and live well despite the inevitable junk heaped upon us.

Faith says, "I am grounded in a greater God who is ultimately in control of all things. I am okay with the limited control I have over the infinite amount of contributing factors in our humanity. Combined with hard work, dedication, and the assurance obstacles will be overcome, I have faith in my circumstances working out according to God's plan."

Hope, shouldering its share of weight, looks toward the future. Embedded in the fabric of our DNA, hope, as they say, springs eternal. The human species is born with a hope as real as our head, shoulders, knees, and toes.

Dr. Judith Rich states, "Hope is a match in a dark tunnel, a moment of light, just enough to reveal the path ahead and ultimately the way out."[11]

Finally, grit is a determinant of the amount of success one is able to achieve throughout life. Grit says, "I can persist through any hardship with laser focus and determination to persist toward achieving the good goals I accept for myself." I found out that both Nick and I had hope and waning faith, but were in desperate need of grit.

*Chapter 12*

# Running With
# Scissors

M*y cell phone jangled me out of a rare REM sleep. "By the Seaside"* waltzed across my darkened room, its happy tone a stark contrast to the nauseous fear brought on by a 3 a.m. phone call. Picking up the iPhone with dread, the screen face shouted "Nick." It had been a tough few years launching Nick from teen to young adult college freshman, and the process had left me spent. I answered the happy chirp with my heart in my throat.

Worse than an audio call, this was a rare FaceTime call. His ruddy face sharpened into view. The picture was clear and stark; his wild eyes belied the glimpse of the innocent orange and purple sky behind his head. Panic rattled me wide awake as I saw my child alive but certainly not looking well. Nick had shared everything with me—as an only child he had few options—up until ninth grade, and with a few massive exceptions he still enjoyed sharing his life with me. It was 5:30 a.m. in Clemson and my son was running...for exercise. His face, red and splotchy from the autumn chill of a South Carolina morning, was unaccustomed to meeting the first light of day.

"MOM! I had to show you the sunrise! I am out RUNNING! I couldn't sleep! Been up ALL night! I feel like a million bucks!" he panted between thwacks of shoes hitting cold pavement.

Tucked under the covers shivering, I feared for my son's life. He had logged hundreds of hours speeding along in the hammock of his baby jogger and was seven years old when he ran his first triathlon at a waterpark in Hawaii. Running was good and grounding, something he grew up around. Somehow, though, he grew to hate exercise and actively avoided running for fun. This was not a run to improve his health and well-being, it was a freakish anomaly. This millionth after-hours call in two years was unwelcome.

"Nick, why are you up at 5:30 running?" I said with control.

"This is AWESOME! I am going to get out here more often!" he nearly sang back in delight. "There are only a few people out running this early. Check out the sky!"

The phone released his face for a view of the sunrise peeking up over the hill. I couldn't make out where on campus the shaky glimpses were coming from.

My view was jerked back to his tomato-red cheeks I had once known so well. The camera phone bounced up and down as he ran...faster now, eager to share with me out of habit this most spectacular moment in his life.

Bounce, bounce, bounce, his face came and went on the small screen I clutched in a death grip.

Death grips and parenting often go hand in hand. All parents relate. There is the inevitable first time your little bean goes missing at Dillard's or Home Depot, when you unashamedly shout and scurry around in fear, only to find him under the women's lingerie rounder, playing zoo with a pair of cheetah-print underwear. Then, trepidation comes upon release of your school-age kiddo (decked out in new Gymboree duds) into the first day of first grade, to the care of Mrs. Fukumoto. The death grip surfaces again when handing over the keys to the automobile where he would be vulnerable, within its four sides of metal, rubber, and glass. Navigating caution and joy in equal measure in the upbringing of my child felt mostly doable— always manageable despite the circumstances.

*Safe* was now a wistful memory, as we had launched over Niagara Falls in a rickety boat, crashing into the turbid waters where only the lucky survive. Hanging on for dear life for over two years now, I didn't believe I was one of the lucky ones, and I envied parents whose children were kicking butt and taking names throughout their senior years in high school and into college. Two years hanging on tight to the very life of the child I carried and birthed and loved and prayed over, wishing beyond reason he was only lost in a rack in some department store.

He was altered, and blocking our questions; Ken was awake and excited to see Nick up and running, unaware of the oddity of this spectacle. Nick *needed* me to see his moment. Finally! He had taken up running! "LOOK MOM! I am exercising!" High on something, in the midst of wrecking his life, he still sought my approval.

Reluctantly, I ended the call with his promise to check in before he left for his classes, though I knew he would not remember to check in. These same two years, his lies and empty promises flowed forth like a wide-open faucet. He would probably crash and never make it to class. The child who could not tell a lie had become a young adult compulsive in passing out fake information to placate all around him. Drugs can do that to a person. Reckless pursuit of maintaining his terrible lifestyle blended together with his honed values creating a want for "something more." A hole in the soul can only be filled with God. Everything else is a replacement waiting to expire. A confusing jumble of his inherent nature to pursue goals and achieve but also to party hard and have the time of his life kept him pursuing academics while prioritizing the social aspects of what he thought everyone "fun" on campus was doing. In other words, the goal he doggedly pursued was "fun" at almost any cost. Gravitating toward the "fun" peers, all newly freed from direct parental supervision, introduced a stream of late-night parties, drugs, and dangerous behaviors. An extension of his refusal sophomore year of high school to form friendships with academic-minded peers on the claim that they "just sat in front of the TV; they didn't do anything" morphed into bonding again with less academically minded friends whose primary collegiate goal was trolling their way around the party scene. My child was elec-trified with the round-the-clock options to partake in the seedier side of campus life, eschewing any of the plethora of campus-wide organized events, which I continually urged him to attend.

Text to Nick: "Hey bud. Did you see the Color Run is this weekend? Are you interested?"

Nick: "Nah."

Text to Nick: "Good Morning, Sweetie! Movie night at The Hendrix Student Center! It's *Mission Impossible*! You gonna make it?"

Nick: "I've seen it, Mom."

Text to Nick: "Nick! I see they are organizing intramural Lacrosse. You love Lacrosse! Will you please get over there to try out?"

Nick: "Nah. I haven't played in a while. Those people are really good."

What I see clearly now in the telling is this: If an individual has a passion toward a pursuit, chances are good they are receptive to suggestions. You have to *want* to conform, comply, achieve. You must *want* to inhale wisdom and mentoring, even seek it out. If you don't *want* it, the offerings of help are left to waft by, never gaining passage inside the intended recipient.

─────────────────── **Nick's Perspective** ───────────────────

*When I went for that run and FaceTimed Mom, I had taken an Adderall to prepare for a busy study day. I don't get up early often, and I remember feeling exhilarated like I had not felt in ages.*

I wasn't convinced. The freakish morning run confirmed my suspicion that all was not going well at Clemson, but still my interventions remained anemic. After the run, I insisted he see a school counselor. He agreed to one session on the assumption he would walk away with a prescription for Adderall, the ADHD medication prescribed to half of his friends. It is an amphetamine—speed. Hunting down the experts, I found on WebMD that 25 percent of college students are prescribed ADHD medication.[12] In their unprescribed form they are known as "study drugs." I suspect their appeal to young people to focus on studies for an extended period of time to garner excellent scores is tantalizing. Adderall and Vyvanse are easy to get, according to my young classmates during my time earning my MPH. They are seen as harmless and innocuous given their widespread use for ADHD in the twenty-first century. The CDC reports, "The estimated number of children ever diagnosed with ADHD, according to a national 2016 parent survey, is 6.1 million (9.4%). [13]

Then there was this survey from Ohio State University: "Across the U.S., nearly one in six college students now say they've used stimulants like Adderall, Ritalin, or Dexadrine—drugs normally prescribed for Attention Deficit Hyperactivity Disorder (ADHD)—without a prescription."[14] It only takes a tiny leap to progress from medicating to pass a test to medicating for energy to craving a consistent endorphin high. These possibilities are normalized on college campuses, and I suppose I normalized them as well. We make up stories, I know for sure, to normalize what is tough to wrap our minds around. I think of it as a default that our subconscious sets to lovingly protect us from a broken heart. But the truth is, things just get worse when we refuse to recognize and deal with the truth.

I thought Nick needed a little talking to, a bit of correction, and some stern words. Over Christmas break, he would be home for three weeks—he would be back under our roof, rooted in the familiar comforts of family and love. One lasting message that bears repeating from the headmaster at Franklin Prep after one disturbing discussion was this: "These kids all test their boundaries. They have little failures and big failures. We need to make sure they avoid *epic failures*. They don't bounce back from epic failures," he said. I was receptive to this wisdom but oblivious on how to put it into action. I wanted more than anything to be sure Nick avoided an epic fail.

"Ring, ring" went my phone's FaceTime feature one Sunday morning. It was nine o'clock and I was relaxing on the patio with a second cup of coffee.

"Mom, hey," Nick began when I tapped the green button. "I have something to show you and I don't want you to freak out. I am fine, just so you know." He held the phone away from him, giving me a glimpse of a small refrigerator under the elevated bed of his roommate.

He sounded good, normal even. I took a deep breath. "What's up, bud?"

The camera spun around toward his face. He looked tired, but fine. Then he opened his mouth.

HIS FRONT TOOTH WAS MISSING!

"Dear Lord, Nick. What...what on Earth did you do?!" I shrieked.

A gaping dark space where a lovely tooth once perched stared back at my shocked face.

"Wellllll...after the game last night, John and I were walking back from Walter's tailgate. John jumped over the cement barricade on College Avenue, and I followed," he explained. "Ha! I missed. And fell flat on my face. When I got up, there was blood ALL OVER and I was short a tooth!"

*Dear Lord, please let this level out,* I prayed.

"I wasn't even drunk!" he fibbed.

That Monday we found a dentist to begin the multistep process of replacing his tooth. It was an uncomplicated fix. This time, it was not a massive injury. The reminder of that drunken blunder stares me in the face when my son smiles. The fake tooth overlaps his remaining incisor. Someday, I suppose, he can replace the fake tooth for a better fit.

Thanksgiving 2016, we met Nick in Sumter to spend that first holiday with Tradd and his family and then attend a Clemson game. After dinner, Nick and Tradd met with friends to do the same thing they did in high school—hang out in the parking lot of Beacon Cinemas with all manner of unsavory clowns from Sumter High. I have no idea who these people were, really. I crept out of my house a few times to drive down to Beacon prior to our move, seeking clarity on the same question I pondered at Thanksgiving. Was I paranoid or was Nick on a path of destruction? Were these familiar mama bear defenses deserved? We drove back to Clemson on Friday night, in time for Game Day with the Clemson Tigers vs. Georgia on Saturday.

Game Day is more than a football game; it's a visceral experience, as I mentioned earlier. These are moments in time most Clemson alumni and residents fervently cling to year after year—from birth to graduation to death. Orange and Purple explodes throughout the small town, creating a conglomerate of blending experiences. School flags wave high on cars, dorms, and Clemson campus structures. Tiger Paw–festooned canopies cover BBQ grills and Yeti coolers. Early in the day, the fragrant waft of BBQ permeates campus. A welcome interruption in the midst of the tailgating is the Tiger Walk, where all the Clemson football players and coaches donning suit and tie calmly unload from purple buses to stream through the crowds and into the locker room. As the day bleeds into sunset, Orange-and-Purple people line up for the parade, led by the marching band and cheer squads, toward the stadium. Then, hours later and minutes before game time, the uniformed team and staff load back onto the buses where the belching caravan inches its way to the iron gates in the back of the stadium, spilling players into Death Valley. From the stands, we see the orange paw-stamped helmets bouncing up and down, the players crowding and swaying as one to lay hands on the iconic Howard's Rock. The "Tiger Rag" song belts out of the bandstand as the massive players in random sets of two and three race down the grassy student section, high-fiving the drunk, purple-faced and bare-torso-painted students. Then the run onto the field, steam-rolling in for "the most exciting twenty-five seconds in football." Party, party, party! Game Day is a giant party.

Stalking my child on iPhone finder began in high school, but the obsession with his whereabouts peaked the third month of his first year of college. My crazed brain ruled my knee-jerk actions and disturbed my peace of mind. Parents raise their children with the assumption—no, the expectation—they will be okay and thrive. I yearned for this natural outcome of doing a decent job raising my child. I was excited to launch a life for myself after almost two decades of living at the whims of military assignments and motherhood.

Back in New Mexico, days spilled out in front of me to pursue my goals free from time-consuming obligations. I enrolled in a master yoga class in preparation to couple my degree in public health with yoga. I would work with clients out of our home studio, helping them achieve total wellness. That was the goal. Then, life got in the way when my mother and brother-in-law dealt with debilitating strokes. And Nick—he went off the rails. God had other plans.

Looking back, when a second child was clearly not going to be our blessing, I had doubled down on sibling and buddy mode with my son. It took time and excessive energy to play mom and pseudo-sibling in Nick's nomadic life. I had my run with a career from the age of nineteen until I became a mom, quite by surprise, at thirty-four, when fertility prospects begin a downward plunge toward menopause. I worked adjunct positions offering flexibility, and grabbed the chance to earn my master's degree while doing a decent job as a mom. I poured into my son, grabbed chances for self-improvement where possible, and took a backseat to my husband's career. We traveled, explored, served, and lived well. All I ever really yearned for, though, was for my son to thrive—to be independent and filled with purpose and good health. The nightly stalking in Nick's room to check his breathing—which began in infancy (post-Bobby)—was me not letting go. But when I thought I was ready to let go, my son would not let go—he would not thrive. I could not let go of him until he let go of his destructive path—and stopped roping me into involvement in his crooked ways. Teamwork! We were a team and instead of a resounding "STOP!" I seemed to be saying, "Sign me up as a helper!"

Texting him in rapid-fire missives to LET ME KNOW WHEN YOU ARE IN BED plagued my every sleepless night. Boom! Boom! Boom! I fired off the texts until the location finder showed him back in Holmes Hall. As noted earlier, I often pulled up the public webcam aimed directly at the front door of his building, wondering if it was in real time, because I rarely saw him or any human filling the midnight-to-two-o'clock stream.

---

### Nick's Perspective

*I obviously knew Mom and Dad were following me on the iPhone tracker. It was one of the conditions for going out with my friends at night. One time my mom asked why I was coming home a different way than usual, and that confirmed she actually was tracking me. It did not prevent me from doing anything, and I turned it off when I wanted to go anywhere bad, like South Sumter. As for the stalking on the webcams? NO! I did not know she was doing that. Ummm, it's a little creepy, Mom!*

One shocking midnight phone call came in while I held my phone, stalking him. It was Nick, drunk and sad, and odd, as Nick was not the type to get melancholy when he drank. He was either happy or angry.

"Hey Mom, whatcha doin?"

"Talking to you, Nick," I said.

"I wanted to tell you—I am sitting on a headstone in the cemetery. It's really cool!!" he slurred.

"Nick! Please get to bed. Walk home. Now," I insisted with fear rising in my throat.

"I am lost...I don't know where this cemetery is." He sounded confused.

"I will pull up your location. You can get back to Holmes, bud!" I began directions from his location back to his dorm.

"Mom. I am really lonely. I feel so sad." He was crying now.

I talked to him, tried to soothe him. He was messed up, and rational thought was beyond him. I talked him through the cemetery and back to his dorm. He was calmer when we hung up and so was I. He was okay, in for the night. I could sleep.

I woke up an hour later, just to double-check his position. It was not uncommon for him to manipulate my stalking, to appease me by arriving home and then heading back out. His location finder showed him on campus, but not at Holmes. I called him. He answered.

He was *not* okay. This was something different. He was not drunk. Sentences fell off as he spoke. He mumbled something unintelligible before hanging up. I called again and again...no answer. I texted his roommate. After no response from anyone, I called his suitemate in the connecting room, Robert, whose number I had gotten the first week of school. It had sat idle in my contacts until now. He answered.

"Robert, this is Nick's mother. Something is not right with him. He is wandering around campus." It was 1:30 a.m. as I pleaded with him to go out and find Nick.

Robert agreed, left the room, and went downstairs, out to look for Nick. I knew this because I had the webcam pulled up.

Lying in my dark bedroom, Ken snoring beside me, my phone vibrated with a call from Nick. Robert had found him at a shuttle stop on campus. They'd hopped on it, returning to the dorm and their suite. Nick was still slurring his words when we spoke.

"Mommm...I feel sick. I can't breathe. Mom, I'm scared," he cried and blathered into the phone. "I'm layin' on the bathroom floor." I heard him vomit into the toilet.

Panicked, I told him to stay on the phone with me until he felt better. When I had hung up after his cemetery crawl he sounded calm and somewhat sober—what had he taken before he went back out into the night, alone?

"Nick—don't hang up. What did you take?? Nick...Nick?!" I was shouting now, awakening Ken. I turned on the bedside light.

The phone call was still connected, but I did not hear my son!! I received no response as I shouted his name! WHAT DRUG WAS HE ON?! HAD HE OVERDOSED!!

"NICKKKK!!! ANSWER ME!!" I shouted. *HOW do I help him? He said he couldn't breathe!!*

Robert failed to answer my calls and texting. Nick could be dead!

I phoned the after-hours number for Holmes Hall. I was directed to the all-night security team who patrolled the campus. They would go to his dorm for a welfare check. *Oh shit. Oh shit. Oh shit. He will be furious with me, if he is alive and fine.*

My phone vibrated twenty minutes later. Was it Nick or Clemson security?? I couldn't bear to look at my screen as I answered. *Dear God,* it was my son. He was okay. Oh heavens, the relief I felt.

"Nick!"

"MOMMMM!!! I HATE YOU!! I HATE YOU!!! I F******* HATE YOUR GUTS!!!"

He could not be calmed. Years of rage unleashed from his ransacked dorm room to my quiet bedroom in New Mexico. I remained calm as he leveled his tirade, taking chunks out of my soul. My soothing words belied his rage in a useless attempt to bring him back from the brink of some evil, awful force.

"NO...YOU LISTEN!!!!! I AM DONE WITH YOU! STAY OUT OF MY LIFE!! I NEVER WANT TO SEE YOU, HEAR FROM YOU AGAIN! I HATE YOU!! YOU CALLED THE COPS ON ME! THEY CAME IN AND TOOK ALL MY LIQUOR! THEY TOOK THE TEQUILA BOTTLE I GOT IN NEW MEXICO!! I AM IN TROUBLE AND MAY GET KICKED OUT!! DO YOU HEAR ME?! LEAVE ME ALONE!!!!!"

I handed the phone to Ken. Nick would talk to him for another five minutes as I shivered, curled up beside my sleepy husband.

There would be hoops to jump through to keep Nick on campus. He was assigned a student "lawyer" and a court of students would convene to decide his fate. This being a first offense, he received only a two-month probation. The ding on his academic record fell away just in time for the next blowup. Wouldn't most parents just stand back secure in the ignorance provided by protective blinders shielding them from the tumult of their child? I couldn't. I was not, am not, that parent. Nick seemed incapable of not sharing most of his life with me. Habits are hard to break. He was still seeking me out for comfort, in whatever that looked like through his hazy perspective, pulling me into his escapades before shutting me out time and again. I engaged as a willing participant in this sicko dynamic. More to make myself feel I had a grip, I crafted and mailed a letter to Nick the next day.

*Nick,*

*I write to you with love and confidence in the man you are struggling to become. But, I have a unique viewpoint watching these last two-plus years of your life and how far you seem to be removed from who you really are and Gods purpose for your unique gifts. I know you better than anyone, I think. Therefore, I am qualified to weigh in.*

*You are not trying your best at Clemson, academically. I know if you were, you would be passing all your tests and classes. You would pass up all social life until you had your head above water. You would realize you have every tool and support at your disposal to succeed—and utilize every single one.*

*It boils down to this my sweet son: How bad to you want to stay at Clemson? How bad does it hurt to know you won't be there next year when John and Tradd rise up from Bridge? How bad do you not want to surrender your blessing to be a Clemson Tiger on a free ride no less? Can you never again let lazy and fun drive your choices?*

*If you want it badly enough, you WILL stay and thrive from now on as a Clemson Tiger. Because that is who you are. EVERYTHING you have ever really yearned for you have successfully earned. Right now, you are majoring in Fun 101. That's easy...but Nick, in life easy NEVER lasts long or tastes anything but bitter in the end. A degree in Fun is a semester long, one and done. It's okay to be miserable and tired and frustrated toiling away toward your purpose...it's expected.*

*I love you and I will help you. Everyone will help you get back on track IF you want it badly enough to endure the pain and come out stronger on the other side. Your life matters. The decision to work without relief when necessary to thrive at Clemson is ultimately yours. I hope you make today your "one day."*

*There really are no free rides to a beautiful life. Yours can be spectacular! But the joy will come through pain, passion, hard work, and sound character with God. The party happens only when there is no more toiling to do!*

*Baby, I pray you choose hard work; it is the only way out of your pain and to a truly wonderful life. If you don't learn this now, I promise God will hand you this same icky lesson time and again, harder each time until you get it.*

*- Go to your profs, schedule appts*

*- Go to your advisor, schedule that NOW. Get back on track*

*- Go to resource center...sign up for classes and get tutors*

*- Give up fun for now to stay there for fun down the road to happen*

*- Talk to Dr. Cummings*

*- Work out—lots of options*

*- Find a church youth group*

*IT WILL BE WORTH IT*

*I believe in you, we love you, and God's got you, too.*

*All my love and support, Mom*

Writing the letter gave me a sense of "parenting" him away from danger and a pep talk to get him back on track. Futile. I often wondered if he read my bits of wisdom contained in all my texts and letters.

──────────────── **Nick's Perspective** ────────────────

*Mom, I read everything. I read your cards, texts, and letters. The question should be if I internalized any of it, and the answer is probably not.*

Some monster dwelling inside my child unleashed a wrath—a wrath that would simmer and boil over in the coming months. My unforgivable, in his eyes, transgression offered an all-access pass to finally and completely hate me. Did he hate me for the sin of our life-long entwined love, grounding him and giving him an unconditional support and ally? Tepid, tiny efforts to free himself from my love and care ended now. Seemingly subconscious—and long-familiar—efforts to please his mother ended, granting him permission to fully live on his own terms. After this night, there was no qualm about hacksawing me off of him, creating a gaping vacuum for the dark enemy to enter into and grab his soul for full destruction.

Clemson, I suspect, has at any given moment—during, before, or after game day, out in the expanse of its grassy campus, in the darkened dorm hallways, in the bustling stretch of bars and shops on College Avenue, and in the beer-soaked frat houses—students hell-bent on scoring more. More fun, more peace, more success, more altered states, more sex, more fitness, more-more-more. A community, a village, dominated by your peers! Campus life intoxicates a young brain, and it is exploding with Tiger students, past, present and future, full of dreams and freedom.

There will be a match for everyone—someone during your years at Clemson looking for the more that *you* are seeking! Mile after mile of gleaming buildings, hallowed halls, perfect hedges, dining halls, stores, roads—all here to s*erve you*! It's heady, exhilarating, to enter this hormone-filled, hedonistic land which exists to serve these burgeoning adults, who a year or two before were mere children living by their parents' rule of law. "There for the education" is the half-truth some parents buy into. My child wanted more fun and freedom and less work. High school was a training ground in abandoning ambition in favor of *fun*. Freshman year provided the backdrop for him to major in spreading his wings and crashing.

A February call came early one evening, Mountain Time. I had been tracking Nick. It was a weeknight. Most kids were in for the night, but Nick had found some die-hard fun seekers looking for more. He and another guy drove over to the community college to drink with Nick's best friends and soak in their common-area hot tub until lights out indicated the amenities were closed. They returned to his Clemson campus parking lot—I was happy to see an early night. My child was in his parking lot, one hundred steps away from Holmes Hall. All good.

I had just gone to bed when Nick's unique ringtone shocked me.

"MOM!!! Help!" Nick was screaming. I heard some official voices speaking firmly, in the distance.

"NICK! Are you okay?!" Panicked, helpless...again...I sat bolt upright.

"Get your hands off him! You leave him the f*** alone!" Nick howled. The phone was away from his face but every word launched its way to me.

"NICK!! NICK!! NICHOLAS!! TALK to me!!!"

"Son. Put your hands above your head. Get up against the car. NOW!" Nick was being arrested.

The phone closer to Nick's face now, I heard him clearly.

"MOMMMM!!! Help!!!" He pleaded. "Get your f****** hands off me!"

"Nick! Give the phone to the officer!!" I screamed. I heard scuffling sounds and more voices in the distance. Nick was silent. "Ma'am? This is Officer Jones. Is this your son?"

"Yes! What is going on? What is he doing?" Ken had come into the room at this point.

"Your son is in possession of alcohol and marijuana. He attempted to assault an officer. We are taking him to the Clemson precinct; it's likely he will remain there tonight." The call ended.

I reluctantly hung up and went into the living room to turn the lights back on. I sat on the couch and waited.

An hour later, Ken's phone rang. Nick was allowed one phone call and used it to dial his dad. They were booking him and he would be out the next day. He needed a lawyer. I pulled out my laptop and booked a 6:00 a.m. Delta flight to Atlanta. It was almost midnight. How would I live through the hours before reaching

Clemson? Was it an option to let him deal with the arrest, find his own lawyer, and figure out on his own how to remain at Clemson? No. It was not an option. For eighteen years, I had helicoptered myself above his life. He called me to witness this horrific moment in his life. HE. COULD. NOT. STOP. SHARING.

It was the longest flight of my life, after the longest night I've ever known, all handed to me by a person to whom I was utterly committed. In his fit of fear I saw the massive mistake in making my child the center of my life. Two-plus years of repressed anger crashed up against my utter fear for his well-being. Prior to boarding the plane, I placed a call to a lawyer friend whose children attended Franklin. He had arranged bail, and Nick would be back in his dorm by the time I arrived in Atlanta, rented a car, and drove like a demon the two hours to Clemson.

Pulling into town and approaching the campus allowed me a minute to finally exhale from the sleepless night and tense hours of travel before I saw Nick. I waited outside Holmes Hall. Nick had been released and texted me his intent to shower, eat, and go to class by one o'clock. I needed to lay my eyes on him. So I waited. I parked in a metered space for visitors and got out of the car. It was an unseasonably pleasant February day, so I wandered, almost calmly.

"Mom." I turned around to my scowling son. He allowed a one-way hug. Though I detected how his weight had plummeted since Christmas break, he looked well-rested and...fine.

"Hey, Nick. How are you?"

"Mom. It's fine. You did NOT need to come all the way out here."

"Bud. You called me WHILE you were getting...being... ARRESTED! What was I supposed to do?" I exhaled again. Exhausted though I was, I wanted to know my child was safe. And then...I could get a good night's sleep.

"Well, sorry. I am fine now. You can go home." He made a move to leave. "I have class now."

"Nick! I am not going home. I am staying at the Courtyard. What time is class over?"

He paused, sighing before answering. "I can meet you there at five."

"Great. We can go to dinner. I will see you soon." I hopped into the rental car before he could object and set off to the Courtyard to grab some food and sleep until dinner.

I drove us in the rental car to nearby Anderson for dinner at Olive Garden. Conversation was awkward. He was sitting in the passenger seat, plucking away at his cell phone. I thought about my afternoon spent not napping but in the lobby of the hotel, creating an agreement Nick would sign in exchange for us allowing him to stay at Clemson. I yearned for one of our family dinners, to get him—us—back to normal. I hoped to reveal my recovery plan during our meal and snap him back into his usual logic.

Over summer break before college, Nick had one of his Arkansas IDs seized courtesy of a weed shop on our trip through Aspen. He and John, with too much transparency, conveyed to us the plan to buy weed in the ski town. We encouraged them *not* to. The first attempted purchase was from an "upstanding" pot purveyor who instantly recognized Nick's ID as fake. If Nick and John left the store without the ID, he would refrain from calling law enforcement.

The night of Nick's arrest at Clemson, the second of his two fake IDs caused more trouble than the apprehension of the first. Nick had used his actual name on the ID, altering only the address and date of birth. This error, in a string of errors in judgment during the parking lot arrest included a charge for possession of illegal identification. If the phony driver's license had displayed a random name, no charge would have been brought against him. Nick was without a fake ID when we met for dinner, thus he could not order a drink like we had shamefully allowed at Christmas break in Red River, New Mexico. Most of his anger about the arrest was over the officer "stealing" his free pass to obtaining alcohol. He would proceed to immediately order another set of fake IDs with a phony name for future use. I would continue to pretend it was okay with me and allow their use in my presence.

Driving back from Olive Garden, Nick began to unwind a bit, sliding slightly into the comfort of our still deeply rooted—but somewhat withered—relationship. He agreed to come up to the room to watch *The Amazing Race* on TV. We climbed onto the bed, sitting against the headboard with snacks bought in the hotel lobby's mini market.

"Mom. I don't feel good," Nick groaned. He had settled under the covers.

As I felt his forehead out of habit, looking for a fever, he felt clammy. Gone was the agitated, passive hate that began as a nasty spark in high school, fanning into the current wildfire of hate after the recent welfare check.

"You don't have a fever, Tiger." With a reflexive familiar show of love, I pushed his blond hair back from his forehead. His toxic energy evaporated, leaving in its wake a sad, spent child.

"Mom, I feel exhausted. Out of body, like I want to pass out." He was afraid.

I paused, understanding the weight of the moment.

"Tiger, just sleep here tonight. You have your backpack with you—you can shower and head to class in the morning." The pain of being his mother had reached a crescendo with last night's arrest. But this type of helplessness was somehow worse. Like his broken foot encased in a cast to heal after the middle-school football practice.

"Nah, I have to go. Where are my keys?" I had put them in my purse, hiding them I guess. He rolled off the bed, reaching for his shoes.

"Nick...just stay," I begged.

"No, Mom. You can't hold me hostage here." His anger resurfaced.

He sat up, paused, and then reached for his shoes.

"Keys, Mother. You can't make me stay here. Give me my keys." He stared me down. I handed over his keys.

"Nick, I fly out tomorrow night. Let's have lunch between classes before I go." He had not signed the agreement to meet my conditions to stay in Clemson. I had mandated he live at home with us and attend a school in New Mexico if he didn't agree to my requests.

"Fine. I will see you tomorrow." He bolted toward the door, flung it open, and headed out to meet up with his friends. I stalked him until midnight, insisting he go home or else. Stalking him five miles down the road rather than 1,500 miles away brought no difference in the irrefutable fact evading all logic and location—Nick was headed for an epic fail.

He didn't sign the agreement the next day. He tuned in for a brief second after lunch and before I headed back to Atlanta, agreeing to see a counselor, just once, to see if he could get a prescription for Adderall. Our collaboration at the start of the year to buy Neural Boost supplements on Amazon had failed to give him the focus—and high—he craved. In hindsight, he was short on cash and could no longer purchase contraband from his friends or whoever else sold that on campus.

During Nick's junior year of high school, a student he knew, who was also a fraternity brother to his cousin had overdosed from a cocktail of drugs. A good student, a motivated kid by all accounts up until his death, it was revealed that he had created a lucrative side hack selling cocaine. Some kids would do anything for money to feed their desires.

### Nick's Perspective

*We were at a hot tub party at High Point. We were in our bathing suits, no shirts, and drunk. About midnight, being a weeknight—we left for campus and parked in the student parking lot. About thirty cop cars park in that area! Then, Austin got out of the car and began urinating in the parking lot.*

*Of course, there was an officer in one of the cars, who came over. Two officers asked Austin to turn around and put his hands behind his back. Well, he was obviously very drunk—public drunkenness. I was standing outside the car when they put him in handcuffs. So, I called my mom. I asked her what I should do. While I was on the phone with Mom, I went up to the cop to plead on Austin's behalf. I put a hand on the cop's shoulder while he was facing away. He spun around and threw me up against my car. I resisted arrest—I was drunk.*

*Austin and I were placed in separate cells. He ripped his clothes off, and they gave him a jumpsuit. We shouted out in solidarity about the harassment from the cops. I had no contrition. I did not deserve that arrest, in my mind. To this day, in my mind, I was only trying to help. My epic mistake was placing a hand on the officer.*

## Chapter 13

# Can't-Cun

"*I am going to Florida for spring break, Mom,*" *Nick declared over the phone.* I had been home from Atlanta for less than two weeks. "With all due respect, sweetie," I breathed, "what will you be taking a 'break' from?"

He knew where I was headed with this line of questioning. Majoring in engineering proved boring and time-consuming, interfering with his priority to have fun at any cost. His grades were in the toilet, and taking a "break" from all this fun was riddled with irony.

"Four of us are going to rent a place in Panama City. One of the guys going with us is twenty-one, so no problem!" he said.

A Google search on spring break stories transports a concerned parent to either worry or denial. Decades of reports reveal documented arrests and tens of drinking-related deaths. The past few years of parenting a noncompliant teen had revealed my lack of control over my child. His hormones reflected a grown man's testosterone, yet his unformed frontal lobe processes still operated as they would in a child.

Sitting in my living room in Albuquerque, 1,500 miles away and fourteen days past the arrest, I countered Nick's determination to head to Florida. He met my plethora of fun itineraries with disdain.

"Listen, Nick. Why don't we just plan a spring break trip with the three of us? Skiing in Utah, maybe?" I asked hopefully.

"Mom. No. I want to go with my friends."

I thought for a minute before blurting out, "How about a family trip to Cancun for spring break?"

I looked into options as I spoke to him and saw how affordable it was to book last minute. Spring break in Florida was almost a done deal, and there was no way he was getting himself to an airport for a flight to us. Here's the thing: Noncompliant Nick chooses the difficult path of experiencing errors for himself. Once he digs in and commits to a decision, change happens quickly. But no single influence will sway him. And I obviously was still not in touch with the tough love side of parenting, or with just letting go and allowing the potential for an epic fail.

Noncompliant people don't present with some diagnosable thing you can just "fix." They struggle more, are less coachable, adhere less often to wise advise. In general, noncompliant people have more stress. My son is flat-out stubborn and bullheaded. Stubborn is hardwired into his DNA. The excellent flip side actually presents as an asset leading to career success. Luckily he has sweetness, compassion, and morals that temper this innate willfulness. Or he had those qualities growing up and they were then on pause.

I recall clearly the uncertain window of transition between Ken retiring from the military and stepping into his second career. After attending six schools in eight years, we felt strongly that four years in a single high school would offer Nick an excellent launching pad into college and a stability he had never known.

I knew my son had latched on tight to the type of spring break I had always feared. It would happen one way or the other. Just like all his notions in the past, he would hunt down this plan with rabid intensity. We could demand he come back to Albuquerque and spend the week working with us in a knock-down, drag-out tussle. But in the end my fear got the best of me (Bobby was always on the fringe of my crazy thinking), and spun me to rationalize the irresponsible decision of financing a family beach trip. If I was *there to show him* how to drink respon-sibly on spring break, I could be some type of drinking ROLE MODEL. I hear the judgment from myself and those who have not parented through dangerous defiance. My heart goes out to you if you personally relate to the negotiations and rationaliza-tions my psyche made logical.

Cancun made sense for many reasons. First, the drinking age was eighteen and no chance existed for another MIP or arrest...for underage drinking. Nick drank often at school and regardless of my interference, excess spring break party time would occur. Second, the price was right and we would be staying in a Marriott, what I understood to be more "American" and less "spring breakish." Lastly, we reserved adjoining rooms and could keep tabs on Nick and his two best friends. We laid out the conditions: they would eat breakfast and dinner with us, and other than texting a few times a day and being back in their room by midnight, they were on their own. After his friends' quick assurance to follow the rules, Nick followed up with an eye roll and grunt of agreement.

We flew into Cancun on a Saturday from Albuquerque and would meet up with Nick, John, and Tradd, who had taken a direct flight from Atlanta to Cancun earlier that morning. We arrived on the shuttle from the airport four hours after the boys, handed off our bags to the bellman, and strolled into the massive, cool lobby, complete with huge Vegas-style columns and marble floors. I was expecting a low-slung roof, open breezeway with glimpses of the beach, and huarache-clad bellman—light and breezy. This setup, however, was dark and foreboding.

I gave the front desk my name and asked if the rest of our party had checked in.

"I want to be certain you received the request for the adjoining rooms?"

"Yes, the gentlemen in the connecting room have checked in," he responded. "I show already a balance on your room. Would you like to leave the charges for both rooms on your credit card?"

"There is a balance on our room? That must be a mistake." He rotated the screen to allow viewing on my side of the desk. I saw about seven bar charges totaling over $200. They had been there for four hours.

From leaving home, to the quick flight to Cancun, to the shuttle to the hotel, I allowed a dormant sense of hope and peace to share space with the percolating fear for my son. Cancun seemed like a chance to arrest a spiral that was rocketing south, out of my field of influence. For one week in the midst of the shenanigans of my son and his friends, I could be the proverbial slap to the face of my unconscious son. This honestly seemed logical—I alone had the magic that could mentor him out of this truancy. I imagine many of us know our child intimately from birth. We know the soft goodness of that same person as he slowly morphs from child to independence, but still we always glimpse moments of Little League, moments snuggling after bath time with a book and a bedtime prayer. We see this adult before us as our child who didn't make friends in middle school and looked to us for comfort. This child of mine was a creature I assumed I knew, that would respond to me the same way he mostly had until he was seventeen. The connection might have been cracked from more than a year of his wild behavior, but this trip could cement us back to whole. We could "fix" it!

I prepared myself for the sight of my son, fully drunk. I had seen him drunk only once before, at the Clemson football game, and it was only by rationalizing that "all the other college kids are drunk" that I managed to cope through that inebriated weekend. And here I was again, only this time I had actually planned the whole shebang.

What happened in Cancun was stupid, ridiculous even, and fueled the fire of his quest for fun. The first night at dinner after that full day of drinking, Nick barely tolerated my presence, and sat as far across the table from me as possible. The server knew about an all-access pass to a massive all-you-can-drink pool party in downtown Cancun. The only way in was with this pass, suspended on a lanyard that granted special access to a back room and front-of-the-stage placement to see a band. Nick spent the time at dinner tracking down the information to procure these "golden tickets." Attempts to persuade the boys to stay at the hotel the entire trip were futile. Staying ocean-side on the Gulf Coast along a seven-mile stretch of beach known as The Hotel Zone, stuffed with college kids, should have been sufficient fun. That plan fell short of the pinnacle experience that Nick had envisioned. He was seeking wild fun, not a beer at a beach bonfire and watching TV after midnight in his hotel room while sipping the tequila he had chilling in the tub.

"We want to go downtown one night! All the college kids are down there. It is just a town of college kids at spring break. Perfectly safe, Madre." The bartering for the passes continued through dinner. I learned the next morning that they had gone to meet the server's brother to pay for the passes. Meeting up with Nick that first full day for lunch, after they returned from downtown, consisted of a flow of cocktails that seemed to raise even Tradd's eyebrows. Nagging at Nick to slow down initiated hateful glances. I modeled excellent poolside drinking, sipping only a few cocktails served in plastic cups each day.

The past months had unsettled me when my son was in sight, and my spirit churned still when we were apart. There was no peace.

No place for my soul to rest. I sought a new routine in attempting to build a life in New Mexico, find a friend group and meaningful work, and seek out a church family. I threw myself into church, but the persistent call to parent my son had choked off the inroads I made. The new routine became fielding frightening calls and texts at all hours of the day and night while trying to focus on the new obligations I was mapping out. Cancun could be my chance to find peace...I thought.

I spent the first few days actually enjoying Cancun's lovely weather and beautiful beach. Our adjoining rooms were situated on the fifth floor in the bottom part of a U-shaped structure facing the pool with the swim-up bar and the ocean. The generous balcony offered up two lounge chairs and a table. The second afternoon, around five o'clock, I came back from a massage to find a security guard leaving Nick's room. I hurried into my room as Nick was making his way back through the connecting door.

"Hey!" I exhaled a breath. "What's going on? Why was a security guard here?"

Ken rolled his eyes. "Tradd climbed over the balcony. He was dangling over the rail when someone spotted him. What a moron!"

I opened my mouth to speak, but nothing came out.

"It seems he dropped Nick's cigar off the edge of the balcony and it fell onto the balcony below. Tradd swung over the edge and lowered down one floor. Not sure how he made it back up to their balcony. I must say, I am impressed. Didn't know Tradd had that level of athleticism in him," Ken said as he walked over to knock on the now-closed connecting door.

"Nick! Open up, bud," Ken demanded. The door opened.

Walking into the dark room, my senses were assaulted with wafts of stale air and dirty feet.

"Tradd. Bud. What would your mother say with you hanging off a balcony?" I said. "I need to bring you home alive."

"Yes, ma'am. I know. It looked doable! I have jumped out my bedroom window many times and felt safe with the maneuver," he reasoned. "The security guard gave us a warning and we are good to go!" Consequences for Tradd's wrongdoing stuck like a Band-Aid on a wet finger. Pulled over by police numerous times, his slaps on the wrist involved mere counsel to head on home and be safe. I had heard secondhand accounts of his slippery good luck, and one episode I had witnessed in person.

My attempts to chaperone a spring break for my son had dated back to his junior year in high school. Tradd's mother, Mary Kate, and the mother of one other boy agreed to join me at John's beach house on Pawleys Island on the Atlantic coast just north of Charleston, to watch over the boys and their group of friends. Rules were laid out, the presence of alcohol ignored, and strict instructions not to drink and drive gave us a framework for a fun vacation. The third night of the trip the boys had gone to dinner in Myrtle Beach, meeting up with Tradd's girlfriend.

Mary Kate, the other mother, and I were enjoying a glass of wine and some small talk when Mary Kate's phone rang. It was 11:30 p.m. and Tradd was still in Myrtle Beach. Nick and the other boys were on their way home. According to my iPhone tracker they were about three miles from the beach house. The phone call was from a Myrtle Beach police officer.

"Well, Officer, I appreciate your making this allowance for Tradd. We will be about thirty minutes," Mary Kate said. She was calm; all must be well. "Yes sir, we will be sure to speak to him at length tonight. Thank you."

She turned to me. "Tradd left his car door open when he dropped off his girlfriend. There was all manner of empty cans and bottles littering that boy's floor. Well, shoot. I need to rouse up Hailey"—Tradd's younger sister—"to drive me over to Myrtle

Beach." She paused to walk over and holler up the stairs for Hailey to come down.

"The officer is cutting him a huge break by not arresting him. He was sober, the officer said. No MIP or DWI this time. But I agreed to drive that truck home." Mary Kate herself was just south of sober, so she needed her daughter to drive her to Myrtle.

Tradd had a lifted Ford F-150, dropped in the back, with a light bar across the roof and tinted windows so dark as to be near illegal. Mary Kate—with Tradd passed out in the passenger seat—inched along for twenty miles with her head out the window in order to see the road. She finally learned the hazards of driving that truck with its blackened windshield at night. She confiscated the keys to his truck after spring break, promising their return when he removed the tint. We made it through the week with only one more child being pulled over, in front of the beach house. He got off scot-free too. He was stupid drunk. But the officer shirked his due diligence in not insisting on a field sobriety test and let the friend turn the car around and drive the block back to the beach house.

Tradd would go on to dodge arrests a handful of times over the next few years, released always with a verbal or written warning and advice to be safe. He had a goofy kind of sweetness and a kind personality that I believe prompted adults toward forgiveness of his "unintended" transgressions. He just graduated from college and to this day no police officer has cited him for any illegal activity. I have yet to understand why one teen is held accountable and for the same crime others are let off with a warning or a phone call to a parent.

I recall again the headmaster of Franklin Hills Prep sharing his wisdom. "Nick will run the course of this behavior. Many kids make it through the gauntlet unscathed. But I have to be blunt here." He paused, looking at Ken and me intently. "There are some kids running wild who have what I call an epic fail. This season of life for these kids who rebel is dicey, and they need to avoid the epic fail.

The wise words stuck with me. Is it all hit-or-miss whether your teen will "make it through the gauntlet" or fail epically? An epic fail is an arrest that leads to a police record that sticks. An epic fail is killing someone. An epic fail is death at the hands of your own stupidity. An epic fail is an untreated eating disorder. Bobby had an epic fail. That is what I thought as the headmaster was imparting his knowledge for our benefit. We would be left to wait it out, for years perhaps, to see if Nick survived the gauntlet. After that talk, I had scrambled to pull Nick away from his own demise, his own epic fail. I judged harshly my erratic efforts to "save" him from himself, blaming and shaming myself as lacking courage to act boldly. But wait. What if all my mama-bear crazy *did matter?* What if the combination of all I didn't do and the actions I did muster up pulled him back from a permanent epic fail?

In the stinky room in Cancun, I looked at Tradd and his "Aw shucks, yes ma'am" manners and understood the slippery nature of being agreeable and thus avoiding paying the price for wrongdoings. I scanned the small, dark space. Empty liquor bottles, cigars, and clothes littered every available surface. Where are they getting entire liquor bottles? I looked in the bathroom.

The bathtub, once a place to actually bathe, was liberated to serve as a giant Yeti Cooler, its generous size filled halfway to the top with ice and bottles of tequila, vodka, and beer. How many trips to the ice machine did they log to fill the tub that high? In addition to the bar tab tally, now halfway to $1,000, there was this makeshift bar *in their hotel room.* My husband laughed and applauded their ingenuity. A "boys will be boys" assessment of the scenario concluded with Ken smacking John on the back with glee.

The last night of spring break was a Friday. That morning, Nick showed up at my request, sporting gym shorts and a bare, sunburned torso. Silent, he glowered directly at me from his perch on the tiny couch. Sitting in the chair opposite him, I implored him to just be content staying in The Hotel Zone. Too many reliable stories of missing and injured college kids partying in downtown Cancun left me desperate to change his mind. I could have just forbidden he go downtown and kept the boys locked in their room. At some point, though, Nick would find a way to satisfy his burning curiosity to fully attend a spring-break party in Cancun. Tradd had just saw fit to monkey himself around the outside of the twenty-story hotel. Would they all shimmy down to the ground below to freedom?

"Nick. There are thousands of parties you can walk to, right from our hotel. Why not just stay near the resort?"

He whipped his head to me as he clenched his fists into red angry balls. Wild eyes shot bullets of hate as he spat his response. "We will be fine. We *are* going downtown."

Tears sprang up in my eyes. My son was gone and the devil had taken up residence in his heart. I don't know how else to explain the hate pouring out of him. Seventeen years of fully knowing his unconditional love for me had me searching hard for our unique bond, that despite any confrontation, always surfaced. At that moment, no doubt remained that the college antics, the casual drunken arrest and slap on the wrist were the tragic start to an epic failure. I saw clearly that the flip side of love is hate, and the animosity for my presence in his life had morphed from nuisance to hatred.

We all met for dinner at Gustino's, in the Marriott. The boys were sober, and Nick was calm and talkative. I thought he had reversed course on heading downtown, and asked him if they wanted to spend this next-to-last night with us. We were heading to the Flamenco show after dinner and there was a night club planned for later.

His eyes widened. "Ummm, Nooo. Sorry, Madre. We have our passes, all-access, lest you forgot! We will be living like Gucci Mane tonight."

Radric Delantic Davis, aka Gucci Mane, I knew had been in and out of prison, making him only more heroic to young men. "Bud. Just stay with us tonight, it will be fun!" I pleaded from the clueless bubble I alone had constructed.

"Naw. We will be fine. As agreed, we will text you a few times and be in by one!" He was back to his cheerful nature.

We parted ways around 9:30 p.m. Ken and I headed to the hotel's Flamenco show and the boys grabbed a cab downtown. The hotel was huge, with wide hallways and twenty-foot ceilings connecting ballrooms to conference rooms to dining areas. We wound our way through the quiet maze of space, arriving at the lounge overlooking the pool and beach to grab a seat for the show. We ordered a margarita and relaxed. Nick texted mid-show that they were downtown, and all was good. There were crowds of American college kids milling about and they had run into a group from Clemson. My worry subsided and I focused on the show.

A vivid memory came to mind. Flamenco dance originated in eighteenth-century Spain. We had seen our first show in Spain at the Parador de Carmona, where we had booked a room for the night before driving north to Seville the next day. The building is a stunning, fourteenth-century Arab fortress standing high above the town. It offers a fabulous swimming pool, terraces with views of the fragrant olive orchards below, and a delightful interior courtyard oozing the character of its Moorish past. It was there that we enjoyed the flamenco show.

Nick was four years old. We had flown from our home in Lajes Azores to a medical appointment at the naval base in Roda, Spain. Families needing medical care beyond the usual are flown via military planes to either Spain or Germany for treatment. The plane rotates only once a week, which leaves the patient and whomever they choose to accompany them an entire week to visit the sights. We always tried to schedule our appointments on the front end of the week, leaving the entire back half for traveling. We squeezed in the dentist appointment we needed on the first day after our arrival, leaving six more days to see the Andalusian region of eastern Spain. The first stop was Carmona and a night in the former castle, then an upscale Parador.

After enjoying locally seasoned olives and tart, refreshing sangria made in-house, we ventured down to the flamenco show. In the open courtyard fronting the lobby and shops, we sat mesmerized watching the flips of legs, quick turns, and bold moves of the regional dancers. Nick loved it all. He loved being in Spain, traveling and eating olives and drinking "virgin" sangria. I wished he was with us, enjoying this show.

Back in our room, drifting in and out of sleep, I woke up at 12:47 a.m. I knew Nick was not back from downtown yet; it was too quiet next door. The bright outline of the numbers of the clock ticked off the minutes, as I listened intently for the sound of the boys returning next door. Still quiet. At 1:00 a.m., I texted Nick. I waited for the blurb saying, "Read," assuring my message was received. Another text, this time with a "Not delivered" exclamation point. I re-sent it as a "text" option; still not received. My heart was racing to a familiar beat: loud and stupid and full of regret and pain. Familiar from so many nights wondering if my kid was alive.

After 1:00 a.m., I heard the boys' door open and someone banging around in the room. Relief flooded my soul. I knocked on the connecting door. A ragged-looking John answered.

"John! Where are Nick and Tradd?"

"They did not come back with me. I caught a cab after I threw up downtown," he slurred.

"John! You were all to stick together! That was the deal! That is why we agreed to you going downtown! How could you leave them?!" I was livid.

"Ma'am, they would not come and I have a girlfriendddd! I had to come back." We went back and forth for a few minutes and then said goodnight.

Five minutes later he opened his side of the connecting door; ours was wide open.

"Ms. Suzanne. I need to tell you that it is not okay for me to get in trouble for leaving them downtown. They would not come back. I came back, like I was told to. It is not fair that I get yelled at for that," he said, his head held high, gaze holding steady with mine. Wow. I didn't know he had this conviction in him.

"I understand, John. You did the right thing coming back on time. Thank you."

At 1:15 I scrolled to Favorites and paused. If the call went straight to voicemail, I knew his phone was off, or dead, and I had no way to know where he was. It wasn't that going out in Mexico with a few friends was necessarily riddled with potential for danger. Rather, my son's impulses were without regulation, his dangerous bent was "have fun" and transcend "normal," resulting in the potential for horrific outcomes. I punched his face icon with my thumb and waited. The call went to voicemail.

Fear rose in my throat at 1:30 a.m. as my many regrets surfaced to remind me of this avoidable agony. The culmination of all my less-than-courageous moments heaped onto this one as I death-gripped my cell phone in the dark.

I searched for Tradd's number and texted, "Are you with Nick? Get him and get back to the hotel NOW." Delivered.

A minute later Tradd responded, "Yes, ma'am!" Whew. My pulse slowing, I hunkered down to await their return. I distracted myself watching a video on my iPad.

Knock, Knock, BANG, BANG! I bolted out of the bed, crashing into the table as I launched into the dark to answer the door. I was overcome with relief and calm with my child outside the door.

Snapping on the hall light, struggling with the safety latch, I opened the door to find Tradd, barefoot and sweating, looking high as a kite on a windy day.

I poked my head out the door. "Where is Nick? Tradd?" He stumbled into the room.

"Ms. Suzanne! He wouldn't come with me. I swear I begged him...told him to come on with me. He refused!" he panted.

"So you left him in downtown Cancun?! We told you guys to stay together, no matter what!" I flung my arms around wildly, pointing toward downtown.

"Ma'am, you said get back NOW and here I am! I couldn't find a taxi, so I RAN all the way back!" He looked absolutely gleeful. He was unconcerned that he ran all that way barefoot. Well, this is what compliant disobedience looked like. He showed up when pressed despite being drunk and strung out.

"He has NO PHONE, Tradd! I am unable to reach him!"

"Yes, ma'am, his phone died!" Tradd was shuffling over to the connecting door, with a big, casual yawn signaling he was coming off of whatever and ready to call it a night.

With sickening dread, I punched in Nick's number for a text, hoping he had found a charger. Undelivered.

"KEN! Wake up!" He had slept through all my struggle like the devout believer who knew, that ultimately, one Person was in charge and it was not we the parents. Truthfully, Ken's comfort level during the past few years had been safely ensconced under layers of optimism, denial—and understanding that God has a plan for all of us, and we are commanded in the Bible not to worry or be anxious for anything. So, he slept well and wrote off as teenage discovery all of Nick's rebellion, which offered him countless good nights' sleeps and peace of mind.

"Nick is downtown, BY HIMSELF, with no phone!" I said, yanking open drawers, pulling out clothes for both of us. "Get up! We are going to find him!" Ken went along with MY worry and anxious actions despite wishing he was back in bed.

"Suz, I am sure he is fine. They went to some college party. He will be back soon."

"Tradd just came back WITHOUT NICK!" Have you not heard how sketchy Mexico is outside this American bubble of The Hotel Zone?! Kids DIE here, Ken!"

Marching over to the front door, I threw it open and waited for Ken. We stepped off the elevator into the grand lobby. Bustling with energy when we had entered a few days earlier, it was now eerily still. The bellman jumped off his perch on the outside bench to hail one of the idling taxi cabs that would take us downtown. A brief unguarded moment allowed me a glimpse of why Nick was so drawn to the wee hours of the night. Two a.m. was quiet, with almost a trill of illicit anticipation in the atmosphere. I got it, for just that second, before my intuitive reminder: no good happens after midnight for any lawless fun seekers or college freshman. Perhaps there is good in the night for expectant mothers in labor, an all-night study session for a crucial test or certification, or perhaps the graveyard shift at a busy airport. But not for my son, not for someone with no *off* switch and a badly damaged moral compass.

Before Tradd had weaved his way back through the connecting door to his room, he highlighted the route they had taken, places they had been, and the last place he had seen Nick. Stress level in check by *doing something* to *save* my child from himself, moving toward him in the back of the cab also brought a measure of relief. Darkness in The Hotel Zone slowly gave way to traffic and lights. The streets were littered with college kids and Mexican police strolling, smoking cigarettes with watchful gazes among the kids. Parked police cruisers with kids in the backseat dotted the curbs. We pulled up in front of the club Tradd and Nick were at when I'd phoned Tradd.

──────────────── **Nick's Perspective** ────────────────

*I don't remember the name of the club where the pool party was. We started the night at a hookah lounge, as I recall. I have a clear memory of that and then the next location, Señor Frog's. We had downed vast amounts of tequila shots there. We must have hung out there for quite a while, before we met some girls who were going to a disco club down the block. We danced there, and drank more tequila shots.*

*Did we do drugs? No Mom, we did not. There was a sketchy man on the beach who sold us some awful weed. It was a very sketchy situation all the way around. That was it though. Tequila was the choice of drink all night long, and the reason I can't recall much of the night. John had had enough after throwing up all the tequila from Senor Frog's while we were dancing with those girls. He called it a night, then hopped into a cab alone to head back to the hotel.*

*Tradd had received your text just prior to entering the pool party spot. He bailed after that. He said, "Nick, your mom just texted and wants us back now, dude. I am heading back…now." I refused to go with him, and after multiple pleas for me to head back with him, he took off running and I went into the party alone. I was drunk and unafraid, ready to meet some people, do some more shots, and dance.*

*He ran back without shoes on? Wow. No, I have no idea how he wound up without shoes, but he happily relayed the news the next day that he ran the three miles back.*

After sliding out of the shelter of the cab and paying the driver, we wound our way toward the racket coming from around the corner. The outdoor nightclub was set back about twenty-five yards from the bustling street, offering a tiki-themed arch and barricaded exterior. If that was not enough to keep out random fun seekers and concerned parents, the rotund bouncer was.

"Look, we don't have a ticket. We are here looking for my son. Just let us come in and look around." I should have grabbed Tradd's all-access lanyard before I left.

"No, bueno! You must have ticket purchased prior to this moment," the gatekeeper relayed to us.

"Do we look like we are here for the party?" We argued with the bouncer for close to five minutes. In addition to juggling his ticket checking and ID duties, he had time to be sure we did not slip through the tiki archway. Over his shoulder I saw a stage, a pool, and a massive firepit off to the side of the stage. I knew Nick must be in there. It actually looked quite innocent...and fun.

"My son has been left alone by his friends! Just let me in and my husband will stay here with you! Certainly you have a mother who would be worried for you, in a foreign country on your own and drunk out of your mind. Imagine her in my situation!"

Random moments of kindness had peppered my life with reprieves for two years, beginning in 2015. With Ken in New Mexico, starting a new business, I had little backup the entirety of Nick's senior year. There were ineffective calls at my request for Ken to phone Nick and "get him in line." But it was Tradd's father who often stepped in, for better or worse, but always with the right intentions to keep my son on the right side of the law. Like wrangling him back home from a party after the baseball concussion.

There must exist a universal pact among kind souls to lend a hand to desperate mothers. The commonality for all mammalian life is human gestation in the womb. We humans are universally wired through this commonality for empathy toward the maternal. The inherent ability to produce life from a physical body, to nurture and selflessly provide for the well-being of the offspring, is the very nature of existence. We all understand this at some level. The delicate nature of keeping the child alive until they are themselves equipped transverses toward an almost divine understanding. Not that my arrival on the dirty threshold of an explosive party scene begging some Mexican mother's son to let in my desperate self was rich with all this nuance, but the guy at the bamboo podium paused, ceased his ID checking with furrowed brows and kind eyes, and stepped aside to allow us entrance. I imagine he cheered on the hope that I would find my son, and rescue him from himself. Or maybe, he knew I couldn't do any of these things, he had seen tons of drunk Americans, and he kindly took pity on the obvious helplessness of it all.

Throngs of charged-up young "adults" littered every inch of the massive outdoor party space. For a brief moment, walking among the mayhem held hope: "Yes! There is no way Nick is not at this party! We will find him soon." After thirty minutes scouring the area and the faces of the drunk kids all around us, poking our heads into the dark recesses of quiet, small huddles in various corners, I knew there was no way we were going to find him. If by the grace of God we did, my child full of tequila and rebellion would refuse to come with us. The hate-shooting eye daggers from his once sweet gaze told me the state of his soul and his stubborn inability to follow our directives would not reverse in that moment. Nothing had changed about the nature of my son since those first months in life when he would not sleep in his own bed. His defiance to not remain content and happy in the Kids Klub at the health club where I worked, or even shrieking in the backseat of the car during traffic jams on the Beltway where a protracted, screamy fit endured for a full hour, existed innately in my son.

I knew what I was up against. The quiet space in my brain met resignation, as I helplessly watched writhing spring breakers up on the stage. We exited back under the tiki arch and hailed a cab. The only solace riding back to the hotel was that I had not witnessed a single kidnapping, drug deal, or murder. We would go back to our hotel room and I would wait.

After two more hours, as I shivered in the dark hotel room, the sheer panic of knowing my son must be dead stripped off the final layer of hope protecting me from reality. Loss happens in an instant, much like a slap in the face or a dive into a cold pool brings shock. Like the phone call when I was at work, telling me my own father was dead. Over and done, what comes next is minor after the initial shock. But the punishing process of loss, real or imagined, usually unfolds gradually, the smackdowns accumulating into one harsh and final twelfth-round knockout. These dark nights of the soul, as St. John of the Cross in the sixteenth century explained, are a passage from dark to light through nocturnal sufferings, sparked by a spiritual crisis.[15] The end result is a union with God. The reward of the struggle brings a delicious peace when the union of mind, body, and soul come together. I knew, even in suffering that night away, that this harsh burning St. Paul described was a bottomless abyss. St. Paul of The Cross is said to have had a forty-five-year dark night of the soul. If I had known the worst was in the offing, that what I called a "dark night" was only in my mind, surely I would not have survived those dark hours of waiting in Cancun.

I woke up with a start and glanced at the digital bedside clock shouting out the time, 5:11 a.m. OH CRAP! I fell asleep. Looking at my cell phone, there was a message from Nick.

"Sorry. My phone died. I'm back."

I bolted out of bed, slowing at the double door as I inched it open. The stench of ripe college kid and liquor assaulted me as I entered the room. I counted the boys. John, sleeping alone, sprawled across one queen bed. Glancing over with held breath, there were two shapes on the other bed. I paused, looking at Nick sleeping peacefully, mouth agape, not a care in the world. A hotel trash can resting empty alongside the bed pierced me with the familiar; something I had taught him to do as a little boy sick on carnival food. Later, we learned that Nick was dancing on a stage abutting the pool all night; we just hadn't spotted him in the crowd of revelers. All my angst and pain was for nothing.

The countless hours over eighteen years where I habitually stood guard over my sleeping child, most often in those first moments in my care, diminish but never cease. That first week of his life, I would lean in and check to see that he was breathing; so slight was his slumber that I would carefully rest my hand on his chest in search of movement. Ken had mostly slept through these nightly check-ins, as he did during the worst night of my life, there in Cancun. He had enjoyed a good night's rest prior to my jostling him awake. For Ken, a fun cab ride downtown to catch a glimpse of the nightlife rounded out what was hitherto a boring, early-to-bed evening. He had mostly slept through, literally and figuratively, the past two years of parenting Nick. The source of his hands-off fatherhood, while he chanted, "Boys will be boys! I made it just fine through some tough spots and so will he!" might've been grounded in truth and experience. But his head-in-the-sand denial, "There is no way Nick is doing XYZ! You are imagining it!" exposed his inability to confront who his child had become. (Only this year did I discover that being raised in the shadow of addiction can lead to an undisciplined mind. Ken has a disciplined mindset; tragic thoughts don't run amok in his brain. The off-ramp to my toxic thoughts was found between the covers of only one book: the Bible. Only shouting the name of Jesus and reciting some applicable Bible verses obliterates the devil's attempts to subvert my uplifted thoughts and behaviors.)

The next day, and our last in Cancun, was brilliantly sunny. The finest weather yet sparkled serene across the placid azure Gulf waters, right outside our balcony door, where I sat, gazing out at the ocean and sipping a cup of strong coffee. Only six hours earlier I believed to my core that Nick was dead. I wondered why I couldn't be sound asleep and unfazed by a college kid sowing his oats. Was I just unable to cease a lifetime of helicopter parenting? Should I mind my own life and surrender to God my son for Him to handle? Of course the answer to those questions is a resounding YES.

Yet: How does a mother go from a necessary vigilance to fully witnessing without interference the tumult toward destruction of their child? How do we know what is potential for an epic fail? When do we rush in seeking to prevent one, and when do we witness it from the sidelines in ignorance or tacit permissiveness? Worse, the sickening mixture of my current calm with a lingering shock after the worst night of my life was coupled with this stark truth: that night and the last few months were just an acceleration to the top of the bell curve of Nick's destruction. I knew, gazing at the calm of Mexico, I had no control of what storms remained in the offing. Still, I tried as the unaware pseudo-Christian I was. God was whispering, and I heard Him asking me to stay close to my son, but completely ignored any heavenly shouts about what that closeness and guidance should look like.

In the hush of the airplane on our return from Cancun, I spoke softly. "Nick. There has to be a plan that allows me comfort in dropping you back off at school. There is no way to my peace of mind with so much distance separating me from your destructive mindset."

I poked him from his fake slumber. "Bud. Listen to me."

Slowly turning his head my direction, hooded eyelids barely concealed his piercing gaze of hate.

"What?" he spat.

He had acquiesced, at Ken's mandate, to take Ken's seat on our flight back to Atlanta. But his physical presence, he made sure, would be the only contribution to these feeble attempts at redirection and "charting a new course, volume 2." More than I had seen in years, his heart and soul were shut off to only me. Connected emotionally as mother and son, and always his favorite confidant, the only way toward continuation of his errant behavior was through a dissonance with the person who most thoroughly understood his divergence from his true nature. I knew my kiddo was down there in his dark depths, dormant but present, thus I continued my efforts via this plan or that plan.

"Nick, look," I leaned toward him as he inched closer to the window.

"If you want to remain at Clemson, I need to know you aren't going to *perish* at your own hand." I had written on my laptop a plan, once again, to stay at Clemson...or else. Ha! You can't negotiate with the devil, and the devil had a firm grip on my child. The wrestle for a sinner's heart can only be won by partnering with the will of God. I questioned whether to release this embarrassing "game plan." On display is my complete naivete and ignorance to the severity of his self-destructive path; and the fact that I was not in control. But below is the plan I outlined.

### Thrive

I. No vehicle

II. Self-guided study in anger and rage management
   A. Check in with me weekly

III. Hire a personal trainer—at least twelve sessions

IV. One yoga class a week until summer

V. OFF Adderall—find a natural supplement regimen (ideally from personal trainer)

VI. NO drugs at all

VII. NO hard liquor

VIII. GO TO CHURCH or a Christian college group with a friend at least once a month there is one mega church that holds one on campus

IX. Refrain from getting fake ID replacement until you soar for three consecutive months

X. Eat at least two meals a day, several times a week on campus

XI. Set a curfew for yourself of 1–2 a.m.(?) until you are stable this summer

XII. Touch base HONESTLY with me (or an other approved adult) as an accountability partner

XIII. Complete checkup with MD

XIV. Negotiable options—just suggestions:

A. Cry daily or weekly (chick flick movie?)

B. Skin care and self-care plan

C. Scream in your pillow while completely sober once a week

D. Hit baseballs and racquetballs, or play some sport where you can safely smash a ball

E. Join a club team

F. Pray daily

G. Read Bible passage daily

SUGGESTIONS FOR Nick—Begin to check in daily. Maybe look to diffuse irritations and manage them in some way. And is your instinct to deal with your past crap through tuning out and disrespecting teachers, police, administrators, and such? If so, can you diffuse? Don't let the devil in :( I think you only hurt yourself by not acknowledging your fears and irritations.

You have this time now to be single, to learn how to perfect being alone—when you stand on your own you can find the perfect partner to do life with.

"Dad and I insist you follow through with this list," I said. His eyes shot over to mine, daggers of hate again palpable in his stare.

"I am sure Dad is not insisting. And there is no way I am finding a 'youth group!'" he spat.

The flight landed after two hours of mostly silence as Nick dozed and refused to participate in the intricacies of my "Thrive Plan." Still, I savored the nearness, my child trapped on a plane, right next to me. For two hours and thirty-five minutes, he was safe. Peace. I wanted *never* to land in Atlanta, where we would part ways and Ken and I would fly on to New Mexico while the boys would Uber over to John's sister's house to pick up their car for the two-hour drive back to Clemson. We paused at the entrance to customs in Atlanta. One serpentine queue to the left indicated processing for travelers headed to baggage claim, while the queue to the right was for connecting passengers. Before we went our separate ways, a joyful John and Tradd thanked us effusively with hugs and words of gratitude, while Nick sighed. He moved into my arms for a brief hug.

"Mom. I am fine. I will see you in a few months." He would be flying home to spend two months of his summer break with us.

He broke away to fully embrace his father. Glancing over, as I made my way through the long line toward my connecting flight, it was impossible to ignore how confident he looked. There was a young man who could handle anything. An elusive hopefulness surfaced in my periphery, that maybe this roughest season was over; no more walking a thin line between *thrive* and *crash*.

Chapter 14

# Faith Is a Journey,
# Not a Destination

*A*wful *stories lurk beyond the computer screen of an internet* search. One easy search presents several click options about a college girl out at the town bars in Virginia. She goes missing after a dubious late-night choice to walk home alone. Another search leads to a cautionary tragedy about a girl, soon to graduate college, ordering an Uber after a night out with friends. On her app she books a ride home, alone, from Five Points in Columbia, South Carolina. Yammering away on a phone call when her "Uber" pulls up, she yanks on the door handle—locked. She pulls again and again. Finally, the door unlocks and she hops in, still on her phone call. Failing to check whether the driver and plates match the description detailed on her app, she hops into the wrong car. She is found in a field days later, her horrific condition bearing witness to her deadly mistake.

Yet another story of a college student succumbing to an epic fail is the fraternity hazing gone wrong and the subterfuge to hide the truth, which to this day is still vague. College freshman Tucker Hipps, pledging Sigma Phi Epsilon, jumps off a bridge into shallow lake water in the shadowy hours between late night and dawn. Calls for help are not placed for several hours, and by the time the panicked frat boys cobble together cogent lies into a cohesive story to liberate them from blame, Tucker has long since perished from his tragic leap. A cross staked into the ground stands to this day on the S.C. 93 bridge where Tucker Hipps fell to his death.

These epic failures—experienced by students who trusted in their own decision-making and perhaps in a fugue of drunkenness—as the headmaster warned, can't be undone. Mistakes of an individual reverberate within their circle of loved ones, heaping upon them a forced circumstance, and no choice but to *deal* with the consequences.

Ken's phone shrilled into the dark bedroom. Calls on his phone at night were expected; we owned a business where emergent issues occurred 24/7. There was a break-in, a door left unlocked, and once a thief was stealing our security camera. *Was the freezer temperature too low?* I had tracked Nick and felt at peace—he was at Holmes, asleep, I was sure.

Ken picked up the phone, then shielded me from the screen. In a calm voice, he asked the caller, "Are you okay?" He shed the covers and strode quickly into the living room. With the expected uptick in my heart rate and pulse, my ragged breathing set in with a need to GET TO KEN ON THE PHONE. Casey snoozed, dead to the world, unperturbed under my feet. I kicked her awake in haste lurching out of bed. Stumbling to the light switch, flipping it on in desperation—I needed light! Ken was hunched over, sitting on the edge of the dining room chair, whispering into the phone.

"WHAT IS IT?! IS IT NICK??" I shout-whispered. He put the phone on mute.

Nick never called Ken to share his shenanigans. Dear God... was it Nick? Was he alive? Ken nodded, yes, my son was *on the phone*. He was *alive*, right?

"Nick was arrested again. He doesn't want you involved," Ken said with his usual "no worries" attitude he often used where Nick was concerned. *Boys will be boys!*

*What...what?!*

Dizzy, I sat down in the adjacent chair, bending over to catch my breath. Nick was in his dorm room! His location finder said so! During spring break, his roommate had moved out to live with a fraternity brother in a dorm across campus. Nick was alone. His suitemate across the bathroom in the adjoining room, Robert—who had helped me locate Nick on that one stressful night—apparently used drugs like I use caffeine. He enjoyed regular LSD, Nick said, to get inspiration for his projects in architecture class. This guy was bad news. The tally of people at Clemson proper who would *care* about Nick was down to zero. His friends "cared," but their lack of wisdom egged on his miscreant ways. I needed to do *something...take action.* I ran into the bedroom for my phone and got busy booking another 6:00 a.m. Delta flight to Atlanta while listening to Ken chat it out with Nick. The conversation unfolded like the countless ones about where to put up a deer stand, or how to hit a nine iron. I could hear Nick talking. He sounded calm and sober. The officers allowed him as many calls as needed. He had already called a friend's parent, whom he sought out his first time in jail at Clemson, who was a lawyer in Charleston.

Fact: My son *was in jail.* Not in his dorm room, asleep where my stalker app *told* me he was.

Clemson's jail is wedged between an apartment complex and a Tigers apparel store, about a mile from campus. The holding cells, I imagine, were filled with college students biding their short stint in the tank until sober. Then, upon release they showered and headed to classes.

The charges against Nick this time were bulky—they could not be swept under the rug. Possession of illegal drugs. Intent to sell them? Resisting arrest. He had fought the officers trying to hand-cuff him.

I recall the horror of that phone call and all that followed. I had a child who was a repeat offender, dependent at some level on drugs and alcohol, who had lost his ability to function lawfully. His good character and values, once sturdy, had drowned under a deluge of temptation from some dark force. His goodness had been ripped from the foundation upon which it was erected and carried off in this massive mudslide of horrific screw-ups.

## Nick's Perspective

*I was smoking weed in my dorm room. There were two Resident Assistants (RAs) on our floor, though I thought there was only one. One RA said to us on moving day, "Smoke weed, I won't report you." The other RA took his job more seriously. He called the campus police when he smelled weed coming from my room. I was with the two suitemates next door and one other guy, in our room smoking. The cop knocked on my door. My friend Steve walked through the bathroom and out through the connecting room to the hallway. He was in the clear. I freaked out and panicked. I rounded up some drugs I had in my drawer and threw that and the weed to Robert and he put that in his safe. Sadly, the campus police saw all that. Robert showed them what was in it—he didn't have to, legally—and he had other drugs in the safe. He was given a ticket and I was arrested. There I was, not even drinking, smoking some weed, and in walks the campus police and they arrest just me. I had a quantity that made it appear I was a dealer. I did sell it occasionally to people for money. I needed money, for who knows what now. But it seemed important at the time.*

*While I was in the Clemson holding cell, I sort of heard a voice. It was not actually audible, but a quiet type of whisper. It calmed me down and without actually telling me to shape up, it encouraged me that the only way out of my current chaos was Jesus. Essentially to take my life seriously and stop making such stupid decisions was the message. I didn't start reading the Bible or walking a completely straight line, but I settled into being the good guy, if I can say that, that I guess my mom raised.*

*Here is the bottom line: I had fun. I loved that time in my life. Mom says I was dancing with the devil. Okay, if that is the word she wants to use. Everyone did coke...everyone did drugs. Most people on my floor and at High Point (where Tradd lived) did drugs. We were all on a GroupMe for where to score drugs. I sold the stuff on GroupMe. I would NOT do any of that again, but I wouldn't change it either. I am GLAD it is over. Not once did I say, "This is wrong." It was a completely different mindset, and anyone reading this certainly won't understand. I am HAPPY it brought me to a better place through the lessons of it all. I am happy I know about all that. Some seemingly successful adults do that still. I won't. I know what the outcome can be to live that way. I don't want to die or risk the good life I have earned. The "no" to doing all that is greater than the "yes" that brings all the risk. I thought of going back to that life: it was fun. I love fun. But, the fear of getting arrested, the risk, and the compromise of my values is not worth it. I did stray; I did more stupid things up until senior year, but nothing, NOTHING, like the crazy antics from age seventeen to nineteen.*

*I hope my mom knows that all of that led me to being the person I know I am today. I think I am, well, pretty awesome.*

# Chapter 15

# Sift Through
# the Rubble

*I*nstead *of backslapping and bonding with his fellow criminals, Nick laid shiv-*ering and shirtless on a cot in his tiny holding cell. In the midst of the long, dark night, his soul settled for the first time in years. Gone was the devil urging his self-destruction. A chaotic restlessness to which he had slowly grown accustomed settled upon hearing the voice of Jesus whispering and soothing his soul throughout the night. Rather than an audible direction to shape up, Nick felt the presence of God claiming him—returning to him his goodness. This arrest brought the end to his tumultuous years dancing with the devil. He had to go through that dark valley to someday stand upon a mountain in peace. This dark night in a jail cell was actually an answer to prayer.

God often answers prayer at His will, dismissing our easy solutions and miracles for which we fervently pray. The answer to my prayer was a far cry from the resolution I imagined, but was certainly an answer to prayer. A few days before this dark night, Dan Cathy, the chairman, president, and CEO of Chick-fil-A, honored us with a visit to our store. At the close of the tour, his four or five traveling companions insisted on assisting customers to allow team members the chance to sit down and chat with Dan. Our small party moved out to the chairs and tables on the patio. After twenty minutes of speaking, and asking and answering questions, Dan turned to me with laser focus, as though he understood my turmoil, and asked a question that would change our lives forever.

"Suzanne. What can I pray for with you today?"

That was an easy question. I needed no time to wonder what one thing I could request.

I teared up and asked, "My son has been struggling with staying on a godly path. He has stumbled and rebelled for a few years now. It's been really tough. If you can pray for him, we would appreciate that immensely."

Dan prayed right then that God move into Nick's life and direct him toward what was good and worthy. I can't recall all of the words, but the prayer was weighty and heartfelt, bringing me to tears. We stood to take a picture, and as we posed, Dan leaned in and spoke softly.

"Tell me your son's name again." He would continue to pray for Nick by name that day, he said.

Within a few days, Nick was taken into custody and remanded to a path of correction. I have no doubt this "miracle" that brought such pain and suffering to me that night and the months after was an answer to Dan Cathy's prayer.

My all-too-familiar Delta flight the morning following this last incident departed on time. The phone calls with our lawyer friend and the two-hour drive to Clemson from Atlanta were calm and tearful. The nagging fear and desperation from his high school days and the battles for control of his behavior through tracking him; wondering where his window screen was and removing his bathroom door; the sunrise campus run; the missing tooth;

hundreds of pleading phone calls and texts from and to Nick; Cancun, and my own dark night of the soul, where I believed him dead; and the first horrifying arrest—all were inevitable. The nearly constant tsunami tormenting the hours of my days and years and the false narrative that Nick's epic fail would mimic Bobby's—who just could not cope anymore—settled into a calm that one knows only after a storm passes. Nick was not Bobby, and never had been. To be sure, sadness rippled my every cell and my stomach churned with agony for my child.

It was a beautiful spring day in Clemson as I pulled off Highway 76 and onto Perimeter Road. I texted Nick, "Seven minutes out!" The campus was in bloom. Magnolia trees guarded sidewalks bustling with students on their way to and from class. Crepe myrtle trees boasted colorful pink and red blossoms as I pulled into a rare open space in front of Fort Hill House. I parked, locked the rental car, and crossed the familiar street. Lowering slowly onto the courtyard bench, I waited for my son. "Hey Tiger, I'm here," I texted. I set my phone down.

My watery gaze locked onto the freshman drop-off spot where a mere seven months prior, with conflicting emotions of hope and trepidation, our cars had spilled the entirety of Nick's contents into the hands of trusted helpers. For seven months my map dot location was New Mexico while my heart and soul resided in Clemson.

Nick had been blessed in this place where he did indeed haphazardly plant some sturdy new roots. This esteemed place— from which many other intelligent, graduating high school seniors were blocked entry—had accepted Nick with a resounding, "You Are Tigertown Bound!" Despite a sketchy senior year of high school, he was *in*—completely in. With God's grace and the smarts bestowed upon him by me, Ken, and God, Clemson had become both his launch zone and crash pad. Thank God. Thank God it all happened there, where the Headmaster's prediction played out to an epic fail that didn't kill him. In fact, it resuscitated him back to himself.

The appointment with the lawyer was later in the day, following Nick's final class. I looked forward to it. I was eager to move through this period of consequence where Nick had to endure all that would come next. Earthquakes rattle and rage, cracking the foundation of a structure, forcing instability. But foundations can last a lifetime. Experts can come in, lift the house, and fix the cracks and flaws. I knew in the marrow of my soul, sitting there in front of Holmes, that *Nick was still standing!* Nature is and always has been beholden to the whims of God. A Bible passage I had come across one day, Matthew 7:24-27, brought comfort.

> Everyone then who hears these words of mine and does them will be like a wise man who built his house on the rock. And the rain fell, and the floods came, and the winds blew and beat on that house, but it did not fall, because it had been founded on the rock. And everyone who hears these words of mine and does not do them will be like a foolish man who built his house on the sand. And the rain fell, and the floods came, and the winds blew and beat against that house, and it fell, and great was the fall of it. (ESV)

Ken and I *did* build our child on a foundation of rock and not sand after all! Tears of relief flowed as I heard God's inaudible message: "Well done!"

The grace found in Clemson allowed Nick to bash it out with nature in a small Southern town accustomed to forgiving the sins of the fathers who came before. I understand his rocky path might have been God's intent regardless of our longitude and latitude. Franklin Prep surrounded my son with a caring and principled staff whose guidance and infrastructure, I believe, thwarted an irreversible epic fail like that of the Uber girl or the boy on the bridge. Perhaps my interventions and all of the stalking, badgering with word and text, endless negotiations, involving time and again myself into his world, and the persistent attempts toward correction all saved him from an even worse outcome. Or perhaps it was all just God's plan? I stayed close to him, kept him under my watchful gaze, even if it didn't look like the exact divine intervention I mostly ignored. I loved him unconditionally and tried to guide him toward a godly path. As this marathon season of parenting was wrapping up, we were on the top of the hill rounding the bend in the twenty-sixth mile and I thought: *Perhaps all the mama-bear crazy, unconditional love did save him from a full-on epic fail.*

With equal measures of delight and agony, I had once run another tough race—a literal one: the Marine Corps Marathon. I gutted out the process when Nick was only two years old. With gusto, I executed months and months of runs and calculated training. On race day, I dug deep into that well of preparation. The hardest stretch of the 26.2 miles was a lonely, four-mile, mid-race slog to Hains Point. Jutting into the Potomac River, the peninsula withstands the crosswinds and unprotected blows from the seasons, and its bedraggled landscape offered no protection for runners on race day. I had made it out to the tip and back again, into the thick of DC with my energy intact. I dug deep at mile twenty-five, buoyed with understanding that crossing the line would bring success and pride in finishing what I had started. I would endure the daunting and arduous commitment. There was no quit in me as I bit into every reserve in my body, when quitting would have ended the pain. No one, no one ever, can take away that achievement. Permanent in my post-race character was a new confidence, an eternal chorus reminding me of my capability to complete something really difficult. Like finishing well that 26.2

miles, I had persisted in parenting my rebel son. It was indeed a marathon.

Sitting on the bench that afternoon at Clemson, I recognized a similar emotion I had felt rounding the final turn at the Marine Corps Marathon. I had clawed my way to the finish and won the race against the devil to win back my son before he did himself in. I followed through when I wanted to quit during those dark and lonely middle miles. My agony throughout that season I chose to keep to myself, like I did the aches and pains of marathon training. Revealing my struggles might have unleashed my darkest fears from their hiding spot in the deep recesses of my soul.

My husband, resting in the comfort of his naivete and faith during those years, came out unscated. Now, he is shocked to know all that went on during those years he spent in the bleachers. Ironically, he would stand alongside me as we watched our son complete community service, serve out his academic probation, and attend court dates. We had arrived at the same place at the end of it all, yet I was bloody and bruised and he bore the unbroken heart of a man in denial. "Why should I stress about it?" I heard him say at the time. "I have my life to live, and no one comes through their boyhood without battle scars."

We were on track to heal from the pain of the past few years. Just in time, he was saved from the horror of what was, or felt like, an epic fail. Could I recover fully from the grueling miles of chasing after my son as he ran faster still toward a brutal finish? I knew many more hurdles and struggles loomed for Nick going forward. Perhaps even more stalking and late-night worry awaited me over the coming years left at Clemson. But, with gratitude and pride, our front-row seats in the Littlejohn Coliseum bleachers gave a remarkable view of his milestone ring ceremony three years hence. Clemson President Clements bestowed Nick his class ring, signaling his imminent graduation. Nick's amazing girlfriend of over two years flanked his side in the post-ceremony picture. Like an angel sent from above, this lovely girl swooped in four months after his final arrest. She inspired him to continue his commitment to a hard-won course correction. She was his blessing. "You become who you surround yourself with" proved irrefutable with his choice of a partner. She was, I wholly believe, a gift from God for me hanging in there, being a devoted mama when every fiber of my being wanted to turn tail and run. She was an unwitting teammate sharing the honor of loving and encouraging my Nick.

I felt blessed. I turned my gaze away from Fort Hill House to Holmes Hall in time to catch my son walking out the double doors. He paused, searching, then strode directly toward me. His soft green eyes looked neither left nor right, but steady, in my direction. I stood. Moving into my embrace, there, in front of his dorm with all the busy students going about their lives, my child hugged me with all his heart and soul. It was an embrace explaining to me his contrition, his remorse for the pain he caused. With an evident softening in his body, he pulled away and apologized for his actions and my struggle to reach him less than twenty-four hours after his rock-bottom plunge. Later that day, he would tell me of his time with Jesus in his holding cell. We would eat a hearty breakfast at SunnySide Cafe, as he shared with me all that had happened. My son draped his arm around my shoulder and, matching my stride, we crossed the street together.

# Epilogue

While it is okay, and even healthy, to acknowledge "home is where the heart is," it is destructive to rabidly pursue correction of someone's actions under the guise of loving them. That behavior took away my peace of mind and destroyed my good health.

This year, my inner hypochondriac won out when I was diagnosed with a rare type of cancer. I have no doubt the stress I put myself through allowed it to form and fester in my own version of an epic fail. By God's good grace it is fully treatable, and with God's mercy and my faith I am in the process of healing. The Bible is the only self-help book that has brought me through many dark and scary moments in 2023. Trusting God—a discipline to which Ken already adhered—has reignited my soul and allowed me joy and peace as I move into a future of wellness—physically *and* mentally.

Nick is thriving in his new career in Florida. He recently adopted a husky puppy named Maverick, found a great girlfriend named Nicole, and bought a house. He and Nicole read the Bible together most nights and most Sundays attend their new home church. Now, it is Nick that is flying out to New Mexico to cook and clean and cheer me up as I make my way through the healing process.

God often separates us from certain situations, places, or people to isolate us as He works to draw us nearer to His divine plan for our lives. It is our spiritual growth He is after by creating this space for us to focus on Him. Living so far away from good friends and all my beloved family has created detachment from their support so that I may completely rely on God. Isolated further now in all the steps I need to take to heal, God has me in the proverbial boat in the middle of a storm to refine and strengthen me. Just as gold is purified through fire, God is refining me and molding me into a warrior for His kingdom. By focusing solely on Him to bring me out of this challenge whole and healed—in complete faith—I am healed. It turns out God knew exactly what He was doing all along and I only needed to crack open the right book—the Bible—and study it diligently to avoid so much heartache in the journey to rescue my son. God, as it turns out, is the only One who can rescue any of us. God loves me, and you, and of course my son. Through all the sin, rebellion, and near-epic fails, God always loved my son unconditionally.

# Acknowledgments

*T*he crazy idea to write this memoir began with the notion of a short  a short story that I thought I would submit to a magazine or add to the pile of my other short stories, printed out and tucked away in a drawer in my study. But I couldn't stop writing. The words kept flowing. The stories that spilled onto the pages were just too important NOT to share with other mothers. I loved the three-plus years of continuously writing and rewriting this book. At the least, I hope you found it a good read. But, mostly, I pray it was an inspirational read, the kind of book you just couldn't put down. I thank all the readers who picked this up and didn't put it down til l the very end.

There are so many people to thank...where do I begin?

My son Nick—You are the sole reason this book was birthed! Because of you I know how to love without a single condition. I admire how you move through life with utter confidence and kindness, completely transparent and without shame or secrets kept close to your chest. One might say you are an open book! You always give people the benefit of the doubt and the shirt off your back, and rarely say no to a request to help or mentor others. I love you unconditionally and beyond measure. You are not just my favorite son whom I love like you are my own child (an inside joke—Nick is my own child), but you are my dear friend whom I turn to for sage advice on just about any topic.

To my husband, Ken, the one who urged me toward a career as an author. You proclaimed I was a writer when you erupted in delight and laughter upon reading my first travel article for a local newsletter. Thank you for your unconditional support and belief in this book. You never questioned that it would be amazing. As tough as it was, you refrained from knocking on the office door, knowing it would "interrupt my momentum." Thank you for loving me and loving this book you have yet to read.

To my three siblings, Bonnie, David and Cindy, and my power-house mother, Audrey, who showed my spunky, outspoken self unconditional love. It is an honest and sometimes tough love from my nuclear family that provided a safety net I could return to time and time again. This family of mine catapulted me toward my dreams and stood aside as I left them to soar into an adventurous life and, of course, motherhood. Thank you.

To say a breezy thank you to the team at Forefront Books seems insufficient. But, a heartfelt load of gratitude goes to this amazing group of professionals. You all saw merit in the book. Despite any of my awkward, first-time errors you got behind my project with gusto. I am deeply appreciative of all you have done to hone the words, promote me and the book throughout this process, and bring it to the public.

Publisher Justin Batt saw something in me on our first discovery call. We quickly formed a rapport and found many entwined connections, one being the love of the Clemson Tigers. Thank you, Justin, for taking on a first-time author, unconditionally.

Jennifer Gingerich. What can I say? If the dictionary contained the term editorial director, your name would come up as the definition. You guided me, encouraged me, stayed on top of deadlines, and became the compass heading for me throughout this entire project. Thank you from the bottom of my heart.

My massive thanks to Amanda Bauch, the editor who worked on the developmental edit of my manuscript. She labored away tracking changes all over my very rough first draft with the discerning eye of a demanding professor grading an undergrad. Though at first a shock, it soon became clear her edits were kind, tough, and necessary to do justice to my memoir. Her expertise was beyond invaluable.

To Landon Dickerson, in-house editor with the coolest name imaginable. Your skill and patience are beyond measure. I don't know how you take an author from droning on and mucking up some passages to cleaning them up and making them look really good. It's truly a skill to be admired. Thank you.

I am honored to have so many friends, family, and loving individuals in my life who thought my writing of this book book was the most extraordinary pursuit. Every one of you who showed an interest and gave me the "atta girl" comments, I thank you from the bottom of my heart. All the encouragement kept me going when I wondered who would want to read this book, and yet people are doing this very thing.

With all my love and gratitude,

Suzanne J. Roragen

# Notes

1 Yasemin Saplakoglu, "Why Does a Mother's Body Keep Some of Her Baby's Cells After Birth?" *Live Science*, June 28, 2018, https://www.livescience.com/ 62930-why-mom-keeps-baby-cells.html.

2 Robert Child, "Brother Against Brother: The Bloodstained Legacy of Bull Run," July 22, 2023 in *Point of the Spear*, podcast, MP3 audio, https://podcasters. spotify.com/pod/show/robert-child/episodes/Brother-Against-Brother-The-Bloodstained-Legacy-of-Bull-Run-e26nc5k/a-aa3rkrb.

3 Lisa Bevere, "How to Raise Kingdom Warriors," *Charisma*, August 22, 2017, https://mycharisma.com/spiritled-living/woman/how-to-raise-kingdom-warriors/.

4 Emily Underwood, "Your gut is directly connected to your brain, by a newly discovered neuron circuit," *Science*, September 20, 2018, https://www.science.org/ content/article/your-gut-directly-connected-your-brain-newly-discovered-neuron-circuit.

5 Dan Buettner, *The Blue Zones Challenge: A 4-Week Plan for a Longer, Better Life* (Washington, DC: National Geographic, 2021).

6 Erin Massoni, "Positive Effects of Extra Curricular Activities on Students," *ESSAI* 9, no. 27 (April 2011), https://dc.cod.edu/cgi/viewcontent.cgi?article=1370&context=essai.

7 Louie Giglio, *Goliath Must Fall: Winning the Battle Against Your Giants* (Nashville, TN: Thomas Nelson, 2017).

8 "The Importance of Fathers and Positive Male Role Models for Children," *CASA for Children*, June 4, 2015, https://casaforchildren.wordpress.com/2015/06/.

9 Interview with Bono at the 1983 US Music Festival, https://bethandbono.com/ 2012/05/05/music-can-change-the-world-because-it-can-change-people/ #:~:text=In%20an%20interview%20at%20the,African%20Well%20Fund%20 for%20their.

10 Miriam Adeney, *Kingdom Without Borders: The Untold Story of Global Christianity*

(Westmont, IL: InterVarsity Press, 2009).

11 "Paul Doran," Artists, Zari Gallery, https://zarigallery.co.uk/paul-doran/.

12 "Vitamins by Condition," Vitamins and Supplements Center, WebMD, last modified 2018, https://www.webmd.com/vitamins/condition-1021/attention-deficit-hyperactivity-disorder-adhd.

13 Melissa L Danielson, Rebecca H Bitsko, Reem M Ghandour, Joseph R Holbrook, Michael D Kogan, Stephen J Blumberg, "Prevalence of Parent-Reported ADHD Diagnosis and Associated Treatment Among U.S. Children and Adolescents, 2016," *Journal of clinical child and adolescent psychology: the official journal for the Society of Clinical Child and Adolescent Psychology, American Psychological Association, Division 53* 47, no. 2 (January 2018): 199-212, https://pubmed.ncbi.nlm.nih.gov/29363986/.

14 Sari Harrar, "Adderall on Campus," *Psycom*, updated October 7, 2022, https://www.psycom.net/the-truth-about-study-drugs.

15 St. John of the Cross, "Dark Night," 1584-1586, https://www.carmelitemonks.org/Vocation/DarkNight-StJohnoftheCross.pdf.